MW00800573

1. Boys Town

BOYS TOWN
Revolution in Youth Care

"City of Little Men" Becomes "Family of Boys and Girls"

BOYS TOWN
Revolution in Youth Care

Msgr. Robert P. Hupp
EXECUTIVE DIRECTOR EMERITUS, BOYS TOWN
with Hollis J. Limprecht

ALBA · HOUSE   NEW · YORK

SOCIETY OF ST. PAUL, 2187 VICTORY BLVD., STATEN ISLAND, NY 10314

Library of Congress Cataloging-in-Publication Data

Hupp, Robert P., 1915 —
   Boys Town : revolution in youth care / by Robert P. Hupp.
      p.   cm.
   ISBN 0-8189-0641-3
   1. Father Flanagan's Boys Home — History.   I. Title.
HV876.H85   1992   91-46629
362.7'4'09782254 — dc20   CIP

Designed, printed and bound in the United States of
America by the Fathers and Brothers of the
Society of St. Paul, 2187 Victory Boulevard,
Staten Island, New York 10314, as part of their
communications apostolate.

PRINTING INFORMATION:

Current Printing - first digit   1   2   3   4   5   6   7   8   9   10   11   12

Year of Current Printing - first year shown
1992   1993   1994   1995   1996   1997   1998   1999

FOREWORD

In 1915, about the time I was born, Father Flanagan, then a young priest, was working with homeless, jobless, and oftentimes alcoholic itinerant men, who ended up on skid row in Omaha. In his "Working Men's Hotel" (little more than an empty warehouse) he fed, clothed and housed sometimes as many as 500 a day. He saw a pattern in the lives of those who eventually ended up in prison. Many of them had been neglected, even abandoned as children. They went on to become delinquents in their adolescence, then criminals. He often wondered how many of them could have become productive citizens in society had he met them when they were boys. This street knowledge convinced him that the youth who makes a mistake, unless given a chance, is like a plant growing in depleted soil and deprived of health-giving sunshine.

He started with five boys, three wards of the court and two truant newsboys.

Relying now on his faith that "this was God's work" and that God would provide, after roughing it with these boys for a time Father Flanagan began searching for something like permanent quarters. He soon found a house at 25th and Dodge Streets in Omaha to serve his purpose. His next move was to locate a person of good will who would provide the first rental payment. This he found in the person of a friend who loaned him $90 and insisted on remaining anonymous. This "loan" was actually a gift.

Scarcely did the boys have time to get settled in their new abode when additional boys began arriving, thanks to the probation office, to the police, and to some kindly citizens, to say nothing of an occasional youth who just wandered in on his own.

From the very beginning, the Home's prime requirement was that a boy must "want to be here," as Father Flanagan said. The front door was never locked, nor is there a retaining fence of any kind anywhere on the grounds to this day. "I'm not running a prison," Father Flanagan said. "This is a home, and you don't wall in the members of your family."

By the first Christmas over two dozen boys were living there, a large family by any standard. There was no money to buy even an ordinary meal, to say nothing of the traditional fare for a holiday feast. But once again, God provided. Just in time for Christmas, along with a few other food items, a barrel of sauerkraut rolled in, thanks to an Omaha merchant who had heard of the plight of the boys. But, it was really the love, care, patience and understanding there that put the trimming on that sauerkraut menu.

Soon the family outgrew this house. Father Flanagan was unwilling to accept the limits that this house and his meager budget imposed. As long as there were needy boys, he said, God would provide — and God did — because, soon a spacious two-story building became available, ten times the size of his first house. It had a huge porch and plenty of playground. The rent was low because it was the German American Home which, in the rage of World War I, was forced to close.

The program continued to expand as did the number and appetite of the boys, this latter bordering on being bottomless. A variety of sports, elementary as they were, taught the valuable lessons of winning and losing gracefully. A band was organized and after nine months in the new home, not one boy had relapsed, to the pleasant surprise of Flanagan's key volunteers: William "Bill" P. Lynch, Leo Hoffmann, and Con Heafey, who offered a variety of services to the young priest in his work with juveniles.

Father Flanagan knew the importance of offering some kind of meaningful recognition in the life of a lad whenever possible, so, among other things he took every advantage to create a good public image with the boys by joining public parades and community gatherings.

But, his policy of admitting boys, regardless of race and

creed, along with juvenile delinquents, gave the neighbors the jitters. Their complaints finally reached the pitch of outcries that embarrassed the boys and eventually forced Father Flanagan, in 1921, to purchase and move to a new home that was called "Overlook Farm," 160 acres of promise, ten miles west of the city limits of Omaha. This was to become the permanent location for the "City of Little Men" later known as "Boys Town," an incorporated village in the state of Nebraska and only recently designated a National Historic Landmark by the U.S. Department of the Interior.

Now, let it be noted here that not everyone in society distanced themselves from Father Flanagan and his boys. Volunteer groups began to organize to assist in every way possible. Father's mother, Nora, and his sister, Nellie, organized a "Mother's Guild and Sewing Circle." There were men and women who gave of their evenings and weekends to help with all manner of chores. They would do anything, it seemed, to help the zealous priest rekindle the spark of goodness that was only smouldering in the lives of these little men who had been neglected, and in many cases abandoned.

Most notable among those who stepped forth were two professional men, close personal friends, and they were: Dr. Harry Sullivan, a medical doctor, and Dr. Henry Schultz, a dentist. They came to Father Flanagan and offered their services gratis. A couple of years ago when visiting with Dr. Schultz I inquired of him the extent of the services they offered. He said, in his dry inimitable way: "We took good care of all the boys. Harry cut out their tonsils and I pulled their teeth." And this free service they continued for many, many years.

When the local schools were not eager to take these boys into their classes, Bishop Jeremiah Harty loaned Father Flanagan two nuns and a novice from the Sisters of Notre Dame, but, he cautioned that financial aid was out of the question. This marked the beginning of a real school at the Home.

By this time Father Flanagan's idea of "God will provide" took on an added dimension, that of the Lord helping those who help themselves. So, the boys were taught to raise chickens, milk cows, raise a garden, and work in the fields. With the addition of a few wooden barracks, a couple of pot belly stoves, and a pile of cobs, the new home was complete — Mother Hubbard's cupboard and all.

As capital needs increased, God again provided. This time it was a team of long-standing, local friends of Father Flanagan, including: *J. E. Davison*, business executive and member of the Masonic Order; *Henry Monsky*, respected Jewish attorney and civic leader; *Morris Jacobs*, publicity advertising executive and prominent Jewish leader; *Francis P. Matthews*, respected Catholic leader, later Secretary of the Navy, and then Ambassador to Ireland.

This team organized a fund-raising campaign called "Committee of 1000." The net result was the ground breaking in March 1922 for a five-story permanent building that would serve as a school, dormitory, gymnasium and workshop.

As time went on, Father Flanagan himself began building more support for the Home by weekly broadcasts over the first radio station in Omaha, WOAW. He also went on extended bandwagon trips in Nebraska and neighboring states with some of his boys who offered a variety of entertainment along the way.

In 1938 the famous movie "Boys Town," starring Spencer Tracy and Mickey Rooney was made. It was this movie that helped make Boys Town a household name. Demands for Father Flanagan's appearance soon began to mount. General MacArthur sent him to Japan to consult with people there regarding the problems they were having with their youth. It was during this time that the reputation of Boys Town began spawning other Boys Towns around the globe. I have in my files today records of some thirty-five such homes in various foreign countries.

Upon his return to the States, President Harry S. Truman lost no time in sending Father Flanagan as an emissary of the State Department to consult with European countries about youth problems that were plaguing them. It was on this trip in

1948 that Father Flanagan was stricken with a heart attack in Berlin where he died at the age of 63.

Well, in spite of his herculean efforts to enjoy some kind of solvency, he died while his Home was still in debt. But, a better financial climate was on the horizon.

A new era began when Monsignor Nicholas Wegner, experienced in administration and management, was made the second executive director of the Home. It was during his years that the program pioneered by Father Flanagan began to flourish. Athletic teams of the Home rose to national prominence. A concert choir, organized by Monsignor Francis P. Schmitt in 1941, came into its own, conducting annual tours around the country with tours to Japan, Cuba and Canada.

Although Father Flanagan conceived the idea of a Foundation Fund, and started one in 1943, it took some years for it to come to life. He had hoped that the fund would someday become large enough that the revenue from it would cover all, or most of the operating expenses of the Home, thus making it possible for him to spend less time on the road soliciting funds and more time with the boys. It was not until Monsignor Wegner's time, however, that the fund grew to a current $200 million, thus making it possible to begin long-range planning, and enjoy some continuity in the programs.

In 1973, when I came upon the scene, it was no great feat to move ahead. We see far, you know, when we stand on the shoulders of giants. It was the charismatic program innovator, Father Flanagan, complemented by the administrative executive, Monsignor Wegner, who provided the frame for me to climb.

From an address by Father Robert P. Hupp to the Newcomen Society on April 25, 1985.

PREFACE

The first time I encountered Boys Town was in the early 1940's.
My high school basketball team from Trinity High in Sioux City,
Iowa took the 100 mile trip to Omaha to play the Boys Town
Team. As I remember, we lost, but vivid in my memory is Father
Flanagan's greeting to the team and the lunch that was provided.

Boys Town was famous even then. When we played Boys
Town, it was like playing in the big leagues. Boys Town has been
in the big leagues in child care since Father Flanagan brought
reality to his dream of providing a decent life and a sense of hope
to homeless and neglected boys.

Great insitutions, however, must survive and develop from
one leader to another, one generation to another, and often from
one crisis to another. Father Robert Hupp, a priest with a capital
P, took the reins of Boys Town at a difficult time. A better person
could not have been found to take charge because Father Hupp is
a sensitive, caring, sensible and thoughtful leader.

I have known Father Hupp from my very first days at Creighton University. Along with Dan O'Brien, Ed Fitzpatrick, and a
few others, we served Mass for Father Hupp at the Good
Shepherd Convent where he was Chaplain following his World
War II naval duty. My motivation for serving Mass might have
been a little more than religious, because along with Mass came a
wonderful Sunday breakfast and being on the GI Bill made that
meal a particularly happy reality.

My relationship with Father Hupp became more personal
when, in September of 1949, he officiated at Mickie's and my

marriage ceremony. He was equally skillful in that assignment, for after 43 years the contract is still intact.

This book chronicles a fascinating chapter in the life of one of America's finest institutions. But more importantly, it details a significant chapter in the life of a wonderful human being, a great priest who left an indelible mark on Boys Town.

DONALD R. KEOUGH
President
Coca Cola Company

ACKNOWLEDGMENTS

In every furrow of this book is sown seeds of gratitude to God Who has been extremely good to me, to my mother and father, who taught me that the family is the best health, education and welfare system in the world, and to my eight younger brothers and sisters who practiced with me what our parents preached: Joseph Sr., Marie, Maurice, Ferdinand, Mildred, Andy, Jim and Betty.

My thanks, too, to Lilyan Dewhurst, my dedicated and faithful personal secretary since 1977; to my collaborator, Hollis J. Limprecht, and to his wife Marjorie for her sharp-eyed proofreading. Last but not least, my deepest gratitude to several financial supporters who prefer anonymity.

CONTENTS

BOYS TOWN
Revolution in Youth Care

CHAPTER One

IT was Thursday evening, the day before Reverend Edward J. Flanagan, the fabled Father Flanagan of Boys Town, was to leave on a trip to war-ravaged Germany in 1948. Just by luck, I happened to be present at what soon became known as "Flanagan's Last Supper." It was on this trip that Father Flanagan was stricken with a heart attack while in Berlin and died at the age of sixty-three.

The founder, in fact the very soul, of Boys Town was dead. Boys Town, of course, survived, just as Father Flanagan always maintained it would, for he had let it be known at that memorable meal: "This work will continue, you see, whether I am there or not because it is God's work, not mine."

That this gentle, kind, but definitely charismatic man would no longer be in charge of Boys Town never occurred to any of us that night. In 1947 the U.S. State Department had asked Father Flanagan's help in solving the problems of orphaned and displaced children in post-World War II Asia and Europe. He traveled abroad on the USS Fall River to Tokyo, where he met with General Douglas MacArthur to discuss the details of his Far East mission. He visited Hiroshima and Nagasaki, both devastated by the atomic bombs that ended the war with Japan, and he toured orphanages and detention centers in Japan and the Philippines. His recommendations for war-torn Asia so impressed President Truman that the President asked him to do the same for Europe, especially West Germany.

While packing his suitcases late the afternoon of the day before his departure, he was briefed on the affairs of the Home by his assistants, Fathers Edmund Walsh and Louis Demers, and others. He could then give final instructions to his staff before departing on his latest mission.

As a parting gesture he asked the priests on his staff to dinner at which time he would let his expectations and plans be known. I was visiting the campus on my afternoon off and was invited to join in the evening's activities.

As Father Flanagan was making the seating arrangements for dinner, I noticed that the total number of priests present was twelve, including myself. Just to make conversation, because I wasn't one of his inner circle of confidants and advisors, I posed the question to him: "How does it happen that you have only eleven apostles here this evening?"

"The Lord Himself had only eleven good ones," he replied with a gentle smile.

After an improvised invocation we were seated and Father Flanagan began commenting on the changes he had in mind for Boys Town after his return from the European trip. When he got back he was going to pursue the concept of developing a family environment for the boys. In each of the new cottages the residents could get together in the evenings, like a family, with everyone sitting around talking and visiting, eating popcorn and listening to the radio while a log burned slowly in the fireplace. This family setting would replace the relatively cold and rigid atmosphere of dormitory life.

A major plant expansion was almost completed, including the construction of twenty-five individual cottages rather than more dormitories. Father Flanagan told those of us gathered around his table that some day he hoped to have a priest in each cottage to live with and supervise the boys. He wasn't thinking of professional social workers as counselors, and he hardly had in mind assigning a married couple to each cottage to instruct on family living. This was many years ago, but even the thought of having a priest supervising a family setting with the boys was a radical departure from everything known about caring for homeless children in those days. Orphans lived in dormitories — that's just the way it was.

He revealed for the first time that he had learned of the possibility of obtaining a few war-surplus Quonset huts from the government. These he would locate away from the cottages, perhaps down by the Boys Town lake. The unruly boys, boys who did not appreciate and take care of the fine furniture and furnishings in the new cottages, would be housed in the Quonset huts until they decided to appreciate the finer things in the homes.

Father Ray Lisco, who at the time was living in and was in charge of one of the units where the bad actors were assigned, debunked the idea by commenting that those who were banished to the Quonsets would literally destroy the hut unless someone responsible were with them.

"They will burn the place down," he said. "Who is going to be down there with them?"

"I had thought of assigning you to that job," said Father Flanagan with a wink to the rest of us. Needless to say, the rapid exchange reduced Father Lisco to total silence the rest of the evening.

I listened to this banter with detached interest. It never dawned on me that some day I would be assigned to Boys Town, or be in a position to do something about Father Flanagan's second dream.

His first dream, of course, had been the Home for Boys itself, a dream I discussed in a speech I gave to the Newcomen Society of the United States in Omaha on April 25, 1985, and which is reprinted here in the book's Foreword. You may want to refer to it if you missed it. It tells how and why Father Flanagan's Boys Town is a worldwide household word.

His second dream was interrupted by his sudden death during his global mission on behalf of battered and forgotten children everywhere. But as he told us the night of his last supper, "the work will continue." His prophecy did come true alright, but not until many years and countless crises later.

His successor, the priest who was given the task of continuing "God's work," was the highly respected Monsignor Nicholas Wegner, who had ministered for many years to the children at St. James Orphanage from his post as chancellor of the Archdiocese of Omaha.

Monsignor Wegner's experience in administration and management, gained through those years at the Chancery Office, was the answer to Boys Town's need for financial solvency and program stability. Father Flanagan, in spite of his herculean efforts to put the Home on a financially even keel, left it in debt because of several vast post-World War II construction projects.

A better financial climate was on the horizon as Monsignor Wegner stepped in as Boys Town's second executive director. It was during his years, 1948 to 1973, that the program pioneered by Father Flanagan began to flourish. Athletic teams of the Home rose to national prominence. A concert choir, organized by Father Francis Schmitt in 1941, came into its own, conducting annual tours around the country and in a few foreign countries.

After years of living from hand to mouth, Father Flanagan understood that financial security was necessary, and in 1941 he had conceived the idea of a Foundation Fund, but it was not until 1943 that the fund became a reality. He hoped that the fund would become large enough so that the revenue it generated would cover the Home's operating expenses, allowing him some day the luxury of spending more time with his boys and less on the road raising money.

But it was not until Monsignor Wegner's tenure, however, that the fund grew large enough to make possible long-range planning and to enjoy some of the continuity of a well-organized program.

Once the fund-raising program was in place and functioning, it became successful beyond anything Father Flanagan could have imagined. In the twenty-five years after his death it became too successful, too fast perhaps; outstripping the administration's preparedness to expand the program wisely. And therein lay the ammunition for an explosion that rocked Boys Town to its foundation and created an atmosphere of distrust that threatened the Home's integrity and its financial stability. It was this exposure that ultimately brought me to Boys Town as its third executive director — a job I not only did not seek but one I tried my darndest to avoid.

Let me set the scene.

In the early 1970's Monsignor Wegner indicated to his Board of Directors that Boys Town was in a financial condition to warrant expansion, and that thought should be given to taking care of more than the 787 youths already living there. The Board decided the thrust should be to provide care for mentally handicapped youngsters because, as someone suggested, a member of the Board had such a youth in the family.

Monsignor Wegner had other ideas.

"That's not the way to go," he told the Board. Competent help for such an undertaking would be hard to come by, he argued. Furthermore, Boys Town would eventually become little more than a glorified baby-sitter.

But the Board persisted, and in a rare instance of disagreement with Monsignor Wegner, instructed him to draw up a plan for construction of facilities for the mentally handicapped, along with staff and programs to tend them. The location would be on 240 acres across West Dodge Road, the northern boundary of Boys Town itself. It would be a campus setting similar to the existing Boys Town, which by now had grown into an incorporated village with its own post office, athletic fields, a high school, a grade school, a vocational training school, two dining halls, a beautiful chapel, a farm and a lake.

Monsignor Wegner felt he had to seek help in running such a program, arguing to his Board that the current Boys Town staff was not equipped for such a change in direction. He had many friends around the country, especially among the clergy, and eventually was led to two Religious Brothers of the Third Order of St. Francis who agreed to come and handle this new program. The two Brothers went to Chicago and began a training course in the care of the mentally handicapped. All seemed in place.

Muriel Humphrey, wife of Hubert Humphrey, Senator from Minnesota and later Vice President of the United States, and a devoted worker among mentally handicapped, turned the first spade of dirt on the site. Her husband was the commencement speaker at Boys Town High School graduation the same day.

Then fate interceded. The two Franciscans, shortly before they were to leave for Boys Town, were killed in an auto accident.

"The Lord is trying to tell us something," Monsignor Wegner said to his Board. The idea of an institution for mentally handicapped youngsters lay dead in the water. Reporters besieged him.

"What will you do now?" they asked.

"At this point I don't know," Monsignor Wegner replied.

"How much money do you have on hand?" they persisted.

Monsignor Wegner said, "No comment."

The major local newspaper, The Omaha World-Herald, accepted Monsignor Wegner's answers, but a suburban weekly by the name of the Sun Newspapers, which published a variety of neighborhood weeklies variously called the Dundee Sun, the North Omaha Sun, the South Omaha Sun and the Benson Sun, was not satisfied. Its editor, a former World-Herald reporter by the name of Paul Williams, decided to see what he could find out through sources other than Monsignor Wegner.

He would follow the Boys Town money trail.

Being a former Chancery official — a place where you are told nothing that the ecclesiastical powers think you need not know — Monsignor Wegner refused to cooperate with the Sun's dogged reporters. His lips were sealed tighter than a clam eating alum.

But editor Williams and his top investigative reporter, Mick Rood, had a recently-enacted federal law on their side. In 1969 Congress authorized the Internal Revenue Service to be the repository for a lengthy financial report required of every charitable institution in the United States. Previously, Boys Town had folded its annual report into its report to the Archdiocese of Omaha, thereby camouflaging the publication of its true worth.

Now, Boys Town's Form 990 was there for anyone with the patience to wait for the IRS to respond to an inquiry, a process that took three to four weeks. Williams had that patience.

In early March of 1972, sensing that a disclosure by the Sun Newspapers was forthcoming, the Boys Town Board of Directors authorized Monsignor Wegner to "engage a reputable and qualified firm to make a complete and in-depth study of, and make recommendations in respect to programs, activities and facilities at Father Flanagan's Boys' Home, its operations with respect to the care, maintenance and education of boys in its care," as the minutes for March 8, 1972 stated.

Too little, too late.

Twenty-two days later the Sun newspapers were delivered to an estimated 35,000 Omaha homes with the blazing headline: "700 Boys with $209,000,000."

The Sun newspapers had obtained a copy of IRS Form 990 and revealed its contents. Even those close to Boys Town who figured the Home was not a candidate for the poverty program were astonished to learn there was that much money in the till. Although I was not directly affected, that disclosure got my attention too.

At this time I was a small town country pastor in charge of a new parish, Christ the King, in southwest Omaha, a job I thoroughly enjoyed. My relations with Boys Town had been about that of the average parish priest who is busy with his own matters and only knew about and respected the work of the Home.

Some time later Reporter Mick Rood, whom I knew personally, asked what I thought of the Sun's blockbuster. I surmised that the disclosure probably would help Boys Town in the long run. Unfortunately it was a much longer run than I anticipated at the time I responded to Rood's questions.

The Sun's special report covered eight full-size newspaper pages. Friends of mine in the news business have told me it was vastly overdone; that a couple of pages could have held most of the important information. But the hefty package had impact, and the Sun Newspapers won a coveted Pulitzer Prize for community service, rare for a weekly newspaper in an urban market. The Pulitzer gave the report more credibility and importance than it probably deserved, and it certainly gave the report national distribution it wouldn't have merited otherwise. The Sun's investigative reporting consisted of little more than extracting the damaging numbers from Boys Town's Form 990.

Beyond that though, the Sun's reporters interviewed a number of the Boys Town's seventeen Board members and found a woeful lack of information about the workings of the place they were supposed to be directing. Almost without exception, they admitted they had no idea the bank account totaled $209 million.

I learned some time later that Monsignor Wegner held the Board in the palm of his hand, never trusting too much information to them. All prominent people, mostly from Omaha but with a smattering of out-of-towners, they met once a year. Monsignor Wegner would produce a single copy of the one-page agenda, pass it around the table at the annual meeting and then "file" it.

For his twenty-five year tenure as executive director of Boys Town, no written record of Board minutes has ever been located.

The Sun Newspapers' most damaging thrust was that Boys Town "is a money machine that brings in some $25 million a year from the public.

"Boys Town," it said, "increases its net worth by $16 million to $18 million a year, three to four times as much as it spends to take care of the boys.

"Boys Town still continues to send out some 33 million letters a year telling Americans it needs their money ('$1, $2, $5 or any amount you care to give') to keep the wolf from the door," stated the Sun.

"In short, Boys Town has more money than it knows what to do with. It may be the richest city in America. Based on the 1970 census figures and its 1970 financial report, it had a net worth of over $190,000 per person."

Beyond the figures, the Sun editorialized regarding Boys Town's mission and its future.

"Equally unsettling, Boys Town finds itself out of step with the times. Its boy population is falling, and it is being reluctantly forced to accept some boys it wouldn't have taken a few years ago. Indeed, its whole concept — the large custodial institution — is under question, if not direct attack, by many nationally respected agencies and theorists in the child care field."

But mainly the Sun concentrated on money — and Boys Town's consistent efforts to raise more. It reprinted the letter sent to 33 million Americans the previous Christmas — there were Christmas and Easter appeals — which began:

"There will be no joyous Christmas season this year for many homeless and forgotten boys to look forward to with eager anticipation as the more fortunate boys do. For some of them it will be the first time, while others, due to parental neglect, have never known a happy Christmas."

With $209 million in the bank, a happy Christmas was certainly not beyond the reach of Boys Town's 787 citizens (the census varied almost daily).

The letter concluded: "You can help bring happiness to other homeless and unwanted boys by sending me in the enclosed envelope $1.00, $2.00, $5.00 or any amount you care to give and our boys will make you an honorary citizen of Boys Town and I will send you a certificate with my acknowledgment. The enclosed Boys Town Christmas seals are for your use. Thank you, and may God bless you and watch over you and yours forevermore. Sincerely — Father Wegner."

Devastating as the Sun's stories were, there was absolutely no evidence of cheating or pocket lining by anyone. Monsignor Wegner was uncomfortable with the rapid growth of the fund. He wanted to do more, but was not quite sure what to do. A dual communication problem seemed to plague his administration. One mistake was his failure to confide implicitly in his Board and staff; the second was even greater, and that was that he obviously did not always read each campaign letter before signing and sending it out. Routinely signing a letter without reading it still occurs on occasion in many a busy office. This happened in Wegner's case and was understandable, though not excusable, when it became known that he was in poor health, having had sixteen major operations late in life. This situation coupled with his super-conservative nature gave the Sun ammunition to shoot at him.

The Christmas letter was definitely a mistake. Monsignor Wegner had been appointed executive director of the Home when Boys Town was under financial stress and it was his mission to put the Home on a financially sound basis. Too sound, in the view of some people. However, let it be noted here that Father Flanagan himself was forty years ahead of his time. Today many colleges, universities, even high schools, are starting to build trust funds as he did to insure future operations against economic fluctuations.

Reaction to the Sun's disclosures was immediate and almost disastrous. Donations fell by $15 million in the year following the special report. Further, strong pressure was mounted on Monsignor Wegner to resign, something he was reluctant to do despite several years of ill health. He was concerned about who his successor might be.

Here, with extreme reluctance, I became a major player in the drama. I had watched from the safety of my parish perch. Beyond the feeling that perhaps Monsignor Wegner should have been more cooperative with the press, I had no further comment at the time. With no related responsibility, I could afford to be a disinterested spectator. I had no idea that some day soon the whole kettle of fish would be mine to sort out.

First, let me say a bit about myself and my career. I was born on July 3, 1915, the first of nine children to a farm couple living in the corner of Holt, Antelope and Wheeler counties in Nebraska. As a young boy I helped the family with farm chores, attended classes in a one room schoolhouse and dreamed of being a musician.

My high school days were filled with baseball and football

practices, playing the trombone, taking part in traveling shows sponsored by the parish church and probably the most fun, hunting with my Lutheran grandfather. He was a big man, six feet four inches tall and well over two hundred pounds. I had a Catholic grandfather too, but he died before I was able to know him.

No one really knew how much I wanted to pursue a musical education but for lack of funds I was frustrated. Given the opportunity to earn as I learned, I decided in favor of a higher classical education. I attended Junior College in Conception, Missouri. It was then that I decided to study for the priesthood. I attended Kenrick Seminary in St. Louis, Missouri and on May 18, 1940, was ordained in St. Cecilia's Cathedral in Omaha. Later that day I returned home to celebrate my first Mass.

Early in World War II there was a call for Chaplains. When asked why I enlisted in the service, my standard response was threefold: First, I said that I am patriotic and I love my country. Second, I wanted to do my part. Third, they came and got me — "they" being Bishop James Hugh Ryan and the Military Ordinariate. My first assignment in the United States Navy was to attend Chaplain's School at William and Mary College in Williamsburg, Virginia. From there I was sent to the U.S. Naval Disciplinary Barracks and Prison in San Pedro, California. I lived and worked behind bars in this former federal penitentiary for a year and a half, ministering to the overcrowded population. When a report of excessive rackets existing in the prison broke, revealed by New York City gossip columnist and radio personality Walter Winchell, I was one of a very few officers not disciplined or transformed as the Navy moved in with heavy brass to clean house.

After that experience I requested sea duty, and subsequently was assigned to the aircraft carrier USS Corregidor, where I was privileged for a year and a half to serve aboard ship, to offer Mass at sea, and occasionally on the hood of a jeep in the war-torn islands of the South Pacific.

After the war I returned to Omaha. I received the assignment of Director of the Catholic Youth Organization (CYO) and

Chaplain at the Good Shepherd Convent, a home for neglected girls, many of whom were wayward.

In the CYO I dealt with a lot of young people who were trouble-free, and also many who weren't. The task of organizing, scheduling, and keeping pace with some fifty basketball teams playing in the ghetto of North Omaha and ethnic neighborhoods of South Omaha during the winters and almost as many baseball teams in the summers kept me busy. That was to say nothing of the fund raising and counseling chores involved. The job put me in touch with most of the city's parish priests and many of the city's coaches and athletic directors, including those at Boys Town — associations that were to be of some help in later duties.

My first parish was St. Mary's in Wayne, Nebraska, after which, in the early 1950's, I was given the task of founding a new parish in the rapidly growing southwest section of Omaha. It was to be called Christ the King Parish. The only thing royal that could be said about us in those early days was the fact that our "church" was in the Royal Ballroom at Peony Park, a dance hall in the middle of an amusement park. I took care of more dead soldiers there on any given Sunday morning than I did in all of World War II. But through hard work and sacrifices by members of the parish, we built a large grade school and a beautiful church, going cautiously into debt at times to accomplish these ends. We worked our way out of debt in twenty years, and I was looking forward to an around-the-world cruise, a twenty-fifth ordination anniversary gift of the devoted people of the parish.

I was about to call the travel agency for cruise assistance when the ripples of the Sun Newspaper's exposé began to lap around my tired feet.

Late in the winter of 1972-73, nearly a year after the Sun stories broke, Archbishop Daniel E. Sheehan approached me at a wedding reception. The bylaws of Father Flanagan's Boys' Home made the presiding Bishop of the Omaha Archdiocese the president of the Boys Town Board of Directors.

"I'd like you to think about going to Boys Town," the Archbishop said. My remark was appropriately flippant, I thought. "Sure, what else is new?"

I was planning a trip. I wanted a vacation. But about every time the Archbishop would see me after that brief exchange he would bring up the subject.

Serious damage had been done to Boys Town and the situation was stewing. I became more convinced than ever that I wanted nothing to do with it. It was my intention to pay off the debt at Christ the King and take the vacation I had been anticipating. I had absolutely no intention of getting involved until one Monday night Monsignor Wegner called me.

"May I come over and see you?" He sounded stressed and urgent.

"Sure," I said, "when?"

"I will be there about eleven o'clock," he said.

Well, my usual retirement time was after the ten o'clock news but I would wait up for him anytime.

He arrived on the dot, hardly able to walk into my room, so weary and crippled he was. He dropped into the chair nearest the door and said, "I will not stay long. I guess you know, they've been wanting me to resign for years now and I've always been afraid some liberal might take over."

A few of the local clergy had let it be known they were interested in taking over at Boys Town to test some of their theories of child care, theories some might consider to be too radical. Wegner certainly was one of the conservatives who felt that way.

"Someone may come and spend our bank account," he said. "I can't see that happening. Money is too hard to come by. If you would agree to take over I will go to the Chancery Office tomorrow morning and resign."

My response to him was the same I had given Archbishop Sheehan many times: "Not in your life."

But Monsignor Wegner persisted. He kept assuring me that I could do it, and do it well. He kept giving me his vote of confidence which, coming from him, meant a great deal.

His plea was so passionate that, to pacify him for the time being, I finally said, "Alright, why don't you go to the Chancery Office in the morning and resign. Certainly you ought to step aside for your own sake. In your condition a resignation can never be seen as a cop-out."

With obvious relief he said, "I'll go down and tell them you . . ."

"Wait a minute," I interrupted. "Tell them nothing. In the first place, I don't want the job, and in the second place, you don't have the right to name your successor."

"I have something to say about it," he said. "The Archbishop and his Board will listen to me."

Finally, to ease the situation I said, "O.K., you can tell the Archbishop to throw my hat in the ring." It was my understanding that a few priests had been interviewed by the Search Committee. I figured that the selection had already been made and that my entry would only be a formality. Wegner left with a lighter step.

The next morning, about 9:30, my telephone rang. It was Archbishop Sheehan. "How long will it take you to get to Boys Town?" he asked. That was rather direct.

"What do you mean?" I countered, knowing full well what he meant.

"You're it," he said in his best fraternal tone. "The new director out there."

"Not me," I said.

"Yes," he said. "Monsignor Wegner has just resigned and we need someone out there as soon as possible."

"That calls for a face-to-face meeting," I said, stalling for time.

No sooner had he agreed than I was on my way to the Chancery. It was a drive of less than fifteen minutes, just time enough for me to plot how I could alibi my way out of this trap. Two thoughts entered my mind. First of all, I was being treated for high blood pressure. I was sure my doctor would not let me step into a cauldron. Second, I would lobby for a definite term of office — a short term.

Then fortified with these two arrows in my quiver I entered his office.

"Well," the Archbishop said, "let's talk.

"First of all I must get permission from my doctor," I said, with great confidence in my voice.

"Sure," he said. "That's fair enough. Visit your doctor this afternoon and get back to me. What else?"

"I will consider it if a definite term of office is involved. No open-ended arrangement, or, until I die."

"Sure," he said. "What do you have in mind?" He was far too patronizing. I began to feel uneasy.

"Well, what are you thinking of?" I countered.

"Five years," he said.

"Nothing doing. Forget it. I'd consider one year."

"One year," he said, his voice rising. "That's not long enough to get your feet wet."

"You might be surprised what could be done if my time was limited to twelve months," I said. From there on my case seemed to deteriorate. In desperation my final offer was, "O.K., I'll compromise. I'll go for two."

"Two, with an option for two more," he countered.

My next move then was to Dr. John Gardner's office. That afternoon as he wrapped the blood pressure cloth around my arm I told him my story and added: "You don't think I should accept, do you?" It was more of a statement than a question.

He squinted at his gadget and said, with a hint of a smile, "Believe it or not, this pressure reading shows a green light. Yes. Go ahead."

"Hey," I snapped, "I thought you told me I have high blood pressure."

"You do, but your medication will take care of it."

"I think I'll change doctors," I said, which of course I never would.

Resigned now to leaving my beloved Christ the King parish and its outstanding flock, I returned to the Archbishop with my surrender with this question: "When am I to report?"

"How about a week from today?"

"Not possible," I said. Our bargaining began all over again, but realistically I knew I was riding the crest of a slump. "Give me ten days."

He agreed. Well, I was in the Boys Town front office the very next day delivering my signature card for the bank and poking through some official papers. I was there for a short time every day before officially moving in ten days later.

For the record, Monsignor Nicholas Wegner officially resigned on October 3, 1973 and was further honored with the title, "Executive Director Emeritus."

Inasmuch as Boys Town had no provisions for a director's retirement, members of the Board suggested we continue his salary and build a new residence on the campus for his retirement years. But, modest to the end, he rejected the idea of a new house and moved into a furnished apartment in the clinic.

In March of 1973 the Board had named the grade school the "Monsignor Nicholas Wegner Elementary School." As usual, he protested but the Board held fast and Wegner School was so named at a later day. He always felt comfortable with the grade school crowd, a reflection of his years at St. James Orphanage, and you may notice that in many pictures of him at Boys Town he is with the younger boys.

Monsignor Wegner was a good and honest man who for a number of years was in the poorest of health and then just happened to be in the wrong place at the wrong time after having secured a financial base for Boys Town. He died on March 18, 1976. In May of that year the Board established two full-tuition academic or vocational scholarships to Boys Town High School graduates as an ongoing tribute to Monsignor Wegner. The announcement was a fitting finale to the celebration of his golden jubilee as a priest, and to his dedication to the Home.

Meanwhile, I didn't realize what a hornet's nest of intrigue and clannishness I had inherited. A.F. Jacobson, the president of Northwestern Bell Telephone Company, and a member of the Board, had been in charge of the Search Committee. Shortly after

I moved into the executive director's office — the official date of my appointment was October 3, 1973, the day of Monsignor Wegner's resignation — Jake came by to visit with me.

Now, Jake was a down-to-earth type, a man of good common sense. Before saying a word he conducted a complete search of my desk, other furnishings in the office, including the pictures on the wall.

"There are a lot of leaks of confidential matters around this place," he explained as he dusted off his hands. "You don't know who can be trusted."

You think I wasn't headed for trouble? Had the doctor taken my blood pressure at that time his decision might have sent me farther west than Boys Town.

CHAPTER TWO

E VEN before my first official day on the job as executive director at Boys Town, I had an inkling of the problem I faced. I mentioned in the previous chapter that I stopped by the director's office nearly every day for some minor shuffling of papers and to familiarize myself with the location of the rest rooms, dining halls and other important installations on the campus.

Before my first day I was asked to sign the employees' paychecks. "Fine," I said, "I'll give you a signature and you can have it engraved and affixed to the check-writing machine."

"No," I was told. "We don't do it that way. You must sign each check individually."

"Seven hundred checks twice a month!" I couldn't believe it. "Why not use a check-writing machine or a signature plate?"

"Somebody might steal the plate with your signature," was the reply.

Because there wasn't time to argue before getting the checks out, I signed my name more than seven hundred times, but I assured the office staff this was going to be the last time I engaged in this exercise of wasted time. I told the finance officer to do what was necessary to install a check-writing machine and that he, personally, was responsible for its security.

There were other mountains to climb. I mean real mountains. More than eighteen months had passed since the Sun Newspapers had carried their "exposé," which I never considered quite that enterprising.

"After all," I used to tell our critics, "Boys Town is just well-managed and well-financed. Is it a sin to be solvent?"

On my first official day at work, October 11, 1973, I called a meeting of all the boys and available members of the staff for late afternoon in the Music Hall. Some 1,050 attended. I had no formal speech to deliver; I wasn't familiar enough with the workings of Boys Town to pass myself off as an expert. But I figured they all wanted to get a good look at the new boy who, in their minds, was going to jolt everyone into a state of attention.

"Look, fellows," I said, "I'm not yet familiar enough with the situation here to make a lot of predictions. But one thing you need to know. I care about every one of you."

The reaction was a sitting ovation. In fact, I think if I had stayed around much longer they might have run me out of the Hall. But I liked the idea of bringing the boys and staff up to date on affairs on the campus, so I scheduled such a gathering every Friday afternoon from then on.

I could hardly blame the boys for not giving me three cheers. Lots of them had good reason for their lack of enthusiasm about the "new boy" because they knew I was going to bring about change, and change is unsettling. Father Flanagan's dream of family life for homeless boys now had become my dream, and I was determined to make it come true. I had set a time limit on my stay — two years with an option for two more — and I wasn't going to wait long to get started.

But first I had to struggle against the staff inertia that had developed through Monsignor Wegner's waning years as executive director, years when he endured a series of serious illnesses that would have floored a weaker man. Because of this drifting on the administrative level, the words "status quo" seemed more appropriate than "He Ain't Heavy, Father, He's My Brother," as the Boys Town motto.

Let me give you a good example of the lackadaisical administrative control which faced me. Take the case of Shorty, a former boy who had stuck around after his days in high school. He was about 40 when I arrived on the scene. He was on the payroll, but I could never find out what he did. Nothing, I think, mostly.

He was shifted from one department to another, with each trying to get rid of him after a few weeks. His finest skill seemed to be that of being perpetually sick. And, of course, a sick man can't be expected to work.

I decided to call Shorty in for a heart-to-heart talk. So crippled did he appear when he entered my office, I got up to help him to a chair.

"Shorty," I said, with all the compassion I could muster, "How do you feel?

"Awful," he said. "I just feel awful."

"You know something," I said. "You tell me how awful you feel. You even look awful, and I just talked to your doctor and he said your prognosis is guarded."

"Yeah? What's that mean?" he asked.

"That means he can't promise you'll live the day out. Shorty, this calls for my talk on the Four Last Things — remember them? Death, Judgment, Heaven and Hell." I usually begin this talk with this question: "Have you made a will?"

After pulling himself together he acknowledged that he had a will.

"Great," I said as I made a pencil note. Then followed a series of questions about whom he wanted to give his eulogy, where he wished to be buried, whether he had left anything to Boys Town? All answers were in the negative.

Without further urging he popped out of his chair and dashed out the door.

"What on earth did you do to him?" asked my secretary, Lilyan Dewhurst. "Have you ever seen him move so fast?"

"You've just witnessed a healing," I said.

The moral here is that Shorty was far too typical of too many employees who felt Boys Town owed them a living. That attitude needed correction.

The Board and Monsignor Wegner had made several gestures toward responding to the Sun Newspaper's criticisms. As I stated in the previous chapter, three weeks before the Sun report was released the Board approved a study of the Home's programs and future actions — a gesture indicative of its intentions to use funds garnered by the mailing campaigns to improve and expand existing programs.

Board members didn't really know what sort of expansion they wanted to support, but they were in a "do something" mentality, and a research program that would study the causes of delinquency and homelessness seemed like a good way to go. Omaha architect Leo Daly was one Board member who knew how to get things done, and he became the driving force behind the project. He was acquainted with a social engineer at Catholic University in Washington, D.C., and made arrangements to form a Technical Assistance Committee (TAC) after the Board, in a meeting on April 7, 1972, gave its approval.

Later that year, Daly was also instrumental in establishing another project that would further prove to the public that Boys Town was serious about putting its financial resources to work. Through his friendship with Dr. T.T. Smith, an Omaha ear-nose-throat specialist, Daly contacted members of the medical staff at John Hopkins University in Baltimore, Maryland to establish the Boys Town National Institute, to be located in Omaha and to serve children with hearing and speech difficulties.

In baseball, batting .500 isn't a bad average, and that's what we hit with the Research Center and the Boys Town Institute, although for the amount of money we poured into the projects, two for two would have looked better on the ledger sheet. The Research Center never really got off the ground but the Institute quickly became world famous.

Besides making these definite decisions on its own, the Board had hired the consulting firm of Booz, Allen & Hamilton to study the Home's operation from top to bottom — education, athletics, dormitory and cottage living, finances, administration — and they released their finding shortly before I took over. Booz, Allen & Hamilton cited chapter and verse of the shortcomings and made a series of recommendations. I was encouraged by this report; it gave me reason to believe that changes must be made and it told me they had to be accomplished soon.

The Research Center and the Institute will be dealt with in subsequent chapters. Both were under way before I moved to Boys Town's hot seat, and both required much of my attention as they developed, but in reality both were back burner items. Out front, already boiling over, were conditions that Booz, Allen & Hamilton — and I — knew demanded immediate attention.

First off, I had to bring order down on what was soon to be known as the "Gaza Strip." That was the name I gave to the east side of the campus, in the valley back of the administration building. Father Flanagan had located twenty-five cottages here and they were designed to change living conditions from dormitory life to a kind of family life. This dream had turned into a nightmare. Over the years the boys had made a shambles of some of the cottages. It's a wonder they hadn't torched a few of them.

These kids were destructive beyond imagination, vandalizing the Home from top to bottom — rest rooms, furniture, walls, locks and other fixtures. And breaking windows! It was routine on Mondays for the maintenance staff to spend the day replacing windows broken over the weekend. I feared for the stained glass windows of the chapel. Fortunately they were spared.

Let me tell you one incident about the windows. I had my suspicions about one lad. I called this little guy, who was about ten years old, into my office one Monday after the weekend window spree and I said to him:
·   "Jimmy, do you have any idea who's shattering all these windows? Every night we have broken windows, but the weekends are the worst."

"No sir, Father, I don't know anything about them."

"Well, I'll tell you what I'm going to do, Jimmy," I said. "I'm going to make you my detective, and I'll give you ten bucks if you can find out who is rattling these windows. You should be able to do this because you're a smart fella and you really get around."

That was the end of the broken window episode; well — not

the absolute end, but from then on that kind of vandalism all but disappeared. And I saved ten bucks to boot.

Jimmy wasn't about to admit any guilt, and besides, I hadn't asked him directly if he had broken any windows so he didn't have to lie. Until then no glass seemed to be sacred except the chapel windows; the bigger the window the louder the noise it made when it crashed.

The young dudes were strong, too. I still have the latch and lock twisted from one of the heaviest doors. Locks of any kind were no deterrent for some of those boys. Some of the more creative examples of destructiveness I brought to my office to keep reminding me what life was like on the "Gaza Strip." The counselors who occupied those cottages were far too permissive, but I must say on their behalf, it was one way to survive.

Daly, the architect, recommended that most of the cottage roofs needed extensive repairs, or in some cases replacement. Many were leaking badly, and that, of course, was adding to the interior damage. In a short time I was fortunate to be able to engage a personal friend of mine, a retired builder, Orrin Shelton, to take charge and, one by one, the process of repairing and renovating the cottages began.

New kitchens, now bathroom fixtures, and air conditioning were installed. All vandalism was repaired. This new look took about a year to complete. As Shelton would announce that one cottage was completed his crew moved to the next. Before-and-after pictures of the worst destruction ended up on display in my office. We had to have decent quarters for the boys if Father Flanagan's dream — and it was now my dream — of providing a family environment was to come true.

Whereas the high school boys lived in the cottages, the grade school boys lived in the older brick dormitories, which had been the original living quarters for all the boys. At one time Father Flanagan considered erecting a new ten-story dorm across the street from the four smaller ones, but somehow, during the early days of World War II, he scrapped the idea in favor of the cottages. Construction on the cottages began as soon as wartime shortages of material eased, and they were finished in 1948. By the time I arrived in late 1973, the cottages showed their twenty-five years of hard, hard wear and tear.

But the dorms, being even older, were worse. I hadn't been on the scene but a few weeks when representatives from the State Health Department arrived for an inspection of the dormitories. Our dorms flunked the inspection. Were they to be closed? The boys moved out? Talk about a bombshell. Where could I find housing for some three hundred boys ranging in age from about eight to fourteen? This called for a trip to Lincoln to visit Governor James Exon, whom I considered a personal friend. I asked him to use his influence and give us a stay to repair the damage and make the dorms fit to pass inspection again. The project would top my priority list. Both of us could see the headlines: "Governor Evicts 300 Boys; Kids Living on Streets." Neither of us wanted that. As a matter of fact, the Governor was very compassionate. He understood our problems and wanted to help. He had a visit with his Health Department bloodhounds. I made some staff changes and the dormitories became a beehive of activity.

The facilities were one thing. A little soap and water, elbow grease and paint could repair them in short order. The boys' attitudes were quite another thing. My popularity in that little village called Boys Town took yet another dip. For a few years I had been riding a bicycle for exercise, one that was a gift of one of my parishioners at Christ the King parish. It was a fifteen-speed technological masterpiece that really flattened those Boys Town hills. Occasionally I'd pedal down the hill to the "Gaza Strip" area, but I soon learned to ride in friendlier territory around the chapel and grade school. Riding on Sudyka Circle on the Strip, or past the High School and Field House, was sure to spark a string of cat calls, Bronx cheers, and assorted raspberries. My Neilsen rating was at a low ebb in that section of town, so I got into the habit of turning my handlebars to the west.

At first mine was the only bicycle on campus. Bikes weren't

allowed for the boys but over a period of time I was able to rescind that rule. In the meantime, though, mine was stolen.

I rode over to the dining hall one evening where alumni were registering for the bicentennial convention. I arrived about 9:30 o'clock and parked my bike out front. Three Boys Town police officers — and this was before that department was organized and certified — were idling by the door. In jest I called them my "Keystone Kops." I asked them to watch my bike.

"Sure," they said.

I was in the building about fifteen or twenty minutes. When I stepped outside my bike was gone. Those three cops were still standing around. They had seen a guy ride off with it, but they had forgotten it belonged to the executive director.

We launched a massive manhunt for my "Huppmobile." About an hour later the culprit was located, along with the bicycle, which by this time had a badly bent front wheel, and my nameplate, which had been affixed to the frame, was missing.

The boy told the cops he'd removed the nameplate at a convenience store off campus and had thrown it in a trash barrel. The cops took him back to the trash barrel and he fished the plate out. Then he was brought to my residence. I was shown the evidence and was asked what should be done with the culprit.

"Nothing tonight," I said. "Bring him to my office at nine o'clock tomorrow morning." He was there on the dot.

"I must compliment you," I said. "You have excellent taste in bicycles. The one you stole is a beauty. Probably the first lesson you will learn at Boys Town is that actions have consequences. Actions determine the kind of consequences you will experience. Now, of all the two-wheelers in the world, you selected mine. From now on that bicycle is yours. But you are going to buy a new one for me."

"How can I do that?" he asked. "Bicycles are expensive and I don't have that kind of money."

"Your counselor will take the money out of your cottage fund and buy a replacement for me identical to the one you stole. Then your counselor will see to it that you work out the cost of that bike."

And so it was. That was one of my early experiences in trying to teach the boys that actions have consequences. When actions are bad, you have to live with the bad consequences, and when they are good you deserve recognition, sometimes compliments.

Later we allowed all the residents to have their own bicycles, if they wanted one and could afford it. All were registered. Mine carried Boys Town license number 1.

Here's another example of actions-consequences. This one wasn't nearly as serious as the bicycle theft, but I think it showed that some of the boys lacked a proper respect for the things we were providing them. This little story involved a breakfast. I went over to the High School Dining Hall one morning and stood in line with the rest. I was practically ignored. The lad in front of me took a stack of pancakes at least eight inches high. There must have been fifteen pancakes in that stack.

I assumed he was taking some for friends, but I noticed he went to an empty table and sat alone. I took my three hotcakes and sat opposite him.

"Boy, you must be hungry," I said. "What are you going to do with all those pancakes?"

"I'm going to eat them," he said, a look of uneasiness coming over his face. "I'm anxious to see how you do this," I said, having heard he intended to sail them.

He stuffed those pancakes in, chewing slower and slower and slower as the pile diminished.

"Nothing like starting the day with a good breakfast," I called as he waddled out the door. He headed straight for the clinic where he sacked out for the rest of the day.

While I was watching the boy down those pancakes I glanced around the dining hall. Nothing had escaped the boys' playfulness. Knives were stuck in the cork ceiling tiles, and somebody had egged Father Flanagan's portrait on the wall. Discipline was conspicuous by its total absence.

One of my embarrassing moments came when the Millard

School District wanted to purchase a large piece of property from our farm. I opposed the idea with the argument that the farm was part of our educational program, hence couldn't be parceled out. Imagine my chagrin to learn that at that time only one boy was working on the farm. That part of our educational program was corrected in a short time, but the damage was done. We eventually lost forty acres of the property, thanks to the power of eminent domain wielded by the Millard School District.

Matters weren't all that much better in the administration building either. Monsignor Wegner, who had succeeded Father Flanagan at a time when the Home's enrollment was much smaller and methods simpler, was too ill in his later days to shift priorities and modify his way of operating. By the time I arrived he was more or less running the place by remote control — out of his hip pocket.

According to the Booz, Allen & Hamilton report there were twenty-one functional areas reporting directly to the executive director. Twenty-one little kingdoms. None would communicate with the others; each wanted a hearing with the top boss. And, besides those twenty-one departments, another ten offices would go to Monsignor Wegner with special requests — usually money.

In my opinion this called for a major reorganization. The Booz, Allen & Hamilton report indicated that the number of departments should be reduced to seven or fewer. Ed Hewitt, my financial genius, and I, after much discussion on the matter, decided on the number five. This would eventually eliminate the little kingdoms, the fragmented areas, and would channel information and requests in an orderly fashion. This improvement was not viewed with overpowering approval. As a matter of fact, opposition to change came in a single voice blasting away at me like a tail gunner.

In the past, if a cottage counselor wanted a microwave oven, he went to Monsignor Wegner and Monsignor gave him a green light. If the baseball coach wanted a new batting cage, he went to Monsignor Wegner. If the math department wanted a new textbook, teachers went to Monsignor Wegner. That describes the system in vogue. By putting a rigid control on what had been a hit-and-miss raid on the treasury, the power and influence of thirty-one little kings was diminished hourly! How they howled. They immediately went to the press where a sympathetic ear was found.

These were the five departments Hewitt and I agreed on: athletics, music, education, cottages (youth care) and administration. At my staff meetings each Monday morning I would get my weekly transfusion of chin music and hot air. Eventually two more department heads were created — the Research Center and the Boys Town Institute. But since they were not located on campus, their deputy directors were not always involved in the Monday meetings.

Prior to my arrival here the Board of Directors met once a year, and as I mentioned in the previous chapter, I have never been able to locate a single copy of Board minutes of those meetings. That called for a change that was made at once; we began meeting quarterly and the Board elected a secretary who did what a secretary is supposed to do — record and keep careful and extensive minutes of Board meetings.

No systematic reporting of program or management information that would provide a review of progress (and problems) had ever been developed at the Home.

Individual departments would develop annual reports and other statistics but these existed largely because of the initiative of the unit head. Traditionally the director had been kept informed of development in various areas of the Home through personal contacts. More broadly, there had been only informal planning that seldom involved the Board except on major capital projects. So among my most ambitious management objectives was the adoption of a comprehensive budget and budgeting system for the Home. This huge task occasioned moaning and groaning that rattled down to the least boy on the campus. We needed a computer. Not even an operation like Christ the King Parish where I had been before could live efficiently without the methodology a computer could offer.

As for personnel records, you could put them in a shoe box. As the late Lyell Bremser, longtime broadcaster of Nebraska football would say, it was "every man, woman and child" for himself/herself when it came to salary. Sometimes two people with identical seniority assigned to the same job would be paid different salaries. How this had happened, or why, nobody knew — or seemed to care. Without financial yardsticks and without clear-cut organizational lines there was no responsibility, no accountability.

Orders would often get lost on the way from top administration to the boys. Over the years, everyone with the least bit of authority decided they needed an assistant, so an assistant was hired. Coordinators were the fashion. There were coordinators coordinating coordinators. We had right here in our midst the world's best, or worst, example of the pervasive growth of bureaucracy. When something went wrong — and it did, too often — it was an exercise in futility to try and pin responsibility on anyone.

Let me give an example that was funny — not funny Ha Ha, but funny strange. One day I stopped a boy on the sidewalk outside my office to visit with him about the way he was groomed.

"Who's your counselor?" I asked.

"What time of day?" he replied. "Morning, afternoon or evening?"

The kid was right. Counselors worked eight hour shifts and then went home. When something occurred that needed attention it had always happened on the night shift, or some other dark time.

It was absolutely imperative to bring some accountability to bear on our employees. Little support was forthcoming from a bunch of men who could have made my job much lighter. I'm speaking of both staff members and alumni living in the region. This latter was a formidable group that took it upon themselves to represent the nearly 13,000 boys who had lived here.

From the day of my arrival most of them opposed every move I made — staffers and alumni alike. They were afraid of change. "If it was good enough for us, it's good enough for the kids today," was their response.

"We never did it that way," they'd say. "It's been a good program for fifty years and now you come along and ruin our home." I had an answer for them.

"You people remind me of the housewife who always cut off the end of the pork roast before putting it in the oven. When asked why she did that, she replied: 'My mother always did.'"

"When the mother was asked why she cut off the end of the pork roast before putting it in her oven, she replied, 'That's what my mother always did.' When the grandmother was asked her reason for cutting off the end of the roast she said, 'My roaster was too small for the whole roast.'"

In the beginning I had told Archbishop Sheehan I would consider a two-year term with an option for two more, but in my own mind I often toyed with the idea of a bail out. Many were the times I felt like it; time after time I'd ask myself, "What am I doing here? Why must I continue with this?" About the time my cup of dissatisfaction would runneth over, some irritant would push my panic button. That charged my chemistry of combat and I'd be good for another six months.

There were, I must add here, two people who in very different ways contributed to my maintaining some measure of sanity through it all.

The first was R.C. "Jim" Brown whose ideas and advice helped me realize that perhaps there could be a dim light at the end of this long, dark tunnel. He was an executive in the New York office of Bozell & Jacobs, an Omaha-based advertising and public relations firm that had served Boys Town Board members for decades.

Jim came to Omaha about once a month to sit in on our brain-storming sessions. He was solid oak in his support of what I was trying to accomplish — full of savvy and common sense, and easy to work with. He would cut to the heart of any problem regarding our tarnished image while the rest of us floundered around. When he spoke, I always listened — and learned.

The other person at quite the opposite end of the public relations spectrum was the keeper of my residence, Martha Promes. She is to this day, at the age of 84, as handy with a broom and hoe as she is with a washer and drier. It's difficult to choose a menu and cook for only one, but anyone can tell that I haven't missed many meals. My residence, adjacent to Dowd Memorial Chapel, was a quiet and comfortable retreat after my fourteen to sixteen-hour days on the job. This was a commodity in extremely short supply, but it was always so, thanks in great part to the housekeeper who came along from the rectory in Christ the King Parish. She is truly a member of a vanishing breed.

But aside from those two, in my early days it was me against the world as defined by the Boys Town campus.

My security blanket was the Booz, Allen & Hamilton report, which I felt would put us on the right track. In addition, I had the complete support of the Board. Its members were in a state of mild panic after the Sun Newspaper's report and with few exceptions my suggestions received endorsement.

The Booz, Allen & Hamilton file became my bible. It harped constantly on the importance of quality care, quality care, quality care. But in my mind I wondered how to develop quality care in a dormitory setting when boys now brought problems the Home had never experienced before? It seemed to me that the recent advent of drugs, student rebellions, parental rejections galore, divorce, and the general erosion of the family called for a more personalized approach to the boys than institutional care could offer.

I could see, from my own boyhood, how a family environment was the best school for learning social skills and family living techniques, values that were not taught in the classroom.

My "bible" told me to cut the enrollment of 787. Reducing the number was the only way to accomplish what the Booz, Allen & Hamilton report called for. Living quarters for the boys at the

Home could accommodate about 400 under the proposed program, the report stated.

Our aim to begin with was something less than the optimum 400. This number could be realized in a comparatively short time, simply by attrition. In the spring of 1974, 122 boys were graduated at which time admissions were closed.

Then, during one of my regular Friday convocations in the Music Hall, I told the boys, "I'm looking for ways to reduce our enrollment numbers and you are going to help me do it."

"I know you are because the next boys who run away are advised to keep running. There will be no return. Whether you will be here or not when the changes are completed is a decision each of you must make for himself. The federal highway, a block or so from this Hall, runs all the way to the East coast and to the West coast and my advice to you is that if you start running, don't stop until you strike water.

"Once you hit the road, good bye. There will be no reentry."

Well, as usual, there were always the adventurous few who would test the system. Sure enough, the next morning about fifty boys were gone. The staff was instructed to report the names of the wanderers to my office. First of all we contacted the agencies or courts responsible for their being here. If the boys returned to the Home we sheltered them temporarily until we could return them to their point of origin. The prime requirement on the part of the boys has always been that they must want to be here, and not on their terms, but in line with the rules of the Home. When a boy ran away he was voting with his feet to be elsewhere. That administrative move effected a reduction in enrollment by almost fifty in one day. Adjustments were made when there was no responsible agency or court involved, because naturally we didn't just dump boys on the streets of Omaha.

Besides overcrowding, Booz, Allen & Hamilton listed other problems that needed to be addressed:

* Lack of a systematic follow-up program for Boys Town graduates

* Failure to consider programs for girls
* Lack of clear job descriptions, and in-service training for employees.

And there were others.

Not all was disappointment during my first months on the job. Little by little progress was being made, mostly in administrative areas. For instance, a catering firm, ARA, was hired to replace the existing food service arrangements for staff and boys. This eliminated a great amount of overtime pay. A budget was prepared, a seminar for youth care management personnel was held, and a training program for counselors and case workers was set up.

Within a year the number of boys dwindled from the 787 on record the day I came on October 11, 1973 to 450. This was seen by my many armchair generals around the place and elsewhere not as a sign of success, but as an indication of the deterioration of the Home. What these people failed to realize is that many things are relative. For example, one night I went bowling and came the closest to a 300 I've every bowled. I hit 125.

Because of the reduced number of boys in high school we made a formal request to the Nebraska High School Athletic Association to be dropped from Class A competition in sports to Class B. That really stung many of the alumni who were still living in the "age of the giants" when the Boys Town Cowboys were racking up state championships in one sport or another. But those were memories of another day. Winning seasons had ceased in the early 1960's. My comment: "From now on we may be Class B competitors in athletics but we will be Double A in child welfare."

Was I whistling in the dark?

A frequent question was: Why doesn't Boys Town have more boys?

As I have already mentioned, the youth of the early 1970's required more than a place to live, good food to eat, a school to educate them, and activities to keep them occupied in their free time. Boys Town for some sixty years was a recognized international leader in providing for these needs of indigent lads. But society was changing, and to remain at the cutting edge of youth care a more sophisticated program was called for. Emotional and psychological problems had entered the picture, thanks to the drug culture.

It was my assignment to address these new dimensions. It seemed to me Father Flanagan's idea of putting a boy in a family surrounding was an idea whose time had finally come.

Remember, Father Flanagan had scotched the idea of adding more dormitories in the 1940's in favor of building the twenty-five cottages. Building materials were hard to come by and construction took longer than anticipated. Before Father Flanagan could develop his program of family living he died, and his dream was laid to rest along with his remains.

Now, perhaps, it was time to resurrect the idea of a town of families and make Father Flanagan's dream a reality.

I was determined to move in that direction! It was no great feat on my part to do so. As I said in my Foreword, we see far when we stand on the shoulders of giants. It was the program innovator, Father Flanagan, complemented by the administrative executive, Monsignor Wegner, who provided the ladder for me to climb.

The time had come for me to climb.

CHAPTER **Three**

FATHER FLANAGAN made many memorable remarks during his lifetime, but probably none reflected the public's perception of Boys Town as eloquently as this one: "There is no such thing as a bad boy."

What most people who quote this statement don't realize is those words are taken out of context.

What he actually said, with one deep breath and in one sentence, was: "I have often thought, providing we give him the proper leisure time program, so that he will not have idle moments to get into mischief, my statement will ring true: There is no such thing as a bad boy."

You can hear Father Flanagan's recorded voice saying those words in an exhibit in the Boys Town Hall of History.

The previous chapter contains frequent references to the "Gaza Strip" and the destruction and chaos created by some of the boys. At first glance, that sort of behavior would appear to knock into a cocked hat Father Flanagan's belief that there is no such thing as a bad boy.

But Father Flanagan understood that boys had to have proper guidance and proper care; that their idle time should be filled with useful activities. And as times changed after Father Flanagan's death, so did the kind of resident admitted to Boys Town. The new resident was a "social orphan," not the conventional fatherless and motherless street waif Father Flanagan gathered under his wings.

Father Flanagan thought that the so-called "bad boy" is only a good boy reacting to a bad environment. Move that boy into a healthy and wholesome environment and he has a fighting chance. Our "Family Concept" does that for the modern troubled youth. It makes transition back into the real world after graduation from high school less difficult.

The family is the best health, education and welfare system in the world, but most Boys Town residents lacked the advantages of a normal family life. With few exceptions, youths who now were coming to Boys Town had some kind of behavior problem. For one reason or another their behavior and attitudes were not what they should be and it was the Home's task to improve both.

When a lad came to Boys Town it was our responsibility to educate and train him — correct his irresponsible behavior, teach him personal accountability and send him back into society where he could begin giving a good account of himself and make a creditable contribution to the community where he lived.

But how were we to do this? Mark Twain once said, in jest of course, that when a boy reaches the age of twelve you feel like putting him in a barrel, sealing the lid and feeding him through a knothole. When he turns sixteen, plug up the knothole.

Seriously, what he was describing was how turbulent are the years of an adolescent. Generally, you might say, that if a lad has enough spunk to get into trouble, he has a good head on his shoulders. It's surprising how many are real sharpies. To develop their talents and direct their energy into meaningful channels is our eternal challenge.

The Booz, Allen & Hamilton report mirrored the view of a number of federal agencies and experts. In an effort to deal realistically with youths who have a number of complex problems it is necessary to encourage the development of programs that represent the least restrictive type of care. Not all troubled youths need a lockup facility. Various types of problems call for various kinds and length of treatment. It is not practical nor desirable to separate a troubled youngster from society any longer than necessary.

Creating a family environment for the boys seemed logical to me. We would do this at Boys Town and call it the Family Concept.

In my early days on the job I neglected taking the kind of notes I could use today. I was too busy in what I called "putting out brush fires." While studying the voluminous Booz, Allen & Hamilton report, which occupied a lion's share of my time, it occurred to me that boys at Boys Town had for the most part never had the opportunity to learn and enjoy the privilege of a normal family life. What are the social skills, the family living techniques that are generally not taught in the classroom but are learned at the hands of loving and caring parents?

The feeling of belonging, one of the essential elements of self-worth, is rooted in the family. In a home parents show their love for their children and convince them of their importance when they spend time with them. A good way to encourage feelings of self-worth is for parents to praise a child when he does something well, or without being asked. Such ordinary things like picking up litter in and around the yard, treating things in the home with care, and being on time for meals. "Catch them doing good" and noting it is far more important in the long run than catching them involved in some kind of mischief.

Armed with a clipboard which became my constant companion, I began jotting down the practical lessons I had learned at home until I went away to college. Being the oldest of nine children, my experiences were too numerous to count at this time. Dormitory life, as I viewed it at Boys Town, or anywhere else for that matter, could no longer be the solution for boys who came to Boys Town with the bag of problems society was now handing them.

One of my early moves was certain to raise a howl from most of the boys. The day of the clique was over, and cliques — or perhaps to put it in more scientific language, peer groups — were common. Living with peers was the rule. Football players lived together; choir members lived together, and most "un-family-like" of all were the groupings by age. While members of a fam'ly vary in age, in our dormitory units and cottages all boys in each unit were of similar age. Grade school and high school youngsters were not living together in any housing unit.

Breaking up the cliques and assigning an age and ethnic mix to each dorm unit and cottage was the goal. This would provide the basis for a family setting. An early note on my clipboard read: "Train the older kids to teach and share with the younger ones like brothers do in a family."

Each unit then would require a trained married couple to take charge, a couple who would live full time in a cottage. No more eight-hour-a-day counselors coming and going. Recruiting those married couples and giving them very basic instructions to begin with would enjoy the highest priority before a family unit could be set up. I surveyed the staff, and discovered only three of the current married counselors and their wives who were willing to cast their fortunes with the new venture. These three couples and I got together and began forming a program for Family Teachers. These couples were Ron and Annette Herron, Jay and Pat Murphy, and Mike and Betty Pyykola. Soon to join these pioneers were John and Cynthia Barksdale.

From the very beginning Father Flanagan was totally color blind when it came to boys he accepted. The only racial problems he ever encountered were occasioned by groups in society when his choir or athletic teams were on the road. Here again he was years ahead of his time and his legacy in that regard would be the lifeblood of the Home. So, an age and ethnic mix in every family group on campus only carried on the tradition.

Other problems, however, were never in short supply. One major obstacle reared its head even while I was contemplating what we should do and how we should do it. This problem came with the person I more or less inherited to work with me in youth care, a man by the name of Herbert Sigurdson. Sigurdson had been recommended for the job of Deputy Director of Youth Care by the Technical Assistance Committee, which had conducted a search before my arrival at Boys Town and had committed the job to one Herb Sigurdson. He would report in January of 1974, a complete stranger to me since I had not been privy to his resumé and interview.

Sigurdson was a congenial, likable and accommodating person. Tall, very presentable and in his late thirties or early forties, his manner was easy and he tried his best to work with me. He tried to understand my strategic plan and I made allowances for his inability to read the ideas churning in my mind. He was not able to overcome the drag of two serious drawbacks: his background and a man named Michael Casey.

First, his background. Sigurdson came to Boys Town from a job at the Soledad, California, prison. He knew prisons and prisoners, and all of his experience naturally led him to view Boys Town as a mini-prison, albeit one without bars and fences but nevertheless a prison; and to treat all the boys like junior delinquents.

Members of the committee, one of whom was an official with the Federal Bureau of Prisons in Washington, D.C., thought that since the boys were, in many instances, wards of the court, juvenile delinquents, a person with a prison background would be best; that prison techniques and procedures would fit in pretty well in what they seemed to think was a traditional reform school.

Sigurdson's second major problem was Mike Casey. Whereas Sigurdson knew prisons from outside the bars, Casey's familiarity with prisons came from behind the bars at the California Institute for Men, Chino, California, where he had served time. Sigurdson and Casey knew each other from opposite sides of prison walls in California, and when Sigurdson advertised nationally for an administrative assistant, Casey responded — on the back of a restaurant place mat. It may qualify as one of the weirdest job resumés on record but it cut the mustard. It was unconventional and it was attention- getting. So was Casey, as it turned out.

Meantime, while I was trying to digest the lengthy Booz, Allen & Hamilton report and decide how to reconcile it with my goal of family life for the boys, my deputy and his assistant in

Youth Care were working at cross purposes. To my chagrin, I
soon learned that at least Casey was.

For some time I was never quite sure what Casey was up to
other than creating chaos and bringing attention to himself.

Sigurdson assumed, and rather innocently so, that he was
hired to offer a better institutional care for the boys — to
perpetuate a restrictive atmosphere in a dormitory-like setting. It
soon became evident that he certainly was not the person to carry
out my ideas. He expressed a willingness to change, but that
would mean training him to do an about-face in leadership while I
was making up my own mind about how to install a family living
environment. He might have been able to grow in the job, but all
along he was saddled with Casey's hare-brained schemes. Sigurdson even brought in a new chief of police, but the new chief,
like Casey, did not fit the mold required for the task. Schooled in a
tough California community, the new chief, John Newton, was too
much law-and-order for our purposes.

Like Sigurdson, he was really a misplaced person at Boys
Town, as were four or five others he had brought in. Sigurdson
knew his penal work well, and he was willing to help me reach my
goals, but he had not hired the right people and he was not able to
convince them to share either his efforts or his workload.

Sigurdson had arrived at Boys Town on January 15, 1974 and
resigned the following September, returning to his former employment in California. It was an amicable parting of the ways; we
both realized almost from the start that the relationship had little
chance of success. Mike Casey's separation came a month
earlier. But whereas Sigurdson's departure cleared the way for
progress toward a family life environment, Casey's departure left
a wake of rubble.

Casey was a disarmingly charming person at first blush. He
was good looking and glib — one of the smoothest talkers I have
ever met, always pleasant and respectful to me. He loved to call
me "boss," and he quickly gave himself a title: "Director of
Special Projects." As I look back, I must say that was an accurate
description of his activities. Trouble was, what was "special" to

him usually turned out to be salty for those of us who would wear out our erasers. He liked to say, "Boss, I'm a catalyst for change at Boys Town."

It was hard to argue with that. He changed things alright, but most of his changes did nothing but create confusion. He had no game plan other than to create chaos. He acted like he knew what he was doing, but if he did his plan never surfaced.

He would create a situation and then try to manipulate people to make the situation work. Casey, in my opinion, never showed his full hand. He intended to dismantle the current system and then put it back together in his own image, whatever that was. He never lasted long enough to reveal his reconstruction secrets.

Casey had been here about a month when one afternoon at four o'clock I glanced out of my office window and saw boys standing out on Highway 6 on the north edge of the campus, thumbing their way downtown. The scene resembled a picket fence. You would have thought all 700-plus boys were leaving town like knights of the road. It took some time to find Casey and inquire what in the name of common sense was going on.

"Well, boss, you're talking about the family concept, and to me a family concept means an open campus," he said. "Members of any family are not restricted to their homes' back yard. So I just opened the campus at four o'clock and told everybody to be back by eleven tonight."

That was my introduction to "catalyst Casey." I don't recall how many boys failed to return that night or the next day, but some never returned. Talk about a permissive society! From an institutional atmosphere on the one hand we now had no discipline or control at all. Casey's philosophy seemed to be, "Destroy everything and then pick up the pieces and build from scratch." When on the next day I cancelled any future open campus, you can well imagine what happened to my popularity among the boys.

So much for Mike's March project. We are now in the month of May when I heard that everyone on campus was "invited to be the guest of the Mayor of Kansas City for the second weekend in May — staff and boys alike." I asked Sigurdson, "What is this rumor all about?

"Casey is making the arrangements," he said.

"That's like sending a demolition crew to Kansas City," I replied in utter disbelief. I phoned the Kansas City mayor's office and talked to the mayor's office manager. "I understand we're to be the weekend guests of the mayor in three weeks," I said. "Tell me more about this."

"Well," she said, "I've been able to arrange for only three hundred tickets to the Royals baseball game that weekend and I'm having trouble getting any more."

"Where will we be staying?" I asked.

"I have no idea," she said.

"Let me talk with the mayor."

"He's out of the country and won't be back until the first of June."

I thanked her with a promise to get back to her before the end of the day.

Casey had lined up enough buses to take everybody to Kansas City and to return in two nights and two days, but had not yet booked hotel space for the trip. All of this without any knowledge of it on my part. I summoned Casey and without ceremony ordered the trip cancelled. My popularity index took another dive.

While all this was going on Casey opened what he called an "intensive care center" in what had been the Orientation Center. This was an idea he borrowed from hospitals. Rather than terminate a bad actor, or send him to a psycho ward, Casey devised a scheme to "handle him in-house," as he said. It sounded good, he thought, but actually he was putting boys in isolation so he could deal with them using prison methods which he knew very well. When I questioned him he justified it all by saying we could save psychiatric and hospital fees.

How he would convince a boy so confined to "say uncle" as he said, was another matter, one he hadn't yet had time to work out.

In fact, he had no plan for these boys at all. Apparently he thought that being in isolation alone would dissipate a boy's desire to behave irrationally. Suffice it to say that Casey's experiment to circumvent professional treatment ended promptly by executive order.

Within a month's time Casey's next move came to light. He felt that he could convince Hollywood movie-makers that it was time for another "Boys Town" movie, this time about our bad actors. About that time a number of files dealing with a few of our trouble-makers disappeared from the locked cabinets in the administration building.

These files contained some highly confidential material and their disappearance could have placed us in jeopardy. Fortunately, nothing came of this rifling of the files, here or in Hollywood, and ultimately most of them were returned. Casey had to go. But before the end I called him in for a chat.

"I understand you're making book on which week I'm going to leave Boys Town," I said.

"Well, boss, there's a lot of unhappiness and dissatisfaction out there," he said. "Everybody is wondering when you're going to throw in the towel."

"Mike," I said, "I'd like to have a piece of that action."

He declined to discuss the matter further and the subject was dropped with a thud.

Since Sigurdson had hired Casey, it was his privilege to give him his last check. Sigurdson vacillated for a week or ten days and I could see that he did not have the courage to terminate his friend Casey.

Without further delay I summoned Casey to my office again and asked him whether he wanted to resign or be fired. As was his custom, he would not give a categorical answer. It was then that I set a deadline for receiving his decision. "Four o'clock this afternoon," I said.

A few minutes before the witching hour he walked into my office as pleasant as ever with a letter that explained how his work was completed and that it was time for him to leave.

I thanked him and commented favorably about the great possibilities in his future.

"You haven't heard the end of me," he said without a smile.

"I can believe that," I said. "I can see great things for you in the future."

"That ain't what I mean, boss," he snarled and out the door he went.

I soon learned what he meant when he said I hadn't heard the last of him. Although Sigurdson returned to California, Casey stayed around Omaha for a while. He had found a willing ear on the editorial staff of the Omaha World-Herald and he continued to feed innuendo and rumors to a reporter, bringing more unfavorable publicity to Boys Town and to our efforts to modernize our youth care program.

The World-Herald, which had jumped onto the "Bash Boys Town" bandwagon in the wake of the Sun Newspapers Pulitzer Prize-winning reports, said in an editorial: ". . . the new approach (Family Concept) at Boys Town is too permissive . . . there is reason to wonder whether the change is toward permissiveness or toward more personal responsibility."

The editorial writer needn't have wondered; our aim always was toward more personal responsibility. True, we weren't going to accomplish that aim with our present personnel, but a solution to that problem was on the way. The imminent departure of Casey and Sigurdson was an important step in that direction.

Casey left August 30, 1974, and Sigurdson departed less than a month later, which meant Boys Town had to start over again finding a Deputy Director of Youth Care. But this time at least I would be hiring my own person, not somebody fobbed off on me by a committee that knew little or nothing about the heart of Boys Town.

But before a search could be organized it became obvious that two of my top assistants, both members of the clergy, were maneuvering and scheming on ways to discredit me so that one of them could be appointed executive director. They hardly trusted each other it seems, so they tape-recorded their plans. After one of them was terminated very unceremoniously some of those tapes were unintentionally left on a window sill behind the curtains. These tapes were discovered by a cleanup man who gave them to me. When the other conspirator learned of the gross negligence he resigned.

Then there was the matter of telephones. The only phones on the campus were those in the administrative offices. At one of the weekly meetings with the boys in the Music Hall, in order to get their attention, I announced we were going to install telephones in the cottages.

"How soon?" came like an echo.

"Well," I said, tongue in cheek, "as soon as the phone company can stock enough pay phones. This will take time."

"Pay phones?" they shouted with a question in their voices and a blare of boos, moans and groans.

"Sure," I said, "Every phone is a pay phone. In the parish where I was before coming to Boys Town some of the homes had as many as three phones. All of them are pay phones, not the coin operated ones, but the kind that bill you once a month." That marked the rumbling end of that convocation, but each cottage did eventually get its pay phone.

It was also about this time the boys were allowed to have good old American coin of the realm. Previously they had been issued scrip to spend at the commissary. When the boys earned money they deserved to be paid in real money. After all, that is what they would be using after they left Boys Town.

Meanwhile, we moved ahead with the Family Concept, the idea the World-Herald viewed with alarm and plotters thought would bring me down.

It was a team effort of a small number of staffers with solid support of a majority of the Board. Among the very staunch believers on the Board were Leo Daly, the architect; A.F. Jacobson, president of Northwestern Bell Telephone Company and J.D. Anderson, president of Guarantee Mutual Insurance Company. All three were opinion makers in the Omaha community, with tremendous influence among other movers and shakers. And they backed our efforts one hundred percent.

A fourth member of the Board, Dr. Claude Organ, challenged me often at Board meetings but always over an honest difference of opinion. Our relationship went way back to my CYO days when he was captain of the first black team to participate in our city-wide basketball program. He later made his way through undergraduate school and medical college and was now chief of surgery at the Creighton University School of Medicine and St. Joseph Hospital.

Board support was absolutely necessary as I began cutting back the surplus staff. In one instance in the grade school there were five teachers for five students. Even with our concentrated educational program that was a bit over-staffed. Throughout the system it was a matter of being over-staffed in quantity and understaffed in quality. In youth care, competence is more important at the youth level than at the administrative level. There were too many people on the payroll who were not trained to fill the positions for which they were being paid.

Twenty teachers were let go because of the reduction in the number of boys. There seemed to be no plan in the matter of balancing the number of admissions of the grade school and high school boys. Upon my arrival the grade school enrollment was so low that some in the Education Department insisted on closing Wegner School. This, of course, was unconscionable for two reasons: one, the number of grade school boys in society who needed Boys Town; and two, the need for boys of those ages to integrate cottages under the Family Concept.

Once a strategic plan for admissions was agreed upon by all concerned, we next zeroed in on developing details of the Family Concept. Counselors who were working in pairs on eight-hour shifts in the cottages would be replaced by a trained married couple who would live-in around the clock. This would solve the responsibility problem. That is to say, when six counselors or more had shift duty in a cottage it was not easy to find one person to admit accountability for anything that went wrong. It was all reminiscent of one of my dad's comments: "When you send one boy to do a job you get a job done! When you send two on the same job you get half of a job done; and when you send three, forget it. You should have gone yourself."

It was my idea that the trained married couples be called Family Teachers because they were to teach family living skills and techniques along with social skills in the home just as school teachers teach academics and discipline in the classrooms. This ran in opposition to some staff members who championed the title "house parents," a designation familiar in other youth care circles. However, Family Teachers described better the role I had for them in our new program. They would not only teach but train the youth under their care in Judeo-Christian values that escape the regular classroom.

While the program itself was being developed, remodeling the cottages to adapt to family type living got under way. Twenty-five cottages, on what I referred to as the "Gaza Strip," were repaired one at a time. As each was finished Family Teachers moved in with no more than ten boys of an age and ethnic mix. Cost of the renovation was $1,436,000.

Thus dormitory living which had served the boys so well for fifty-six years came to an end. In addition, sixteen new cottages, located in the central part of the campus, were in the process of being completed. They were being built at the Board-approved cost of $6,227,450. Each of the four old dormitories had housed four units. Now that the sixteen new cottages were being readied for occupancy, dormitory living was history. Because of their rundown condition and the neglect of maintenance, an extensive renovation was in order before the dorms could be used again.

Converting the entire campus to the Boys Town Model of Family Concept began in late 1974, as is described later, and the transition was completed in 1975. The program's future gave all sorts of promise, although it was in need of much fine tuning. It was the kind of program that did not depend on a charismatic leader. It seemed to be the kind that could be taught. Many of the internal problems could be traced to staff members who had been retained and given new positions rather than sending them job hunting. Attitudinal adjustments came hard for some, and their feelings were projected, too often on purpose, to the boys. But time heals many things.

Ready and willing to share the good thing we had, we were anxious to set up a pilot program and test our ambitions. This meant purchasing a residence somewhere off campus in an area that could be zoned for a group home. One was located on California Street not far from Father Flanagan's original 1917 home. However, when the neighbors heard about our plans a howl arose.

"We don't want you and your bad boys in our back yard," they said.

I asked for a meeting with the neighbors and was invited to attend one. My appearance before the group was an exercise in total futility. We met in the huge living room of one of the residences. Before long I was backed up against the fireplace and for once wished I had the chimney ability of Santa Claus. I was lucky to escape with any self-esteem.

Boys Town's local reputation at this time had to reach up to touch bottom. I was not about to go before the City Council with a request for re-zoning and incur further wrath of these protesters. It was Father Flanagan who had tasted rejection of this kind that occasioned his moving his boys to Overlook Farm. He decided that it would not be wise for Boys Town to be where it could not find a welcome mat. A higher authority seemed to cooperate and very shortly a three-story frame house on Davenport Street, already zoned for a program like ours, was located. That house and another nearby became the core of our off-campus Family Concept pilot program. Very special care was taken to select boys to live in these residences. Our reputation in Omaha was at stake as well as our plans for future expansion.

We explained to the public on a number of occasions that if a boy in those residences turned out to be a bad actor he would be removed and replaced with another. This was a better promise than any other new neighbor might make. In the course of our pilot program only two boys earned a return trip to the Home.

It needs to be noted here that off-campus homes had the advantage of the Home's residential program but not its highly specialized educational program. For this reason boys who needed special tutoring, especially in reading, were not placed in the pilot program. Boys in the pilot program attended neighborhood schools. Family Teachers developed a working relationship with teachers in those schools, grade and high, as any good parent does. The fact that both Family Teachers were on call if a school problem required their assistance was well-received by the school authorities. Family Teachers were sometimes closer to the classroom teachers than many other parents were.

Prior to the establishment of the Family Concept a serious rivalry existed between staff members in the Education Department and youth care. It has been said that at times there was little or no meaningful communication between the two. Father Flanagan himself expressed concern about this situation. But these two kingdoms were brought together when the Family Concept was introduced. School teachers were required to take the Family Teachers Training Course so that the right hand always knew what the left was doing and would cooperate in this matter of training the boys.

Family Teachers complemented school teachers and vice versa. The goal early on was to give the Family Teacher Training Course to every employee on the campus who would be working with boys.

The old saying about "everybody singing out of the same hymn book" was to effect and maintain an air of consistency throughout the Home. A member of the State Welfare Department once said, after making an official visit to the Home, "many a community in the country would love to have the close relationship between school staff and parents that exists at Boys Town today." A boy leaves his cottage in time to report for class at 8:00 a.m. If by 8:15 he does not arrive the school teacher calls the lad's Family Teachers who at once set out to find him. When the wandering sheep is located his Family Teachers visit briefly with him. If he agrees to stay in school he is returned immediately to his class.

Family Teachers and his classroom teacher then arrange for a meeting later the same day where they work together in solving the youth's problem if it has to do with the school. It is not unusual to find that the boy is only testing the system. At any rate, corrective action is swift because it has always been my opinion that delayed justice runs the risk of being no justice at all.

Now, if the lad refuses to return to the classroom the Family Teachers have an opportunity to test the skills they were exposed to in the Family Teacher Courses they took.

As for the boys in the pilot program off campus, we didn't want them to feel they weren't a part of the Boys Town family, so we would transport them out to the campus for all kinds of activities — athletic events, meetings, programs, church services. Otherwise the houses were run the same way I intended for the ultimate Family Teacher program to be run, with family conferences after supper, chores, shopping trips, homework — everything.

I sometimes felt these kids had a better start on returning to real life in society than the kids on campus did, because they were living in a normal social neighborhood. Some of the lessons we learned in these off-campus houses later became the framework of our program of off-campus affiliated homes in other cities, a program described in Chapter 6.

The first remodeled cottage on campus became available in November 1974 and the day after Thanksgiving Ron and Annette Herron moved back to the campus, down on the "Gaza Strip," and on December 18 we brought in the boys. They spent Christmas together in what was to become the first home for children in the country geared to the new concept of youth care.

But time was against us; we had to move as quickly as possible to convert the rest of the campus to the Family Teacher program. We couldn't be successful with two separate programs

— the new and the old — trying to co-exist in the same place at the same time.

For instance, if a nation were to change its traffic rules from driving on the right side of the road to driving on the left, the change would have to be made all at once, all over the country. You couldn't have some motorists going one way and other motorists going another. It was the same with our change in programs.

So here I was as 1974 came to a close, laying my credibility on the line with a program that had no director. I had to find a youth care expert who saw eye to eye with me, and I had to find him soon — before my critics ruined Boys Town in their eagerness to run me off the premises.

CHAPTER **Four**

BOYS TOWN spent a lot of money on "Help Wanted" ads following the resignation of Herb Sigurdson as Deputy Director of Youth Care. His early replacement was critical as was filling the position of Deputy Director for our new Research Center. We conducted nationwide searches for both. Scores of applications were received with most seeking the Research Center position.

A team of our talented people screened the applications for both jobs, seeking candidates who could fulfill the recommendations as outlined in the Booz, Allen & Hamilton report. Those recommendations were quite specific for the Research Center director but less so for the Youth Care director. Finally, after several weeks of reviewing the applications the screening team turned over to me the names of three selected applicants for each job.

I sat down one night with the resumés, went over them carefully, and to my dismay I was unable to find anybody in the Youth Care group who offered anything other than "more of the same." That is to say, all were experienced in institutional type care.

By telephone I visited with the Youth Care applicants but found each one unimpressed with my ideas. The more I talked to these candidates the more I became convinced that we had not found what I wanted in a director of Youth Care.

There was, however, one resumé that intrigued me. Trouble

is, this person applied for the Research Center position. His name was Elery L. Phillips, 33, an assistant professor in the Department of Human Development at Kansas University in Lawrence. He held a doctorate in Human Development. His academic credentials were impressive, but then so were those of all the other applicants.

Dr. Phillips, or Lonnie, as he preferred to be called, wrote in his resumé that he and his wife operated what they called "Achievement Place" near the KU campus. They had five or six youngsters in their home where they applied some of the techniques that I envisioned for the Family Teacher method of operation here at Boys Town.

I was excited over the fact that his ideas seemed to dovetail with mine, so the next afternoon I phoned him. We had a long talk about his experience. His interest peaked when I explained to him that perhaps his research could continue in fifty cottages here rather than in the one he had in Kansas. His original reluctance to consider the Youth Care position had to do with his disenchantment with traditional institutional type care. I invited him to come for a visit so we could discuss this surprising turn of events.

He came the next day. We exchanged ideas, and the fact he would not be dealing here with a bureaucracy that would oppose the thrust of the program further sparked his curiosity. He hesitated when he realized that here he would be working with high school students also, because his experience so far was limited to the grade school level. My previous experience had included working with high school students so the combination could be a winning team, I told him.

To my way of thinking, Phillips was by far the best candidate for Deputy Director of Youth Care. After a very exhaustive afternoon of discussion, a meeting of minds was accomplished and on the basis of a handshake, Phillips returned to Lawrence, where he was under contract with Kansas University. In May, 1975 he reported for duty at Boys Town, bringing with him the nucleus of a staff to operate his/our program of youth care, the Family Concept. Daily he and I spent hours talking, comparing-notes, and planning. We did not always agree but were always able to move ahead without delay.

He was an able organizer, an excellent manager who knew how to delegate. Responsibility was his middle name. I often heckled him over the jargon his social development people used. This usually ended in a learning experience for both of us.

One of our critical discussions in the very beginning was over the technique of behavior modification. He was "tainted" by his detractors as a behavior mod agent — Pavlov's dog theory of training: that a dog would respond to the carrot and stick method of training without knowing why, and "this shouldn't happen to a human being at Boys Town," they said.

I was being tarred with the same brush because there were some things about behavior mod that I thought merited attention. My critics failed to accept the fact that there is always something good about everything. Or, to put it as the old buccaneer did, "You can't fry my pancakes so thin but that they don't have two sides." We were not about to let our critics get away with the charge that we were teaching our boys only rote-like methods. The boys were expected to behave well; but they also were given to understand the reasons for proper behavior.

"Instead of teaching values," I said, "we need to teach virtues."

"What's the difference?" Phillips asked.

"I'll tell you. Values are objective. Virtues are subjective. A virtue is a habit of doing something with a good motive. The Pavlov's dog affair is too mechanical, objective. Behavior mod alone is surface-oriented. We need something deeper than that. Something that will stick. Teaching a boy how to do something without teaching him why is not holistic," I argued.

I told him a favorite story of mine. When I was a lad on the farm my dad would tell me to do something. I'd often ask why, thinking I could delay going to work. He would say, "I don't have time to explain right now, but when I have time later I will explain. As for now, let's just do it." I'd perform the chore and seldom later ask my father to explain because the question was just a cop-out on my part.

I explained to Lonnie that, as I understood it, the traditional approach to behavior is an attempt to change a person's attitude by explaining why a thing should be done with the hope that good behavior will result. The behavioral approach is an attempt to change his behavior by explaining how to do a thing correctly with the hope his attitude will change. My objective was to develop what we might call the Boys Town Model, a blend of the two, because I thought there was a place for both in the education and training of youth. We spent hours discussing this.

I also pointed out to him that Boys Town was an institution built on Judeo-Christian principles and not simply a behavior mod school. There was never a disagreement on the importance of religion in the life of a boy. Phillips always deferred to me in that matter and was most cooperative in implementing the program with religious teaching and training. He was still searching for the proper way to raise homeless and troubled children, which is why he had applied for the research position. He was pleased beyond measure to see the end of institution type care and to find himself on the cutting-edge of youth care evolution — as radio talk show host Rush Limbaugh would say.

The one area where we agreed one hundred percent was in the important role of Family Teachers. The program would sink or swim with them. They would make the difference between a mediocre program, which we already had in place, and the quality program that was our goal. These married couples needed to be highly trained because every couple in every cottage needed to be going consistently in the same direction. These would be the most critical members of our Youth Care staff.

So Lonnie and I began the laborious task of working out details of how to accomplish our goals. What would the Family Teachers teach? Some things must be delegated, as time went on, to the older boys of the family who in turn would teach the younger ones. A manual, detailing "the how, what, and why to teach Family Teachers" was to be followed with another manual that would outline the how, what, and why to train boys in the basics of acceptable behaviors. Role playing and motivating were to play a most important part in all phases of the Family Teachers' program. "Do as I do" was to be their unfailing motto.

As was mentioned in a previous chapter, our first Family Teacher couple moved into a cottage the day after Thanksgiving, 1974, and the boys were moved in a couple of weeks before Christmas. Since Phillips didn't join us until the following May, we had moved ahead on our own, thanks to the first three couples. They had assisted in drawing up the first guidelines they were to live by, and they were anxious to grow with the program. They were real pioneers in the field of the Family Concept without ever receiving the credit they deserved. It was far from easy for them, but it was enjoyable because they had a part in a dream unfolding and they knew it. When Phillips entered the scene the Family Teachers became his operating arm.

Each cottage provided a private apartment for the Family Teachers, who might have one or two younger children of their own. Very little trouble was experienced where small children were involved; the boys got along with them very well, and watching the Family Teachers act as parents of their own youngsters undoubtedly contributed to their training.

We were careful in selecting the boys who went into the first cottage with Ron and Annette Herron. The number was limited to six and high on the list was a high school senior, a ringleader among members of his class. He could be a leader in the family program if he wanted to. He didn't want to. Instead he came storming over to the administration building to see me after telling Ron and Annette, "I'm going to see 'the man' and get him straightened out."

He was hotter than a two dollar smudge pot by the time he reached my office. He stormed in. I greeted him and he unloaded.

"I want to tell you something," he started. "When I came here I was living with my dad in a one-room apartment. Now you've got me living in a real nice home. That's ridiculous. When I get out of here I'll not be living in a (bleep) mansion. I'll be back in a one-room apartment. You and your (bleep) ideas. And younger kids running around the house."

When he ran out of expletives, I asked him, "Are you finished?"

"What else is there?" he asked,

"Well, cowboy," I said, "by your own admission you have no idea what family life is all about. Be the good Lord willing, and if the devil doesn't object, next June you will be graduated and you'll be leaving. You'll probably be the first clod to go out and get married. God help the girl you marry because you don't know anything about family life and don't want to learn."

"Is that what this thing is all about?" he asked in a more moderate tone of voice. The fact that I mentioned marriage seemed to melt his disposition. After a more moderate exchange of ideas and a bit of counseling on my part he returned to his cottage, became a promoter of the program — and graduated in June.

It has long been my contention that if a boy is treated like the kind of a person he has the potential to become, chances are his response will be positive. Give him a normal home environment and teach him how to care for it — he then has a goal to pursue rather than revert to the bleak existence he experienced before coming to Boys Town.

Phillips and his staff began refining the course that all candidates would be required to take before becoming Family Teachers. In brain storming the kinds of behavior they encountered in their cottages, it seemed the bad outnumbered the good two to one. This seemed to offer some insights to the oft repeated human predicament that it is much easier to get into trouble than to stay out.

The good skills to begin with were listed thus: punctuality, good eye contact, pleasant facial expressions, cooperation, and orderly conduct.

The bad behaviors, listed as unacceptable: talking back, mumbling under one's breath, shouting, arguing, rolling eyes, pouting, boasting, making aggressive statements, telling lies, throwing objects, kicking at objects or persons, and interrupting while someone else is talking.

In almost every case it was a boy's errant behavior that landed him at Boys Town. It was our mission to correct his irresponsible way of living, teach him personal accountability and send him back into society where he came from to give a good account of himself and make a creditable contribution to the community where he will live. This would require unteaching the bad behaviors by replacing them with acceptable ways of responding to situations bound to occur in this life. Here the traditional and the behavioral approach came into play according to the personal style of the Family Teachers who were to be role models in every way.

In the majority of cases, the boys were taught to be achievers. They were instructed what to do, how to do it, and why do it this way or that. The immediate result was the development of self-esteem, self-worth. Household chores were to be rotated for obvious reasons. One could learn from the other, and monotony was kept at a minimum.

With a completely new family of boys it was necessary that the Family Teachers cook the meals. Then the various steps in preparing a meal were demonstrated to the boys and one by one they were given the responsibility of making the toast for breakfast, frying the bacon, scrambling the eggs, setting the table properly, and so on. Preparing lunch was next, and then the main meal. At the same time the boys were introduced to the maintenance skills in the kitchen before and after the meals. There was the cleaning of the surface of the stove, the table, and the refrigerator, proper arrangement of items in the refrigerator, washing dishes and silverware, cleaning the floor — just to mention a few of the many details that make for an inviting menu and a tidy kitchen.

Other chores concerned maintaining the rest of the house, including the entrance hall, the living room, bathrooms, stairs and basement, utility room, closets, and the van — all a part of the learning process and shared by all. Personal hygiene and grooming came in for a lion's share of the training.

The boys accompanied the Family Teachers to the super-market, buying items on the list that had been agreed to previously by the boys themselves. Each cottage had a budget. If they wanted steaks this week they might have to do without ice cream. Or it could be hamburgers and ice cream this week. Each of the boys in each cottage had a vote about what they would eat next week. That's the sort of thing that really gets a kid cranked up; something he probably had no voice in at home.

Usually the boys kept the menus simple, but occasionally they would go for a feast. They learned to eat all sorts of foods because they were making the choices under the guidance of the Family Teachers.

As the program developed so did the cry of the critics. "You and your behavior mod," wrote a priest; "You're turning out a bunch of robots."

It almost goes without saying that when boys come to Boys Town they are in a very unstable, unsettled state. For them to settle down to a classroom routine meant the change of an entire lifestyle and came only with great difficulty in most cases, if ever. To adapt to this reality, Father Flanagan placed great emphasis on a vocational training school. It was much more practical to help a boy harness his hyperactivity while learning some trade, engaging in a varied sports program, or getting involved in music than by confining him within the walls of a classroom. That would come later.

Learning the social skills, a very top priority, brought up an entirely new list of "how to's: how to meet visitors at the door, how to answer the phone, how to meet and greet tourists, how to introduce a friend to another person, etc. This required a good deal of role playing for the boys to become comfortable in making those social skills a part of their life. They were told to practice on each other and use every opportunity to make these a second nature. I became an open target. Well do I recall how a ten-year-old came into the sacristy after Mass one Sunday morning, very confidently extended his hand to me and said, "My name is Eddie Smith and I'm sure glad to meet you Father Flanagan." It didn't seem to bother him one bit that I wasn't Father Flanagan. He had "done his thing," as the boys would say, and had the expression on his face of "mission accomplished." That rated a compliment, followed by a brief and sparkling conversation between the two of us.

The boys were encouraged, when they would see an occasional visitor or two wandering about the campus, to introduce themselves, ask the visitors where they came from, welcome them and then be on their way. What a rewarding experience for boys who were accustomed to being neglected, even criticized by adults in their lives.

Developing a training program and manual for future Family Teachers was the task of Dr. Phillips, his staff, and those who were already Family Teachers. In the early months the pioneer couples relied heavily on the "trial and error" method. As time passed the best of these trials and errors were consolidated into the first edition (1977) of a manual called, "The Family and Living Skills Curriculum." Revisions, additions and corrections of this program were so many and frequent that it was several years later before we decided to copyright the work.

When a boy arrives at Boys Town, generally speaking, he comes with a sort of protective shell built around him. He believes no one, because of the abusive treatment he has experienced in his early life. It's our task to pierce that shell and convince the lad that here is someone who cares about him. I say "our" because teamwork is the crucial theme of our new program. Everyone who deals with the boys in any regard needs to develop the skills and attitudes that contribute to a rewarding group effort, that is, to convince the boys that we really care about them. Not just the Family Teachers, but classroom teachers, the police, the coaches, the barber, the dining room help as well — all must be on the same wave length singing out of the same hymn book. We dare not have a maintenance man losing his temper and yelling at a lad the day after his Family Teachers corrected him for using abusive language at his roommate. Consistency must be a hallmark.

Once a boy is convinced that someone really cares for him he begins relating favorably to others. Gradually he exchanges his bad habits for some good relational skills. Soon his entire life is changed. What would trigger the changes in each life would differ as much as one boy differed from another. What was important was the fact that the program was devoted to changing attitudes of all persons involved.

One alumnus returned a few years after graduation to tell what it was that occasioned him to look beyond his own selfish interests. He told of how one day I had come upon him and another boy trying to settle an argument with their fists. My talk to them was anything but convincing, so I took them to the Field House where each was fitted with a pair of cream puff gloves. They continued to disagree, flailing away until they were completely exhausted. The contest was a draw so I took the aggressor into my office where I explained things to him — things like values and virtues we were trying to live by at the Home. For him it was the trip to the Field House and the following session that caught his attention, although his Family Teachers had already said as much to him.

One of the finest teaching tools in the hands of Family Teachers is the Family Conference. Theoretically this meeting is held after every evening meal at the table when everyone is finished eating, or later in the living room. Family Teachers moderate the meeting while one of the boys chairs it. Each boy in turn around the table is given an opportunity to express his likes and dislikes about his day's activities and to enter in the general discussions. After each boy has been heard from, various topics are discussed such as what happened at school that day, the menu, shopping, recreation and entertainment for the weekend, to mention a few. Working out a schedule of task assignments around the home for the following week always comes in for a share of time at a late week conference.

A typical conference might go something like this: After the opening prayer by the chairman of the meeting, or one of the other family members, the first boy is called on for his report.

Let's say he is a new arrival at the Home and this happens to be his first family conference meeting.

"T-bone," the chairman asks: "What are the good things that happened to you today?"

"Nothing good happened to me today," he says with an inflection in his voice that indicates his displeasure at being here.

"Nothing?" questions the chairman.

"No, nothing?" the newcomer snaps.

A brief silence is broken by one of the little guys farther down the table who says, "I'll bet its been a long time since you had three good meals in one day."

Then the rest of the family chips in, each with a possible good thing that could have happened to him, such as living in a home where everybody cares, where he has a clean furnished room of his own, and so on.

The next question the chairman poses to him goes exactly like this: "Well, T-Bone, what are the bad things that happened to you today?"

By this time he may not be able to remember anything that crossed his path. If he does, he is asked: "How did you handle that? What did you do about it?"

If his response makes sense he is commended. If not, he is sure to hear how one or more of the others at the table learned to react to the same thing that occurred to him, or what he would have done given a similar problem.

This is where the Family Teachers come in. Besides keeping the meeting on track they add their touch of wisdom after each one has had the floor. In the course of the weekly conferences two of the boys, whose turn it is, are designated to help prepare the meals during the next week. They will accompany the Family Teachers on a weekend trip to the grocery store where they learn what it means to "shop."

A schedule of household tasks covering each day of the coming week is arranged. For the good of the house this schedule is typed and hangs on the bulletin board for all to see and consult as needed.

Any topic within reason is subject to discussion at these "family conferences." Here every boy gets an opportunity to be heard by attentive ears. The lad who said, "Nothing good happened to me today," hears the other boys make their minus and plus reports. Before too many days he says to himself, "I'd better be able to report something good tonight or that family is gonna get on my case." So, without realizing it, his attitude is beginning to change as he sorts out a few good things that he can report at the evening conference. This change of attitude for the boy represents the turning over of a new leaf in his life. It is beginning to dawn on him that for once in his life someone is listening to him.. He receives as much attention as the others. He belongs to a family and all that it means to be somebody.

It seems to be a human condition that a person usually finds in life what he or she is looking for, be it treasures or trouble. While serving as a chaplain aboard ship in the Pacific during WW II, one particular individual and his problems kept recurring.

Each time we stopped in a port he would end up in local police custody. It was usually my assignment just before leaving port to request local authorities to release him into my custody so he could leave with the ship. After the war, en route to Newport News, Virginia where the ship was scheduled to join the mothball fleet, we stopped at Panama City for a one-night stand before entering the Panama Canal. This young sailor, who was a real good humor man, was one of the last to leave the ship with his evening liberty pass in hand.

I said to him, "Butch, there's a lot of evil in this city. And these people have a jail. We are leaving dock tomorrow at 0700. We want you to leave with us. If that requires a trip to the local slammer to rescue you I will wrap the first small steel pipe I can find around your neck and lead you back."

"Yes sir, Father," he said. And with a big smile and a small salute he disappeared in the bright lights of Panama City.

The next morning he was aboard ship, on duty, and I asked him, "How does it happen that you went out last night and never got into any trouble?"

"Well sir, Father," he said, "I just wasn't looking for any."

I think that explained the difference. I saw it happening on our campus all the time. A guy who is looking for trouble will find it. And if he's looking for good experiences he will find those too.

"There is no such thing as a bad boy." Father Flanagan used that expression and so have many of the rest of us. Theologically that is true. However, there are young fellas who develop enough kinetic energy that they trample on the rights of others and that's when trouble results. If a boy need not worry about where he will sleep at night, where the next meal is coming from, how to avoid the abuse of an alcoholic and otherwise mean parent, he can begin looking for the finer, interesting and important things in life. Without ever asking a boy, one can tell by the expression on his face that his outlook on life has improved. When that scowl, that frown, that bewildered look he came with turns into a carefree smile and a playful mien, you know that someone on the campus has pierced the protective shell. Someone on the campus was doing his or her job and all others must be contributing.

The underlying lesson being taught in all phases of the Family Concept is that of accountability. In the first place, the Family Teachers must always be ready to give an account of their stewardship, and are expected to teach a sense of responsibility in all things to the members of their household. This latter is an awesome task and requires a constant, unrelenting effort. This aspect of the program alone fills the life of Family Teachers twenty-four hours a day.

Just building the basics of this program took many hours of give and take between Dr. Phillips and myself. Some ideas came from our combined experiences while others were recollections of things we had read or heard elsewhere. It has been said that when you copy from another single source without being authorized to do so, you are a plagiarist. If you copy from many sources, you're a researcher. We were trying to be researchers.

My philosophy has always been that when I could find someone who could perform a task better than I could — a task that needed to be done — I hired that individual. By September of

1975, four months after I had employed Dr. Lonnie Phillips, I knew I had the right man for the Family Concept program for Boys Town.

And it was the right time, too. As Victor Hugo wrote in "History of a Crime," in 1852: "There is one thing mightier than all the armies in the world, and that is an idea whose time has come." The Family Concept's time had come.

CHAPTER Five

"The Boys Town Family Concept is a good idea whose time has come. It helps kids. In the future, even more than now, it will help families." —*James K. Whittaker, professor of social work at the University of Washington on March 14, 1982.*

LONNIE PHILIPPS left little to chance. He kept urging me to commit the principles of our Family Concept to print. This would promote a degree of uniformity in caring for youth at Boys Town.

In a great majority of cases it was a boy's errant behavior that had landed him here in the first place. And it was a history of such behavior rather than an isolated incident that merited attention.

With the advent of drugs in the 1960's student rebellions, with parental rejections resulting from an increased number of divorces, and the general erosion of families in society, a more sophisticated program seemed to be in order. No longer was it adequate to give boys simply food, clothing and shelter, along with an academic education. When irresponsible behavior was the problem, it needed to be replaced with habits of personal accountability if we were to return them to society armed with tools to allow them to make creditable contributions to their communities.

It was our challenge then, to develop what we called the "Boys Town Model." This has already been mentioned as a combination of the "behavior mod" and the traditional way of learning, called by some the Adlerian method.

The Family Teachers technique would be something like this:

"Let me show you how to do this. Here's how you do it; here's how you say it. . . . . Now, give it a try."

This is the HOW approach, the behavior way. Then the Family Teacher says:

"Now that you know HOW to do it let me tell you WHY we do it, and WHY we do it this way."

This is the WHY approach, not really a developed model or system. It's done this way because parents or others have explained the procedure to children in their own inimitable way without ever committing their reasons to print. Sometimes the reason given was "because we have always done it this way." This recalls the young bride who always cut the end off the roast before putting it in the roaster, as noted in an earlier chapter. But it's always good to know that times and customs change as has the size of roasting pans.

Our intention from the outset was to examine reasons why household chores and things in general were done as they were, and to put in concrete form some basic convincing reasons for what was being taught the way it was being taught. This was important for boys who had not had the blessings of a normal home background. Dr. Phillips and his staff had their work cut out for them.

We knew there would be times when our typical model would come upon hard times. I once heard a father, Dr. James C. Dobson of "Focus on the Family" fame, tell how he had trouble teaching his seven-year old son to use a napkin at the table. No amount of wheedling and cajoling produced the desired results. "I forgot," was the routine answer. The father hit upon a little game. To help his son remember, each time he would touch a bit of food before placing his napkin on his lap he was to go in the corner of the dining room, count to twenty-five, and then return to the table. The boy agreed.

"Nobody knows how silly I felt," said the father, "when one day I had to stand on the sidewalk outside a cafe and count to twenty-five before I reentered, all because I had nibbled a cracker before placing my napkin."

Our boys were not napkin happy. For them it had not been a matter of counting to twenty-five but rather receiving a slap in the face or a kick in the derriere. Motivating people to implement our ideas was a real challenge. I repeat, this naturally was in the hands of the Family Teachers.

Given the number of cottages and living units in the dormitories, a reduction in the number of boys was required, as outlined in the Booz, Allen & Hamilton report. Some of the slack would be eliminated by emphasizing what we would call a "program graduation." This meant that if and when a boy got his act together and the situation at his paternal home had been remedied to the satisfaction of the court or social agency responsible for his original placement, he would return to his home to live and continue his schooling there. With the shorter stay at Boys Town, the number of boys benefiting from our program would increase, thus offsetting the reduction in overall residents.

It had often occurred to me that large organizations often became so involved in their internal affairs that society passes them by. This happened at Boys Town and Dr. Phillips later noted it as he wrote in a professional journal, Human Nature magazine: "The dormitories" (at Boys Town) were sterile and uninviting, the central dining hall was massive and the boys were fed cafeteria style. A central laundry handled the boys' clothes, a central bus system handled transportation. For that matter, all services were centralized — a warehouse purchased food and other goods in large quantities, a medical and dental staff offered centralized health care, another staff took care of recreation, social workers took care of special needs.

"Such a pattern of divided responsibilities meant that it was hard to find anyone who would accept responsibility for anything that went wrong. Most staff members shirked responsibility of any kind for a boy not in their unit. 'He's not heavy, Father, 'cause he's not in my section' seemed to be the prevailing attitude."

Changing such an entrenched system was a formidable task. It was necessary for me to be concerned about other departments of the Home while Phillips and three persons he had added to his administrative staff gave it a shot, deinstitutionalizing the Youth Care Department. Within a few months after Phillip's arrival, the four of them — Peggy J. Cunningham, Lou Palma, Richard L. Baron and Lonnie — put down on paper a fifty-page booklet, "Family and Community Living Skills Curriculum."

Major topics in the curriculum covered: Social Behaviors and Social Graces; Greeting and Conversation Skills; Sensitivity; School Behavior; Work Behavior; Maintenance Skills (for life in the cottages); and Independent Skills (preparation for life after Boys Town).

Let's explore one: Sensitivity. The curriculum outlined a trained youth as follows: "The youth is able to show respect for others, their feelings, their possessions and requests. A boy knocks before entering another's bedroom or home, he obtains permission before borrowing or using another's property, he refrains from inappropriate giggling or whispering in the presence of others, he avoids intentional vandalism or destruction of another's property, but if destruction does occur he reports it immediately and replaces it, if possible. He refrains from persuading others to break the rules."

Other topics under Sensitivity: "The youth refrains from swearing in the presence of others, he dresses appropriately for the occasion. He avoids obnoxious behavior in public and is able to ignore others' inappropriate behavior. He is sensitive to handicapped persons and he is able to express apologies."

To the outsider, devoting attention to such minute everyday activities may seem like overkill. But to a youth who had been pushed and shoved around all of his life, who had learned "to the victor belong the spoils," the social graces and acceptable behavior were like a foreign language.

The "Family and Community Living Curriculum" became the Family Teachers' bible. Every day was a "show and tell" time for them from arising in the morning to going to bed at nightfall.

Their task was awesome when you think about it. We were asking the Family Teachers to take kids who had anywhere from an eight to fifteen year history of failure and attempt to prepare them for acceptable adult roles in a period of a couple of years.

Once our centralized system, as described by Phillips, was scrapped, the Family Teachers had the responsibility of providing adequate spiritual and social training, education, religious values, housing, transportation, food, clothing, recreation and health care — all in the context of the family, with the social, legal, religious and moral obligations that anyone accepts when rearing children, especially other people's children.

It's an especially awesome task when you realize that any one of the eight to ten youngsters in each cottage was capable of seriously disrupting a normal family, as most of them had done time and time again, before coming to Boys Town.

The Family Teachers saw to it the boys received everything they needed, much like good parents will do in a normal family setting. They were to provide the care, supervision and training; they were to take the boys shopping for clothes and groceries and gifts; they were to accompany them to school, confer with education teachers and help with homework at night; share in religious training; cheer at athletic events, cry when a youth was having heartbreak and be filled with joy on graduation day.

All of that for eight to ten boys, plus some inevitable turnover. You may understand now why I call the task awesome.

Because the Family Teachers did have so many and varied responsibilities we reorganized our administrative setup to give them support. No more counselors counseling counselors, coordinators coordinating coordinators. Phillips and his aides put together a group of overseers who could help provide the

Family Teachers with the tremendous variety of skills they needed to teach.

Being Family Teachers was a full-time job. To bolster morale and to avoid what was at the time being called "burnout" it was necessary to plan for periods of relaxation for them. Our first step was to organize the cottages into communities with a Community Director in charge. In the beginning the campus was divided into three communities, with a small staff in charge of each. It was the Community Director's responsibility to oversee, tend to the needs and be ever vigilant of the general behavior in the cottages of his group. He/she is the first person in the line of appeal for Family Teachers in any need or request.

Theoretically cottages were organized in groups of five called a "cluster." To each cluster of cottages was assigned an alternate couple who arranged with the regular Family Teachers to live in their cottage one day a week. The idea was to always have two trained adults in every cottage at all times as state law required. This permitted all Family Teachers to enjoy one free day a week. The alternate couple had the advantage of broadening their outlook on the Family Concept by being something of interns in five cottages. The boys too could enjoy a real continuity of program when their regular Family Teachers would leave for whatever reason and would be succeeded by alternates whom they knew.

Accountability is crucial to quality youth care. To achieve it meant a good method of checks and balances which included a system of reporting called "feedback." It had to do with reporting one's own accomplishments and failures to a person who had a right to know. Whether it was a boy to his Family Teacher or School Teacher; Family Teacher to Community Director; or Community Director to the Youth Care Director; or Youth Care Director to Executive Director.

Accountability is crucial to quality classroom behavior also. As mentioned before, all classroom teachers were required to take the Family Teacher Training Course. This was a long drawn out affair in that it was difficult for the people to crowd this into their already full schedule. However, it was absolutely necessary for classroom teachers to know the youth care program to insure consistency in working with the boys. Bad behavior of the boys was as irritating in the classroom as elsewhere on the campus, and it was only by the combined efforts of the teachers, family and classroom, that a boy could be helped. After all, it was the Family Teacher's task to teach the boy good study habits that carried over into the classroom.

In the schools they call it responsibility — the fifth "R". Readin', 'Ritin', 'Rithmetic, Religion, and Responsibility. Both the high school and the Wegner School were fully accredited. The school curriculum went beyond the basics and offered college preparatory courses in math, English, science, a foreign language, and social studies. The Vocational School offered classes at one time in as many as nineteen trades. It was in this latter school that arrangements were made for a trade-off with some of the neighboring high schools for advanced classes not offered at Boys Town. Whatever was best for our students was paramount in our plan.

"Boys are our business," I used to say. We do for them whatever it takes to prepare them for becoming happy, productive, contributing members of society.

Family Teachers are the heart of the Family Concept. They provide the word and example of a caring home environment. For youth who have known little or no order in their lives, an amount of structure was woven into the Family Concept from its very inception. Youth needed to be taught the necessary relationship between behavior and consequences. A handy tool called a point card was devised to keep a running record of each boy's behavior. He would carry this card with him at all times as some day he would carry an ID card or a driver's license. Points were earned or lost immediately following a behavior, and they were so noted on his card by the adult in charge. Positive points could be exchanged for a variety of privileges that would encourage acceptable behavior.

Many youth who come to Boys Town are in no mood to learn or change their behaviors. After all, quality is a hard thing to sell to kids who come from a throw-away society; a society of disposables and instant everything. But once they realize that there are alternate ways of behaving, they begin considering options to solve problems and to build relationships. Natural consequences of their actions are not always evident to them. They need something tangible and understandable to motivate them. It is the daily, the weekly report, as it appears on the point card that the boy carries with him, that gets his attention initially.

Point cards of themselves do not teach the boys. Family Teachers do the teaching by using the point cards to improve and expand their own personal ability to motivate and monitor the behavior of the boys in their home. Effectiveness of the system depends largely on cooperation between the Family Teachers and the boys themselves. "It takes two to tango."

Changes were in order in the Education Department so that it could adjust to its counterpart in the Youth Care Department, the Family Concept. To effect this adjustment, in the summer of 1979 Don Black was hired as Director of Education of the Boys Town schools. Black received his MA in Education from Montana State University. He brought with him three changes in approach to classroom grouping, instruction, and discipline.

Black believed strongly that all students could best be taught in a heterogeneously grouped classroom. That is to say, "special needs students" were integrated in the regular classroom. Classroom teachers were trained by his administrative team to develop and implement individual education plans. This already tested method is called "Mainstreaming."

The next change Black introduced is called "Precision Teaching." This teaching strategy entailed breaking down complex learning objectives into limited and clearly defined components which are then systematically structured for drill and mastery. "PT", as it was commonly called, was incorporated into every discipline and at every grade level.

Finally, the Social Skills Curriculum was the logical complement to the Family Concept already in place in the cottages. This approach, with the point card in hand, gave all who worked with youth — teachers, administrators and support staff — a systematic way to teach appropriate behavior. It was a consistent method for identifying, reacting to, and dealing with positive and negative behavior. This curriculum gave those responsible for student behavior the tools to reduce potentially explosive confrontations to an objective evaluation and to deal with them in an appropriate manner. Whether a student was in the classroom, involved in campus sports, fine arts, vocational career center, work experiences, or in his cottage, the point card came into play.

The communication and cooperation between Family Teachers and classroom teachers that developed could well be the envy of every village in the country.

As a boy learned to enjoy the natural consequences of appropriate behavior, the point system was retired for him. It is consequences that change behavior. This artificial point system has been described as being like a plaster cast physicians use to help heal a broken arm or leg. It is not meant to be a permanent aid. Its eventual removal is a good sign that a healing process is at work.

While Dr. Phillips and his staff were grappling with the problems generated by the Family Concept and revising the program almost every week, I was a cinder in the public eye. The first major criticism of me personally and my proposed changes were published in early 1974 in a Catholic weekly newspaper out of St. Paul, Minnesota, called "The Wanderer." A reporter, Frank Morriss, authored a series of articles headlined: "Boys Town Is Dead." He hung Boys Town in effigy and prepared for the funeral, but we avoided his undertaker.

Morriss interviewed me for only one hour, after which he wrote a long series of articles debunking the new era at Boys Town. Most of what he wrote was parroting the Omaha Sun Newspaper's report of March 1972, with a few of his own barbs tucked in.

"Boys Town Is Dead," Morriss began his first article. "Sure, they still call it Boys Town but it doesn't exist anymore."

Morriss had a runaway imagination. After interviewing me he

spent some time driving around the campus doing his investigative reporting from behind the wheel of his car. Some of his criticism was based on a few visits with disgruntled alumni — I've remarked previously how opposed most alumni of the area were to change as were some of the people who had been terminated for one reason or another.

Several weeks later when in St. Paul to introduce our Concert Choir at the opening of the fall tour, I used the occasion to confront Morriss eyeball to eyeball. Besides confronting him I wanted to talk to the newspaper's publisher to let him know how I felt about the inaccuracies in the series of articles. He turned me over to an assistant editor, Peggy Moen. She interviewed me and wrote a more balanced piece, but, of course, it failed to undo the damage of the original slanders.

Time magazine sent a correspondent, Madeline Nash, from its Chicago office and she, too, came to Boys Town to spend about an hour interviewing me in my office. She then wandered around the campus for most of the day only to be waiting for me at my office at 7:30 the next morning. She had one more question to ask of me.

"How does it feel to be sitting on top of a whole pile of PhD's on your staff without having an advanced degree yourself?"

"Doesn't bother me a bit," I said. "I deal in common sense and they don't give degrees in that."

The magazine ran a full page on Boys Town, with a photograph of me on my bicycle in the middle of the page, but without quoting my response to her final question. Unfortunately, like so many other journalists, she was carried away by the money thing.

In July of 1976, Coronet magazine chewed Boys Town apart in an article. Before we could respond the magazine folded. Cause and effect were not evident but one never knows. About the same time the Readers' Digest came out with an article that was more negative than positive, but its criticisms were mild. Ditto the Washington Post.

The New York Times checked in with an article that was well balanced, listing all the grievances reported by the Sun but also giving me a chance to respond to our critics. Much of the criticism was a take-off on the Sun Newspaper's flippant irresponsible comment: "They have so much money they don't know what to do with it."

It was true that we had a sizable trust fund, but the Board and I knew its history. We wanted to preserve Father Flanagan's idea of building a fund large enough that he could curtail his fund raising trips and spend more time with his boys. This fund would insure the ability to do long range planning, as successful institutions of higher learning were doing, without suffering a severe crunch every time the country's economy would dip. Spending without strategic planning was definitely not my style. Thrift and hoarding are not synonymous in my lexicon.

None of our explanations deterred the Sun newspapers from taking another pot shot at this fat target. Managing Editor Paul Williams had ridden the Pulitzer Prize to an academic job in the journalism department at Ohio State University, but his successor, David Hosokawa, decided in 1978 that it was time to revive the subject and maybe do Williams one better.

His five-page special section was three pages shorter than the previous report, but that is perhaps because Hosokawa relied more on "lampposting" and less on digging up facts as Williams had done in his report.

"Father Robert Hupp, the director of Boys Town since October 11, 1973, is under criticism from his staff and some members of the Board of Directors, and reports circulating around Boys Town indicate Hupp may resign or take an extended leave of absence in the near future," began the copyrighted report co-authored by Hosokawa and reporter Cynthia Pond.

This pair of writers were liberally quoting "one former staff member," "another staff member," "the source," "another source." Two critics actually were quoted by name, Father John L. Farrald, a former Boys Town student and administrator, and Dr. Charles Gershenson, of Washington, D.C., a member of the Boys Town Board of Directors.

I had had my problems with that particular member of the Board. Early on when I questioned the efficiency of our research projects the Board was told that I did not understand research.

"You're not a researcher," he said, and the exchange ended there.

The Sun Newspaper simply was wrong in its attack. I shook it off — it was another of those incidents that made me determined more than ever. I felt that I had the support of a competent brain trust on the Board. Long before I retired both Hosokawa and the Sun Newspaper were history. The newspaper folded in the early 1980's.

I dutifully kept copies of all the shots fired at us, instructing my secretary to keep a scrapbook, which she easily filled. But not all journalists who looked at us hauled out their big guns. In the fall of 1975 an NBC team visited Boys Town and spent the greater part of a week gathering information for an NBC Special, "Giving and Getting — the Charity Business." Boys Town was given very favorable treatment on the NBC program, and on December 22, 1975 Kay Gardella of the New York Daily News wrote in her column "What's On?" the following: "There is no scandal in the Boys Town operation; they are just successful at what they do, and the money is going to good use."

In 1978, the same year as the second Sun report, People Magazine noted that I had been given the assignment of restoring the good name of Boys Town. "He did so, and the crisis is now passed," it concluded. Copies of the magazine were distributed to Dr. Phillips, his staff, and to the Family Teachers. Their self-esteem needed bolstering too.

CHAPTER Six

WHEN Father Flanagan opened his home for boys near downtown Omaha, his flock numbered five. The morning I took over as Executive Director in October 1973, the Home's enrollment topped out at 787.

Monsignor Wegner and his staff were accepting practically every boy who was recommended to them. The philosophy of the Home seemed to be the "bigger the better." The only discernible cutoff point was livable space. In fact, one of the Board's reactions to the Sun Newspaper's critical report had been to consider expanding enrollment to one thousand.

More sober thought, plus the recommendations of the Booz, Allen & Hamilton Report, quickly put an end to such impractical goals, and the trend toward a seemingly unlimited population on the campus was reversed.

The emphasis had to switch from quantity to quality if Boys Town were to survive. As I have mentioned previously, we not only closed the admissions department temporarily, but began reducing the number of residents of the Home and within a year our population was down to little more than half the 787 figure. This was accomplished by attrition. We opened admissions again with an eye toward an optimum goal of about 450 residents.

In the back of our minds — Lonnie Phillips' and mine — we toyed with the idea of some day serving far more than the 450, but we would serve them in or near the boys' home towns, not on our campus. The idea of exporting our Boys Town Model of behavioral treatment was an intriguing one. But first we had to stabilize the situation on our campus. We had to perfect the Model before sharing it with others.

There was never a shortage of applications for the slots that we opened on the campus. In 1975 we tallied 1,400 requests for admission, of which, of course, we could accept only a fraction. In the month of February alone we received 300 referrals by telephone, as well as many more by letter.

Because of our tight enrollment criteria our admissions committee required the expertise of several social workers and psychologists. With graduations, boys skipping out or being returned to their agencies, we were able to accept about one hundred a year during the first two years.

Applications for admission came from a wide variety of social agencies from across the land. Many calls came from juvenile court authorities. Our admission committee members soon came to appreciate the more reliable sources; for instance, at one time we had an unusually large number of boys from Albuquerque, New Mexico because our committee had a great deal of respect for the court officers there. If Albuquerque recommended a boy, we knew he was one we could help.

Most admissions were on an emergency basis. An agency or court official would call us to say, "This boy cannot go back into his home environment. It's too dangerous for him. If we can't get him in at Boys Town his next step is a lockup."

If the boy was out of hand, if his parents refused to take him back, if no foster home was available — that would be considered an emergency. We did everything within reason to find a place for him.

On occasion some prominent person, whose request for his son's admission had been denied, would approach his bishop or some political friend for help in securing admission to Boys Town. After having our admissions committee review the case, only to find that it was not an emergency situation, it fell upon my shoulders to repeat the denial. Rarely did power plays go beyond that.

Believe it or not, there actually were true emergencies — not every day, thank goodness, but on an average of once a month. We were prepared for such eventualities. With the Family Concept we could always tuck such a pilgrim into a cottage until final disposition of his case would be made.

Except for Mickey Rooney in the movie, perhaps the most famous case of a boy arriving unheralded on our doorstep was Mike Romano, a twelve-year-old lad from — wouldn't you know — Brooklyn, New York. This was not his real name we learned later.

Early on the morning of March 15, 1975 I heard on a radio newscast that a certain "Mike Romano" had arrived in Omaha via bus and was entertaining the officers in the police station where he ended up. He was telling how he came to live at Boys Town. I immediately called the police station and asked them to hold him until I came to pick him up. When I arrived at the police station he was charming the police, reporters and photographers with his line. Pinned to his coat was a note, "Deliver to Boys Town in Nebraska." Bashful he wasn't.

"My grandma sent me," he said. "She thought Brooklyn is no place to raise a boy." He went on to say that he, two brothers and a sister were too much for his mother to handle so they were all turned over to grandma.

I began to have some suspicions about the boy's family because he wasn't dressed in tatters like the typical pillar-to-post boy.

"What does your father do?" I asked Mike.

"I really don't know," he said. This told me that his dad was among the living.

"What kind of a car does he drive?" I asked.

"A Cadillac."

"Well," I said, "he's not really camping out then, is he?"

"No," he said.

I then mentioned the names of a few characters whom I had read about, guys who moved about in New York mafia circles.

"Ever hear of any of those people?" I asked.

"Oh, yeah, my dad has often mentioned them," he said.

Ours was a very enlightening conversation all the way back to Boys Town. Later that day I checked Mike out with New York authorities, and a court official told me the Romano parents were fugitives from justice in deep trouble with the law through allegedly fraudulent real estate deals.

Both of Mike's brothers, Jim and Chris, ultimately joined him at Boys Town. Mike and Chris responded well to what Boys Town offered, but Jim, the eldest, was the black sheep of the family and we never were able to keep him from wandering.

Mike's arrival with the note went out over the Associated Press wires and many newspapers used the story, but the New York Daily News gave this home town boy the biggest splash. Mike and I were pictured on Page 1 of the next two issues of the tabloid paper that day. Over the months Mike was with us the Daily News kept alive its interest in him. Every two months or so the New York Daily News called for an update on his development, and Mike would be in the papers again. Within the year Mike returned to Brooklyn at the request of authorities there who were trying to rehabilitate the family, once the parents had been located, adjudicated and placed on probation. Based on his errant behavior at the Home, our Boys Town Student Court concurred in the decision and arranged his departure. This gave Mike further press. Not long after arriving in Brooklyn he was pictured in the Daily News sitting between two inmates of the Green Haven Correctional Facility where he gave a talk on the evils in society. Mike then sort of disappeared from the scene.

Upon opening admissions again and with such a wealth of requests for entry, we tried to tailor admissions to our needs. If a cottage lacked the proper ethnic or racial mix, or didn't have a good age mix, we gave them candidates that filled our need whenever possible. However, our rules were not so hard and fast that they couldn't be bent occasionally.

When an unexpected boy did show up on our doorstep, our normal procedure was to give him temporary shelter until we checked with authorities in his home town. It wasn't all that unusual for a youngster to arrive unannounced, but it was unusual for us to be able to keep him. Either someone came to get him, or we escorted him back home. Unlike Mike Romano's grandmother, we didn't tag the boy and dump him off at the bus station.

Well do I recall one cocky young fella from Norfolk, Nebraska, who had hitchhiked his way to the campus and said he wanted to live at Boys Town.

"I see you have a lot of cars around here," he said. "Do all the boys have cars?"

"No," I said, "the cars belong to the employees."

"The kids don't have cars?" He seemed surprised. "Well, can I bring my TV if I decide to stay here?"

"No."

"What about my six-speaker stereo?"

"No."

"Well, what do the boys do around here all the time?"

It was about time to end this conversation that was going nowhere so we called his folks to come and get him.

Then there was the call one Sunday night from a woman in a little town in South Dakota.

"I called to inquire whether you would take my brother? He's driving me and our dad crazy. He has started to smoke and drink, and now has started running around all hours of the night."

"Well, I don't know," I mused. "How old is he?"

"He just turned 40," she said.

I told her that he was a little old for our program and after a few consoling words terminated the conversation as amicably as I could.

The boy from Norfolk was cocky, but not nearly as precocious as the twelve-year-old from Omaha. His father and I had no idea where he picked up his habits, but this dude was a handful. Nobody had been able to control him. He had been in psycho wards and detention centers. But his grandfather called and asked if we would try to help the boy.

"If someone isn't able to help him we will lose that boy. He has an IQ of 145." I expressed reluctance to admit the lad but because of past association with his grandfather I agreed to do the best we could.

He was assigned to a living unit in the dormitories and I told the Family Teachers if they had any trouble with him to let me know personally.

About a month later they called me to say that they were tossing in the towel.

"What's the matter," I asked.

They listed the troubles, item by item.

"He's the most destructive kid we ever had," they said. "The other day he threw a wastebasket through a closed window. After every meal he stands in the middle of the kitchen and tosses his cup into the sink, a la shooting a basketball, to see how many dishes he can break. Last week he poked a hole in his bedroom wall. He tore out a small bathroom fixture. This morning was the clincher. He took a softball·bat out of the closet and broke the television set."

I hurried to the scene of the disturbance as fast as I could go. When I arrived this young man was sitting on the couch acting as if he didn't have a care in the world.

To start our friendly little exchange I asked: "How are you getting along?"

He looked up and snapped, "I'm not learning a thing in this dump."

"Well, you are about to learn a lesson you'll never forget," I said with a little authority.

"Yeah, what's that?" he asked.

"It's a little thing called a razor strap," I said.

"Yeah. My dad tried that but it didn't work."

"Well," I said, "Then he doesn't know how to apply it. If it's done right it works; it really works. It's a lesson you'll never forget if you live to be a hundred."

"There's a law against that," he said showing just a hint of concern on his face. "You can't hit a man."

"There are two things wrong with what you just said," I replied. "First, you're not a man. Second, it may be against the

law in downtown Omaha, Kansas City, Denver, or New York, but
Boys Town is an incorporated village in Nebraska and I write the
laws here. I'm the mayor, the chief of police, the fire chief and the
director of the Home, all wrapped up in one. I have my own
attorney and my own judge." I had recently hired a retired judge
to work here in the Legal Department. And I recently talked with
the Governor of Nebraska and he told me not to send our garbage
to the state home for delinquents in Kearney.

"Now," I said, "You want to make something of it?"

By this time I had gotten his attention.

"Will it leave a mark?" he asked.

"That's the great part of this treatment," I said. "Your bottom
will get red. But that's not too unusual. You could get the same if
you sat on a heating pad too long."

"It's something like the hot water bottle treatment I've heard
about in some prisons."

He then went on to tell what he knew about the hot water
bottle deal — a beating with a full hot water bottle leaves no
marks.

"Well, this is the junior model of that hot water bottle treatment." I said.

Starting for the door, I told the Family Teachers that the next
time this fellow began destroying property they were to call me.
"I make house calls with that thing," I said.

But before I left the Family Teacher signalled the lad to give
me a tour of the apartment. That was a normal procedure — to
show a guest around, even a guest on a mission such as mine. We
started with the kitchen.

"Do any cooking?" I asked him.

"Oh, yeah. I get breakfast and I baked a cake the other day."

"I thought you said you never learned anything here. You
learned how to cook. I know men in Omaha who learned how to
cook and now they're millionaires owning their own restaurants."

"I sure don't want to cook for a living," he said. He continued
with me on the prescribed tour and we wound up at the bathroom.

"The bathrooms are all alike, but you can look in if you want to," he said.

" Boy, am I glad to see where the bathroom is," I said. I began tapping the plasterboard walls in an effort to locate a stud. I pretended I couldn't find one and I said: "The door frame here will work just as well."

"What are you going to do with the door frame?" he asked.

"When your Family Teacher calls me over to deliver this lesson I want a good solid place where you can rest your head. When you bend over that gives me a good target and I don't want your head to go through the wall when I give you a good belt. That's probably where your dad failed. And with the bathroom handy you can go in and clean up when it's all over. Thanks for the tour."

I left. I had a mighty hard time keeping a straight face during that encounter, let me tell you.

Meantime he was given an aptitude test to determine what his future might be. He could do practically anything he set his mind to. As I recall, he had a particular interest in electronics. His teacher in that field was encouraged to give him much additional work and reading material to keep him occupied.

Then one day he told the Family Teachers he wanted to attend Catholic Mass. The Protestant services were too boring he said. "All they do is sing and read the Bible," he explained. He was Episcopalian and we didn't have Episcopalian services. The Family Teachers sent him to Lonnie Phillips. Phillips heard him out and told him we don't change religions around here, but he could see Father Hupp about it.

"I don't ever want to see that man again," he told Lonnie, but was finally convinced that I could be a nice guy under the proper circumstances.

"How are you getting along?" I asked when he showed up in my office.

"Okay," he said.

"Okay is not enough," I said. "I want some particulars."

"Well, I went home for Thanksgiving and didn't have even one argument with my dad," he said.

"Now that's progress," I said, since he and his dad had great difficulty in communicating.

"What's on your wonderful mind?" I asked.

"I want to go to Mass," he said. "In my church we always had Mass."

"Tell you what," I said. "If you get a letter from your dad telling me that it is alright for you to make that change I will give it serious consideration."

About Christmas time he came back with the letter, and I gave him permission to switch services. About a month later he came in again, this time wanting to receive communion.

"I'm sitting there like a spectator and I want to be part of the action," he said.

"Well," I said, "that's a big request. If you bring a letter from your dad telling me that he agrees, then I will again consider it. But you need to know what you request doesn't come easily. This will require a summit meeting. I'll have to talk to the Pope about this. I don't have the kind of authority your request demands." Just the idea that his request was of such importance really pleased him.

Sure enough, a month later a favorable response came from his father. Now, I thought, is the time to make an important move. I called his father and suggested, "Why don't you come once a month, pick up your son and take him to your church where he can receive communion during Mass. This could be a great occasion for you two people to test your communication skills."

The boy's dad followed through and by the time his son graduated from Boys Town the two enjoyed a normal father-son relationship. Some years later I told this story at a downtown service club luncheon using fictitious names. The lad's dad happened to be sitting at the table. He came up afterwards and said, "You told that story correctly. That was me and my son. He's a different fella now. Boys Town certainly did turn him around."

Everyone must know by this time that under no conditions do

we permit corporal punishment at Boys Town. What this kid didn't know didn't hurt him. State law doesn't permit striking a resident. Our entire staff knew that muscular Christianity had no part in our program. If we couldn't otherwise convince a boy to participate in our program there were other places for him to go.

It was no secret that an occasional youth would test one aspect of our system or another, beyond the limit. Occasionally a staff member might shove a boy around unnecessarily for which he might receive a warning, or perhaps a short suspension to serve as a cooling down period. I am unable to recall a single incident when a staff member was terminated for roughing up a boy. The big stick we carried around was that when a boy became unmanageable we would return him to the agency that sent him here in the first place. In a boy's calmer moments he was not interested in that. That was usually enough to restore peace and order in his home.

Of course, when a boy brought with him a lifetime of hardships, sometimes herculean efforts were expended to fit him into the system. Consider the case of the little black kid from the East, a lad of about twelve, whose physique gave the impression that he might have been carved out of a tree stump. That is to say, he was a husky little guy who presented us with a very unique problem. It seemed that he was constantly getting into fights with white children. It wasn't long until he was hailed before our Student Court.

Dr. Phillips and I were judges on this campus Student Court, a court Lonnie and I organized to handle unusual behavior cases. The justice we dispersed was heavily weighed with mercy and common sense. This was early on, before the Family Teachers had enough experience and expertise to handle difficult situations. If they felt a boy was too much for them they were urged to send him to the Student Court which met once a week, or as often as necessary.

Promptly at nine o'clock on the morning of Student Court this little fellow marched smartly up to the desk where Lonnie and I sat.

"What's the charge?" I asked.

"Prejudice," said the Family Teacher, one of our black staff members. Lonnie turned to the boy, "Do you know what prejudice is?"

"No sir."

Beverly Ayres, an able defendant at all court sessions, interrupted, "Since Jeff doesn't understand the charge this case should be shelved for a week and I will explain the charge to him."

This was agreeable to all concerned and it was so ordered.

Sure enough, the Family Teacher and the boy were standing before us the following week.

"Do you know what prejudice means now?" asked Phillips.

"Yes," said the boy.

"Are you guilty?"

"I sure am." He smiled broadly.

Back in his home neighborhood the white youth were beating up on him daily and he was just programmed to retaliate. He brought that behavior with him and it brought him to Student Court. Here was a case where common sense prevailed. He was warned that he'd better mind his Family Teacher or he'd be right back where he came from, putting up with those prejudiced white hooligans on his street back home. That he didn't want, and after a few more sessions with Beverly Ayres he came to realize that the whole world of Boys Town was out to help, not fight him.

Out of our Student Court experience we formed a task force of staff members who could help Family Teachers in a crisis. Task force members could hurry to a cottage if a really serious disciplinary problem developed, something beyond the Family Teachers' ability to handle quickly and successfully. It was our theory that problems needed to be faced on the spot. I say again, delayed justice is often no justice at all.

For a long time the boys had been given the opportunity to elect an honorary mayor who was usually a senior. To assist him four councilmen were chosen, one from each section of the Home. On his staff too were commissioners, one from each of the 25 cottages and the four dormitories. Chief duties of the mayor and his staff had to do with supporting the counselors in tidying up their own living quarters and the campus in general. Occasionally some of the boys needed to be roped in, even mayors when they let the system go to their heads. Take the case of one of our last mayors. This lad took his job seriously — at least the public part of it. He was everywhere, making speeches, shaking hands, acting the part of a real politician. Trouble is, he got his priorities mixed up, and he flunked civics. One of the city commissioners threatened to bring impeachment proceedings. The mayor finally got the message and resigned before suffering the humiliation of impeachment. He wrote me a letter of resignation which said:

"Dear Father — I've been mayor since last June, and I've learned it's a hard thing being mayor. I'm turning in my resignation because I got my heart into it, but I couldn't get my head into it."

In the long run, I think that boy will go far.

There was hardly a little urchin who didn't test the system one way or another soon after he arrived. The system was explained to them, then invariably they had to find out for themselves whether we meant what we said. Usually a single misstep would settle their curiosity and they'd look for other cracks in our armor.

The most common violations by the boys included sassing the classroom or Family Teachers, being boisterous in classrooms or cottages, fighting, refusing a teacher's orders, or not being punctual. This involved more than the school rooms. In our Boys Town Model every boy had a full schedule every day. The idea was to keep every youngster fully occupied. Each evening's family conference laid out each boy's schedule for the following day.

Every boy had some kind of chore at the cottage, even if it meant just sweeping the sidewalk in front. There were always leaves and debris on the streets, and Boys Town had always prided itself on the immaculate appearance of the campus. And once all the normal chores were assigned, the creative ability of the Family Teachers was challenged. Each cottage figuratively could have posted a sign that read, "There is no loitering here. Idle hands are the devil's workshop."

Making up weekly schedules to fit every individual boy became a complicated task when disciplinary action of one kind or another was in order for a boy. Coaches and choir directors understood that they too were a part of the overall system and when a boy had been a bad actor his disciplinary chore might interfere with his practice or rehearsal time. When it did, the system prevailed. So it behooved the coaching staff and the choir directors to encourage good behavior, even insist on it, beyond their sphere of activity. Boys Town lost a few athletic games over the years because one or another of its star players was grounded for a serious breach of rules that carried with it a strict campus restriction.

As a matter of fact, everybody on campus — coaches, teachers, maintenance people, drivers — were constantly reminded that they were part of the overall program; they realized the common goal was to do what was best for each individual resident. All were forced to think and work in terms of our being here to teach and train boys, not just to hold down a spot in the work force. Boys are our business.

The farther along we went, the better things began to peak as the heart of the Family Concept emerged. Older boys in a cottage helped wise up the younger ones. When Family Teachers needed help, the staff crisis task force and Student Court came into play. When all efforts failed, a call to the agency that sent the boy originally was in order. Someone at the agency then would speak to the boy on the phone and assure him that a return home might mean a lockup. This usually resulted in a marked change of attitude on the part of the boy, and the family atmosphere began to appeal to him. Where the negative attitude persisted, arrangements were then made to return him to his agency.

In many cases, Boys Town was a boy's last chance before losing his liberty. On occasion, when he tested the system of the agency that recalled him and found it to be foolproof, he would request a return to Boys Town. If his place had not yet been filled at the Home, and if in the best judgment of authorities concerned he would cooperate with another chance, it was granted him. He returned to Boys Town with a better outlook on life.

With the increasing number of youth being abandoned, neglected, and abused, we knew that Boys Town would never be able to care for all who needed help. "The more the merrier," the bigger the better," would not be our philosophy. Developing a quality care program was more important, the kind of program we could share with others. Our idea held a great potential now that the "least restrictive type of care" was recognized.

As a boy's behavior improved, restrictive measures were reduced. We were thus able to phase out the Student Court once our Family Teachers grew in wisdom and experience in handling their households.

My concern began to build over recent graduates who had not lived the Family Concept long enough to be self-sufficient once they left Boys Town. After discussing the problem with Dr. Phillips and his staff, a program called "Transitional Living" was developed. It was housed in one of the empty dormitories and was designed to help two types of boys:

* High school seniors in their last semester who would be going into the work world and who needed to be introduced to the real world. They were housed four to a unit, would buy their own groceries, do some of their own cooking, laundry, cleaning and other household chores. Family Teachers watched but from a distance.

* Youths already graduated who found themselves unable to take that initial step into society with full confidence in their abilities. They were allowed to return for a limited period, during which time they received additional counseling and assistance in finding and retaining a job. It was like returning to have their batteries recharged.

From its inception this program was intended to be a temporary one until its elements could be incorporated into our regular training program for Family Teachers.

We were always willing to try something new even if success wasn't guaranteed. That is how we became involved with the Christus House. United Catholic Social Services in Omaha operated in St. James Adolescent Chemical Dependency Center under the name Christus House. We agreed to fund several beds at Christus House for the care and treatment of our residents who came to us with hard core drug problems.

Upon my arrival at Boys Town I found a sizable drug problem — a product of the student turmoil of the late 1960's and early 1970's. Phillips and I agreed that a youngster with a hard core drug problem would require institutionalized treatment which we could not provide. Such a boy was not admitted to the Home. But marijuana, we agreed, could be handled by the Family Teachers if we trained them to recognize a boy who was on the weed and what to do about it.

Our association with Christus House was not one of our great success stories. The program did not prove effective for our type of addict. One year and $100,000 later we withdrew from the program. It was our considered opinion that basically the solution to the drug problem is one of education. We will never eliminate drugs entirely, but we think we will be able to keep it under control with the reins in the firm hands of our Family Teachers.

If the Christus House was no great success, it can be said without fear of contradiction that a program we introduced to the country a short time later would become one of the most important advances ever to occur in the United States. Youth care experts across the nation told us so. I'm speaking of the Boys Town Model that we exported across the country.

Listen to what Dr. Montrose Wolfe had to say. Dr. Wolfe was a professor in the Department of Human Development at Kansas University and Chairman of the Boys Town Youth Care Advisory Committee. When his committee presented its report to the Board, it termed the Boys Town Model "the best in the United States."

Again, our idea was to develop a high quality program and invite others to use it. The Boys Town USA program will be explained in a later chapter, but let me say here that before we could export our Boys Town Model it was necessary to test it in a few existing child care institutions. A key factor in our ability to share our secrets was the fact that the Boys Town Model did not depend on the powers of a charismatic leader.

Let me explain. Father Flanagan was a charismatic figure; he was world famous as a hero and he fit the image. The great success of Boys Town during his lifetime, and later, was due to his leadership, his charisma, which lived on. My critics were quick to point out to me, as if I didn't know it, that I was no Father Flanagan. If our program could work under my direction, it could work under the direction of anyone who cared about children and had a minimum of administrative ability. People could be taught the program. Just like we teach Family Teachers, so someone else could be taught to administer the program.

Not long after our Family Teacher program was developed and people learned of it, institutions and agencies around the country began asking for the secret. The first serious inquiries came from New Orleans where two agencies were operating five different homes, all relatively small. We did not have the manpower to establish a Boys Town in New Orleans, so arrangements were made for them to send people to Boys Town to be trained as Family Teachers.

We shared technical expertise with their staff members, and upon their return to New Orleans we continued to provide assistance and support in implementing their new skills for the benefit of their youth. This wasn't easy; we learned then that it could take two or three years to really convert an organization's program to our model of youth care.

This was our first venture in sharing the Boys Town Model with another community. Although the young people in the care of agencies and courts in other states would never see Boys Town in Nebraska, many would soon come to benefit from our experience. Requests for information soon came from

Massachusetts, New Jersey, Texas, Kansas and Florida, just to name a few. Most were areas where youth correction facilities were overcrowded. At no time did we solicit agencies.

One request came for a social agency in Washington, D.C. With the help of those people we managed to assist in opening a residence in the city's inner city. It was only two blocks from what the neighbors told us was "the crime center of D.C." After a few months this was recorded in my diary as "a noble experiment." The need was there but the environment wasn't.

By mid-1978 there were 27 group homes affiliated with Boys Town in 13 states serving 122 youths. At its peak this program served over 500 youths at one time in 90 homes.

As the Boys Town USA program expanded, the problems multiplied. In some cases the affiliated homes were using Boys Town's name and reputation to raise funds and then using those funds in ways that had nothing to do with enhancing or even operating our Model. Our name was being tarnished. From this experience we learned that to export our program properly it was necessary first and foremost that we have an assurance that Boys Town is "wanted and welcomed" by the local agencies and government (city and state), the general public, and the governing bodies of the local churches. Furthermore there should be no serious objection on the part of local entities to Boys Town owning and operating the necessary group homes and to our program being installed in those homes.

And finally, funding for each project is to be solicited in advance from area resources such as corporations, foundations, grants and selected individuals. Once adequate funds were assured they must be dedicated to the project for which they are collected, separate and distinct from the Boys Town present budget. That is to say, Boys Town's funds, or resources thereof, are not to be used. Boys Town would train the staff and operate a quality program for those who made the facility possible. When people will put their money where their mouth is, everyone gains. We live and learn.

CHAPTER Seven

I'VE mentioned the Research Center (Center for the Study of Youth Development) in previous chapters; how it and the Boys Town National Institute (now Boys Town National Research Hospital) were two projects the Board of Directors turned to, in a spasm of rectitude that followed the "great disclosure" of the Sun Newspapers in March 1972. The Board didn't do too badly, batting .500 — one of two projects. The miss, as it turned out to be, was the Research Center.

Let's turn our attention to the particulars of that bold adventure, a mistake that cost us a substantial sum of money over a period of nearly ten years; a mistake that periodically demanded much of my time when I could have been more deeply involved in our Family Concept of living for the boys.

The idea of a Research Center was a great one, considering the staggering proportion of youth problems in the United States at the time. Approval by the Board was in itself a recognition of the problems; even more to the point, it was a recognition shared by leaders in the field that grave deficiencies in our knowledge prevented us from understanding more thoroughly how to alleviate the extreme distress of the young. It was to be a great investment in the family.

Among the important topics to study when it came to helping needy youth were:

* The impact of poverty on the intellectual, emotional and social development of youth.

* The role of language in a child's psychological development and its influence in adolescent rebellion.

* The role of the church, school and other institutions in re-habilitating young people.

* The use of non-professionals in the youth care field. The drug culture and its impact on youth; the fact that many boys came to Boys Town with needles in their pockets, Demeral in their veins, and marijuana in their lungs.

* The alarming increase in sexual, physical and mental abuse in children.

The good Lord knows those topics needed answers that relevant research might have provided. Unfortunately — and this is the tragedy of the Boys Town Center for the Study of Youth Development, as the Research Center was formally named — it didn't work out that way. Ongoing research at the universities was way off target and there seemed to be no amicable way to get the ear of anyone in the academic hierarchy.

Their well paid researchers ignored the practical matters that would have helped Boys Town in its mission. Instead of practical issues, they turned to basic research; the kind of research that some people think allows academicians to publish scholarly tomes in obscure little technical journals, thus enhancing their own personal status and tenure on college faculties. Basic research is necessary but hardly at the expense of the Boys Town trust fund.

One research center gathered statistics about young people living in South America near the Amazon. Another center sent a team off to South Africa. Neither project seemed to have anything to do with Boys Town's direct needs. But this is getting ahead of the story. Let's backtrack to events as they unfolded even before my arrival on the scene.

The idea for a research center germinated at Board level. After some rather spirited exchanges at a meeting on March 9, 1972, a consensus was reached and the Board went on record in support of "research on the problems of homeless and unfortunate youth." A special committee, chaired by Leo A. Daly, was appointed to study and implement this decision. A month later Daly and his group recommended the Board adopt a two-pronged program:

* Obtain technical assistance as necessary to implement its search for programs of betterment for Boys Town.
* Retain Catholic University in Washington, D.C. to form a team called the Technical Assistance Committee. The team was to be composed of outstanding scholars recruited from varied disciplines in the area of youth welfare.

Dr. James P. O'Connor, Vice Provost and Dean of Graduate Studies at Catholic University, was the first person appointed. He was named coordinator of the Technical Assistance Committee and was instrumental in selecting the other two members: Dr. George H. Weber, Deputy Chief of the Center for Studies in Crime and Delinquency of the National Institute of Mental Health, Department of Health, Education and Welfare; and Dr. James F. Garrett, Assistant Administrator of the Social Rehabilitation Service for Research and Demonstrations of the Department of Health, Education and Welfare. It was an impressive trio from the standpoint of scholarly credentials.

This committee submitted its first recommendation on August 20, 1972. O'Connor proposed the establishment of a "Research Center Complex," and on November 8 he presented a written proposal that included details of the complex.

O'Connor urged that Stanford University and Catholic University be selected as sites for the complex. With a major university on each coast of the United States and Boys Town in the center, the young people of our country and their problems would be well covered. The main center itself would be built at Boys Town, across the South Lake, with regional centers at Stanford and Catholic Universities.

During this November 1972 meeting, while the Board was

voting approval of the Technical Assistance Committee proposals, a crucial amendment was offered by Board Member Harry Cohen, an Omaha attorney, and seconded by Board Member William Grodinsky, also an attorney. It recommended approval of the proposals, but with this clause inserted: "Subject, however, to approval by Father Flanagan's Boys' Home's legal counsel." Those two lawyers wondered whether a program of such scope would legally fall within the Home's charter.

They reasoned that someone who gave $5.00 in response to Boys Town's Christmas letters would expect that donation to help provide food, clothing, shelter and education to needy boys, not pay for some esoteric research done by someone far removed from Boys Town and its mission. Was Boys Town being honest with that donor whose $5.00 was not spent directly caring for boys?

The chairman, Archbishop Daniel E. Sheehan, put the motion to a vote. Five said yea, five said nay, one member abstained and one member was absent. At 5-5 it fell to the chairman for his decision. He did not vote. The amendment was not approved. The research undertaking would not be subject to approval of Boys Town's legal counsel for its compliance with Boys Town's Charter.

So, full speed ahead. The Board voted itself power on December 14, 1972 to purchase and maintain insurance on behalf of its members and members of the corporation, covering any liability leveled against and incurred by them, individually or collectively. A committee was appointed and authorized to investigate and arrange for a Directors' and Officers' Liability and Corporate Reimbursement Insurance Policy with coverage in the maximum amount obtainable up to $25 million. The Board was notified on March 2, 1973 that Lloyds of London had advised that insurance coverage of $15 million would be issued. Thus did Board members think they were protecting themselves, if indeed they were off target.

The Technical Assistance Committee argued, quite persuasively, that the two universities could not be bound by short-term contracts. They needed a long-term commitment from Boys Town in order to attract staff and programming. They received this commitment. Each university was given a 25-year contract that called for a total expenditure by Boys Town of approximately $100 million over the period of the agreement.

Upon reading the details of the research project I was most unhappy. It seemed to me that Boys Town had many more immediate problems than these projects addressed. These contracts gave universities almost unlimited control. They designed expensive facilities to house their centers, hired staff members and put together their basic research programs.

Boys Town Board approved a new Research Center building on the Boys Town campus. It would be located south of the main campus, across the lake, with an entrance from Pacific Street. Its estimated cost was $7,504,000, plus an additional $740,064 for sewers and roads. Meanwhile, each university was to have its own Boys Town Center. The new building at Catholic University was to cost $2,391,000 and the Stanford Center was to be located in a portion of a campus building that would be remodeled at a cost of $1.5 million.

The original expenditures seemed to me to be exorbitant but even more frustrating was the direction of the research. But matters had moved too swiftly to stem the tide, and on May 3, 1976 a time capsule ceremony was held on our campus for the Boys Town Center. The honored guest was Mother Teresa of Calcutta, India, who was to receive the Father Flanagan Award for Service to Youth in a concurrent ceremony.

The capsule contains the following items: Pictures of Father Flanagan, Monsignor Wegner and "yours truly"; bicentennial Boys Town bronze coins and a flag; a 1976 map of Boys Town; the latest issue of the Boys Town Quarterly; a "Two Brothers" statuette; "Boys Town Sings America" 8-track tape; spring letter of appeal; a list and picture of staff members; Father Flanagan Award luncheon program; Mother Teresa card — Apostle of the Unwanted; and a copy of the May 3, 1976 issue of the Omaha World Herald.

Construction of the 140,000 square foot building moved along on schedule. Members of the staff moved into the building in December 1977, and beginning on May 6, 1978 a week-long series of public workshops and discussions with distinguished scholars in the field of youth development marked the dedication of the Boys Town Center for the Study of Youth Development. And by now the price tag of the building, utilities and equipment was close to $10 million.

Former President Gerald R. Ford gave the dedication address on May 11, 1978 at a dinner at Peony Park. Only a speaker of his stature could have followed the "presentation" speech by Boys Town Mayor Barnaby Spring. The young mayor presented a special award to James Paxson, an Omaha businessman, for his establishment of the Gerald R. Ford birth site near Hanscom Park in midtown Omaha. Paxson himself was the product of a boys' home in Fremont, Nebraska fifty years earlier.

Barnaby used the occasion to condemn child abuse. "One of the most abominable things to the students of Boys Town is child abuse," he said. "Child abuse belongs in hell." He praised the idea of the new center·but related the concern of one of the "little kids" of Boys Town who told Barnaby, "I sure hope they don't forget about me."

In his own inimitable way this little fellow was already expressing the great need for research relevant to Boys Town.

The former President, in his relaxed fashion, opened his dedication speech with a prayer: "Oh Lord, please forgive all the nice people of Omaha for exaggerating so much. And Lord, please forgive me for enjoying it so much."

Ford then continued: "It is great for our country to make the strongest aircraft — we are all for that; it is necessary to have them. But this kind of development must be matched with efforts directed at development of youth."

The Research Center building was constructed with two wings extending in a V-shape from the main entrance and lobby. On the right is the office wing with space for the director and his staff, followed by library space and eight modules arranged on split levels. Each module is comprised of a central secretarial area surrounded by five offices.

The conference wing on the left features a 31-room residential section, an auditorium, conference rooms, a commons area and a complete dining facility. At the end of each wing a covered walk joins the two. The walkway is a bridge over a small alcove of the lake. It's a real beauty, and should be, considering the cost.

The man in charge of our Research Center, whose job it was to coordinate research at Catholic and Stanford Universities, was Dr. Ronald A. Feldman. He had been Acting Dean of the School of Social Work at Washington University in St. Louis, Missouri, when he was hired as Deputy Director of Research. He took over in July 1974, and until the new building was completed he and his developing staff had office space off campus.

He was the one I turned to in my frustrations about the programs at the universities. His frustrations matched mine. Authorities at the universities paid no more attention to him than they did to me, and two months after moving into the new building he resigned and returned to Washington University.

In my opinion, Ron did the best he could. He spoke their scientific language but unfortunately couldn't influence the powers at the universities to listen.

Then there was a quarrelsome Board member, the one who loved his doctorate and cast a few insinuations at my lack of the same. To tell the truth, he was right in telling the Board that I didn't understand basic research being conducted with Boys Town's money with no promise of direct results to the Home. Basic research seemed to be just about anything the PhDs wanted it to be. I requested a list of research projects to which Boys Town was contributing financially. Here is a partial list:

* Developmental Studies with Premature and Full-term Infants.
* Development of Sleep-wake Rhythms in Infants.
* Maternal Attachment and Peer Affiliation during the Child's First Two Years.

* Oscillating Waterbed Care for Premature Infants in the First Weeks of Life.
* Sleep Studies in Infancy.
* Birth Hormones, Early Development and Maternal Response.

All were valid basic research projects but of questionable value, if any, to the programs that were developing at the Home. If the public were to find out — and there were a few noises rattling around about our possibly wasting donors' money — we would be in trouble if some controls were not soon established on research.

Far more important than their basic research, it seemed to me, was to make sure our boys knew we cared about them and their futures. It doesn't require a lot of research to figure out that caring about a boy makes a big impression on him. If we showed love and respect, he would get the picture. Compassion rather than basic research was our immediate need. Everything we did had to have a practical application.

It took nearly a year to find a replacement for Dr. Feldman. In May 1979 Dr. Morton Weir came to the rescue. He was Vice Chancellor for Academic Affairs at the University of Illinois, and an expert on experimental child psychology. He accepted the position with the understanding that it might be for a limited time only, pending the outcome of our controversy with the universities. Some progress had been made in convincing the Board that we were not getting our money's worth out of our expensive research undertakings.

Talk at the two universities did seem convincing. For instance, the people at one university told us the focus of their research concentrated on "moral, religious and intellectual development of young people." And at the other, the focus was on "treatment of children who are victims of deprivation, abuse and neglect."

It sounded just like we would receive what we were expecting, but nothing even approached these common sense topics.

Research reports reminded one of the old Arabian proverb: "I hear your mill grinding but see no flour coming out." Members of our Board were now becoming uneasy. A time of decision had arrived.

It had been suggested to me a few months earlier by a couple of close personal friends that a good corporation attorney on my administrative staff would be of great assistance. My prayers were answered when a long-time friend, F. Vinson Roach, chief counsel for InterNorth, the natural gas transmission company in Omaha, retired from the company and agreed to join my staff. Roach had been an expert negotiator for the gas company. Just the man I needed, a man as determined as a little dog shaking a tree root he had dug up. Unfortunately, while moving out of his office at InterNorth, he suffered a slight stroke which affected his right arm. He could hardly sign his name although therapy was expected to do wonders for the right arm. His mind was as clear as ever though and his speech was not affected, so the first thing I asked him to do was read those university contracts and give me his opinion of their relevance to Boys Town.

About two weeks later he came in to see me and advised that in his opinion the contracts gave me authority to pay the bills and nothing more.

"How can we correct that?" I asked.

"Let's get more legal opinions; I could be wrong," he said.

We did just that. We sought opinions from two separate law firms in Omaha, and both agreed substantially with what Roach had said. My next move was to call the universities and ask for a meeting to discuss my concerns. Both responded by telling me they had a contract and that there was nothing to discuss. I had an idea how to get their attention. I stopped payment on the bills they submitted. Suddenly my phone began ringing. Our verbal exchange went on by phone until finally the universities refused to talk any longer. They wanted to meet with Boys Town legal counsel.

Meantime, while all this conversation was going on from my office, another member was added to Boys Town's legal department in the person of John C. Burke, a recently retired judge in the city of Omaha. He had just completed nineteen years on the district bench and was well informed on the workings of Boys Town.

On December 11, 1980 our legal counsel in the persons of F. Vinson Roach and John C. Burke met in Washington, D.C. with the legal counsel for Catholic University to the effect that in Nebraska, charitable donations are impressed with a public trust specifically imposed by the objects and purposes of the charitable corporation, and that the trust cannot be amended by amending the Articles of Incorporation. Any amendment of the objects and purposes of the trust is reserved to a Court of Equity.

Our attorneys invited counsel for Catholic University to review our side of the case, and said they would be happy to review their case. Our attorneys were stonewalled. Back home with our Cowboys, the response I received from the university was, "We have a contract. It's up to you people to live up to the terms of that contract. Just put those checks in the mail."

Our attorneys followed the same approach with legal counsel for Stanford. They made an appointment, traveled there and presented our legal side and invited counsel there to submit their side. Stonewalled again! The objects and purposes of the Home's charter did not provide for the establishment of Research Centers for the expenditures of $100 million, our attorneys said.

"We have a contract," they replied. "It's up to you people to live up to the terms of that contract. Just put those checks in the mail."

No more checks were sent, and in March of 1981 the two universities jointly filed suit against Boys Town in Superior Court of Santa Clara, Palo Alto, California, the home base of Stanford. We were actually on the home court of Stanford's highly touted law school.

Roach and Burke added another California attorney by the name of McGuire to the Boys Town team. More impressive than the towers of Stanford that could be seen from the courtroom was the array of attorneys present for both universities.

The presiding judge entered the chambers, sat down, looked at the stack of briefs before him and asked if anyone could add something not already found in the briefs. One of the attorneys stood up and started to explain a point and the judge interrupted him saying, "Your point is covered in one of the briefs." Obviously, the judge had done his homework. He threw out the case. Later the universities lost an appeal, both at the state appeals level and in the California State Supreme Court.

In a last ditch stand the attorneys for the universities in May of 1981 filed separate suits in the U.S. District Court in Omaha. Boys Town's attorneys countered with a motion stating that the case properly should be heard in the Nebraska District Court.

While this was going on a new president by the name of Dr. Donald Kennedy took the reins at Stanford University. Upon learning of the lawsuit against Boys Town, he called one of the Menninger brothers in Topeka, Kansas, who was serving on Stanford's Board of Directors. He asked Dr. Menninger if he knew anyone on the Board at Boys Town. He knew Robert Kutak, whose law firm had for years been closely associated with Boys Town. He directed Dr. Kennedy to one of his associates, Harold Rock, who was well acquainted with the Home. Rock then suggested Dr. Kennedy call me because I, being a member of the Board, had been designated its spokesman in this matter.

Dr. Kennedy called me and after introducing ourselves and exchanging a few pleasantries, he went directly to the point.

"I understand Stanford and Boys Town are involved in a lawsuit," he said.

"That is correct," I said, and went on to outline the problem as I saw it.

"Two great organizations that we represent should not be wrangling in court," he said. "We should be able to sit down and solve our own problems."

"I couldn't agree more," I said. "That's what I wanted to do months ago."

"If it meets with your approval," he said, "I will ask our

attorneys to call yours and settle this problem out of court. If they are unable to reach an agreement then you and I will."

That was music to my ears.

Two days later attorneys from the universities arrived in Omaha and met with our attorneys. Since Stanford was providing most of the legal expertise, Catholic University agreed to let them handle the negotiations for both schools. Roach and Burke convinced the legal beagles that we needed new contracts. An agreement was reached by which the 25-year contracts were terminated and replaced with 5-year contracts, to run from 1981 to 1986. All research would be relevant to the Boys Town operation. Contracts had a renewal option if agreeable to both sides. Otherwise, lump sum payments of $2,500,000 were made to each of the two institutions to close out the contracts. The remaining payments of $22 million under each contract for the remaining eighteen years were cancelled.

We had provided each of the two universities with the Boys Town "He Ain't Heavy . . ." statues. As the 5-year contracts ran out we asked that these statues be returned to us and that all other references to Boys Town be eliminated from the two universities. Fingering their $2,500,000 consolation prizes, they agreed.

When Dr. Morton Weir returned to the University of Illinois in August of 1982 it marked the beginning of the end of the research component of the Center as it had been conceived originally. His very able assistant, Tom Gregory, was given the unenviable task of terminating the research staff, which he did with compassion and efficiency. When the commission was completed in June 1983, Gregory was retained to become Deputy Director of Development. From this point on all research would be done in, or at least supervised by, the department concerned.

The beautiful Center building, which was tagged by some as "the mistake across the lake," was now ready for new occupancy. Plans had already been drawn for an addition to the old Administration building to alleviate the overcrowded conditions there. The vacated new building across the lake now provided all the additional office space needed. After some minor remodeling in the Center, administration offices were moved into the right wing, leaving the old Administration Building to house the Youth Care Department offices which had been scattered around the campus. The left wing of the Center, with its food service facilities, meeting rooms and motel facilities would continue as a conference center.

Now I could turn more of my attention to the other major project I inherited when I became executive director — The Boys Town National Institute, later named "The Boys Town National Research Hospital."

That department of the Home was an immaculate conception and continues to be a tremendous success.

CHAPTER **Eight**

AN INSTITUTION dedicated to addressing communication disorders in children was one of the Board of Directors' first reactions to the Sun Newspaper's report in March of 1972. The creation of such an Institute, along with a Center for Youth Development, was approved by the Board before Monsignor Wegner retired. The Boys Town National Institute for Communication Disorders as it came to be called was a huge success from the very beginning, while the Research Center had a hard time getting off the ground.

It did not take long for me to become a wholehearted supporter of the Institute after some early misgivings that it may have extended too far the original concept of Boys Town. But once I understood how it fit into our mission I put all my energies behind it. To me it was the proverbial ounce of prevention, with a pound of cure.

The Institute was really the brainchild of three men — Monsignor Wegner, Leo Daly and Dr. T.T. Smith. Daly was the Board's most aggressive member and he had a long-standing friendship with Dr. Smith, a well-known Omaha ear-nose-and-throat specialist.

While attending a medical meeting in Texas, Dr. Smith met with a good friend, Dr. John Bordley, Chief of Pediatrics at Johns Hopkins University in Baltimore. In the course of their visit the plans at Boys Town became the topic of conversation. Dr. Smith outlined briefly the discussions he had with Monsignor Wegner

Father Hupp, newly appointed director of Boys Town (1973).

Franciscan Circle was named after the Franciscan Sisters who served the Home from 1940-1976, working in the clinic, the kitchen, the laundry and the offices.

Father Hupp bicycles with some of his boys (1982).

Barnaby Spring was the Mayor of Boys Town who gave that memorable speech in 1978 when President Ford visited the facilities (see p. 100).

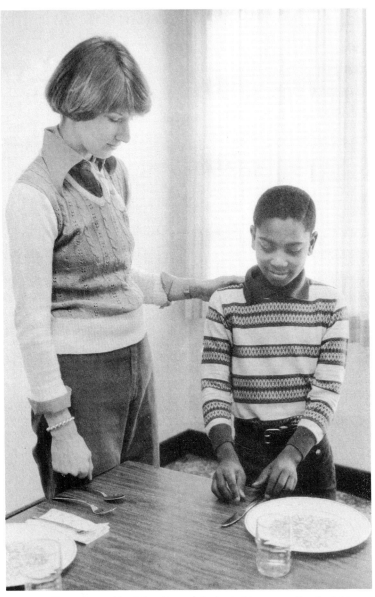

Family skills are learned by doing. Even such simple things as setting the table or making one's bed must be taught and practiced.

Meals begin with a prayer led by different members of the "family" each evening. Discussions often follow this main meal and all are encouraged to offer their insights.

Children share rooms in their new homes and are expected to keep them clean and in order.

Mike and Betty Pyykoly, Boys Town family teachers, with their own two children (on toy tractors) and the rest of their extended family.

Bob and Dorothy De Bolt and some of their "unadoptable" children.

Michael De Luca, Father Hupp, and Paul Mouch in front of the Boys Town pylon (1970). Photo by Tim McCormick

Father Hupp talking to Mike Romano who arrived on the scene on March 15, 1975.

Father Hupp fishing with a couple of the boys.

Father Hupp with the boys around the piano (April 21, 1978). Photo by Barry Staver

Dowd Memorial Chapel forms the backdrop for this leisurely stroll through Boys Town with some of the boys (1977).

Boys Town Midget football team wins the "Badger Bowl" trophy played at Madison, Wisconsin in November of 1973.

Friends honor Father Hupp on his 50th anniversary. From left to right: Father John Farrald, Dr. E. (Lonnie) Phillips, Dr. Patrick Brookhouser, Father Hupp, Bill Ramsey, Dr. Ron Feldman, Ed Hewitt, and Pat Norton.

Father Hupp, Dr. Brookhouser and Dr. Feldman field questions in an interview on Channel 3 TV, Jan. 10, 1975.

The original Boys Town statue.

The one which replaced it.

Father Hupp with two boys outside Father Flanagan's Tomb, Dowd Memorial Chapel (1977).

Paul Mouch and Michael De Luca in prayer before the tomb of Father Flanagan (1979). Photo by Tim McCormick

Youngsters after Mass ask, "Where's Boys Town?"

Boys Town Center (the "Mistake Across the Lake"), now the Administration Building.

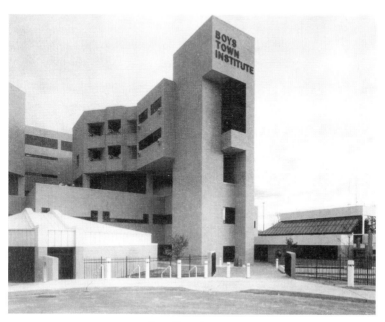

Boys Town Institute.

Institute hearing test brings a smile of recognition and joy to a youngster with hearing difficulties (1977).

Clown Sheldon Bernard visits Steve Ruehrwein (left) and Gary Wise (right) at Boys Town Institute.

After 65 years as a home for boys, Boys Town had its first female graduates in 1983. All from Nebraska, they are, from left to right, Cindy Koppenhaver of Omaha, Jeanette Hoer of Wahoo, Joni Bachelor of York, Lisa Bordogna of Lincoln and Diana Luce of Omaha.

Father Hupp plays the piano for the first Variety Show in the Music Hall (1975).

Two members of the Boys Town Choir in cassock and surplice.

Mayor Ed Koch welcomes the Boys Town Choir to New York (1983).

and Leo Daly in Omaha. Dr. Bordley said he knew the very man to help organize and operate such a communications disorders institute.

He was Dr. Patrick E. Brookhouser, chief of the resident staff in the Otolaryngology Department at Johns Hopkins School of Medicine. He was a native of Missouri Valley, Iowa, just a hop, skip and jump from the Creighton University School of Medicine in Omaha, where he graduated with honors. Dr. Brookhouser required little persuading to accept the position as Deputy Director of the proposed Boys Town National Institute.

His appointment was approved by the Boys Town Board on July 2, 1972, four months after the Sun Newspapers report and more than a year before my appointment. He set up shop in a corner of St. Joseph Hospital on South Tenth Street in Omaha, meanwhile assessing what the function of the Institute should be.

Among the early obstacles Dr. Brookhouser had to overcome was to convince members of the Creighton medical staff, which uses St. Joseph Hospital as its teaching hospital, that he would not be competing with them, nor would the Institute encroach on the School of Medicine's Pediatric Department.

In fact, as a good will gesture on the part of the Home, someone there broached the subject of constructing on Boys Town's property at 144th and Pacific, both the Institute and a department of St. Joseph's Hospital. However, a hospital of any kind that far out seemed to the planners like constructing somewhere west of the sun and so that idea never got out of the chute.

One of Dr. Brookhouser's many attributes is his winning personality; another is his integrity. He quickly won over members of the pediatric staff, and he kept his word that the Institute would not duplicate the treatment and research of the Pediatrics Department.

Dr. Brookhouser prepared a "statement of purpose" for the Board's blue ribbon committee overseeing the Institute. Members of this group were Chairman Daly, Dr. Claude Organ, A.F. Jacobson, Bill Grodinsky and Harry Cohen. The Board sought legal confirmation that the Institute did, in fact, fit the Boys Town mission.

Following, in part, is the proposal by Dr. Brookhouser to the committee:

> "The child born with a communication disorder might live to be 100 years of age, but unless this disorder can be corrected by modern means, he or she will be unable to compete on an equal basis with his/her normal peers. For the more severely handicapped, this is a tragic affliction which deprives children of a normal education.
>
> "In many cases the frustration arising from the child's inability to communicate normally has led to the development of behavior so violent that a child with normal intelligence has been judged insane. Until today many states support institutions for the 'deaf and feebleminded.' They make the decision where to place deaf children on the basis of routine intelligence tests. No deaf child can pass such tests before he learns to communicate, so literally thousands of them have been 'put away' in homes for the mentally retarded.
>
> "Studies have demonstrated that deaf children and adults are severely undereducated with illiteracy rates of thirty percent and average academic achievements no higher than the fifth grade level, and often less. Such people grow up to live unfulfilled lives outside society's mainstream even though they are of normal intellect.
>
> "There is a serious need to develop a center of national stature that can address this problem," concluded Dr. Brookhouser.

You can bet I read this statement very carefully. I felt some apprehension; for one thing, it was going to be permanently located away from the Boys Town campus, and I had to be sure it would be well run without our being able to, in effect, look over Dr. Brookhouser's shoulder.

He and I had many long conversations as I tried to arrive at some kind of rationale for the Institute that would be attractive to the ordinary donor. I asked him to educate me, if he thought that possible, as to the meaning of those long terms for medical problems he would be handling. If I were to market the Institute to the man on the street I must be able to explain in layman's terms how the work of the Institute relates to Boys Town. As old Alfalfa Smith in Texas used to say, "You've gotta get that hay down in the manger where the calves can reach it."

We already knew that almost half of the boys who came to Boys Town suffered from some kind of hearing or speech problem that affected their ability to learn. Whether or not their problem related to their bad behavior was still to be documented.

It seems that a degree of hearing loss sometimes results in a significant number of infants who suffer the normal childhood diseases — measles, mumps, high fevers. For some it may be a total loss if not cared for properly. For others it may be a total or partial loss of hearing in one ear or the other. Without a proper diagnosis parents may be unaware of the youth's partial deafness.

"Sometimes you are the nicest boy," his parent will say; "you pay attention to everything I say. And then again you act like you don't care one bit about what I'm telling you."

What the parent doesn't know is that the son's tin ear happens to be on the side where the parent is. Later, if this lad happens to be seated in his first classroom with his deaf ear toward the teacher it should come as no surprise that he frequently asks the pupil next to him, "What did the teacher say?"

The teacher, without knowing of the boy's hearing problem, faults him for disrupting the class. The boy becomes frustrated, as he has been so many times at home. His frustration leads to depression, even feelings of rejection, and then it's no wonder he questions his self worth.

Who knows how he will act out his feelings? He is almost programmed to be a troublemaker. However, if parents and teachers knew in advance of a child's hearing problem, adjustments would be made and life would be much more pleasant for all concerned. To address this situation, Dr. Brookhouser assured me that it was his determined goal to organize and operate the most complete diagnostic and treatment center in the country. It would address speech and hearing problems of preschool boys and girls.

Dr. Brookhouser had great patience with me as I picked his reservoir of knowledge and experience in the field of speech and hearing problems of young people. As a matter of fact, I found him to be a true Renaissance man, one whom I trusted and leaned on frequently for any information I was seeking, or for just a lively and friendly conversation.

"Lefty" Gomez, all-time great pitcher in the American League, was once asked the secret of his success. He was not only a good pitcher but a very perceptive man.

"The secret of my success," he said, "was a good fast outfield." Those are definitely my sentiments. Whatever degree of success I enjoyed along the Boys Town road I owe to my team.

Like "Lefty" Gomez, I never could have accomplished the things we did by myself. I felt like an orchestra leader who was able to recruit excellent lead men like Ed Hewitt, Lonnie Phillips, Don Black, Father James Gilg and Dr. Patrick Brookhouser. This comparison came naturally because of my early desire to follow a musical career. "Lead men," to use a little musical lingo, are the top performers in each section of the band. The conductor's job is to direct his lead men to blend their individual performances into a symphony of success.

The public was ever curious about the new direction Boys Town was taking. The new Institute piqued their interest, perhaps because every extended family seemed to have or to know some boy or girl with a speech or hearing problem.

It was expected by everyone, it seemed, that I knew all the answers. The eyes of the media were on every move at Boys Town. Since the funds and donations are given to us in trust, this means that every dollar goes directly to help neglected, abused, and abandoned boys. The rationale for including the Institute in our program needed public ventilation. My work was cut out for me.

In October of 1974 a contract with Hawkins Construction Company was signed in the amount of $10 million to build the

Institute adjacent to the new St. Joseph Hospital near 30th and California Streets in Omaha, close to the Creighton University campus.

In September 1975 Creighton University honored Dr. Brookhouser by naming him to the Father Flanagan Chair of Otolaryngology for the contribution already made by the Institute to medical science. Meantime Dr. Brookhouser was organizing what I, in my unmedical background, referred to as a skeleton staff. It didn't take long for me to adjust my vocabulary and call it a core staff. This made it possible to hire personnel and place them as they were recruited. Clinical facilities were moved to the new facility in March of 1977, with doors opening in May of that same year.

The Institute was given a great boost in 1976 when the local Knights of Columbus Council No. 5045 became interested in this new program and began a nationwide publicity campaign with other K. of C. councils, informing them of the facilities of the Boys Town Institute. Councils from around the United States and Canada began calling for admission of children who needed the Institute's care and treatment, and the Councils offered transportation assistance for youth to come to Omaha.

The Home itself gained a great bonus from the addition of the Institute to the Boys Town family. Since 1955 the Alexian Brothers had been operating a health clinic on campus. Theirs had been an incalculable service to the boys and the Home. However, as the number of Brothers and clergy in general around the country was diminishing there was an ever increasing demand for Brothers at their larger hospitals.

In February of 1976 the Alexian Brothers closed the Boys Town clinic and their Superior sent them to new assignments. Fortunately for Boys Town the new Institute was well enough established to begin providing the initial physical examinations of boys as they were admitted and to handle routine medical problems on campus. The Home's rescue squad was now on call around the clock, only minutes away from emergency wards at Methodist and Bergan Mercy Hospitals. Very soon a list of approved physicians and dentists was made available to all cottages. From now on the Family Teachers were to call for appointments with medics of their choice for their boys as parents normally do for their own families. The Institute provided impetus for our comprehensive health care.

National popularity of the Institute was almost instantaneous. By the end of 1976 nearly 4,000 boys and girls had been served, including some from South America. A summer program was started for hearing impaired children allowing them to come and be evaluated and treated without missing school at home.

In a brief and rather informal ceremony in September of 1977 Archbishop Daniel E. Sheehan blessed the new facility. But its official dedication came on October 4, 1978, when the Institute's dedication banquet was held in the Red Lion Hotel in downtown Omaha, at which time "Outstanding Citizen Awards" were presented to Eunice Shriver, Sargent Shriver and Phil Donahue.

The award was given to Eunice Shriver for her generosity and untiring efforts on behalf of handicapped people and mentally retarded children of our nation; to Sargent Shriver for his leadership role in establishing the Peace Corps that has sent thousands of concerned Americans out to help the needy and illiterate young people of the world; and to Phil Donahue for his skilled hosting of a dynamic forum on national television, "The Donahue Show" which helps illuminate complex and controversial, moral and religious issues of our society, especially those affecting children.

The banquet served as a curtain-raiser for a scientific dedication conference that was held on October 5 and 6, 1978, with leading specialists in medicine, education, and research gathered from throughout the United States and several foreign countries. Those two days of workshops and seminars enjoyed the expertise of thirty-two guest faculty and seventeen professional staff of the Institute itself.

"This new project," said Monsignor Wegner in commenting about the Institute which was initiated during his later days as executive director, "is an extension of the dream of service to youth which Father Flanagan had when he founded Boys Town."

From its inception, the Home has continually expanded its physical plans and services in the care and education of homeless boys. Now, in a very special way, we will be serving both boys and girls from all over the country, helping correct their hearing and speech disorders.

"The Boys Town Institute will be dedicated to the goal that every child might hear and speak of the works of God's creation."

Monsignor Wegner's words were prophetic. From the outset, the Institute, the first of its kind in the country to bring communicative specialists of all disciplines together in one hospital, was specially designed for its patients — children. Here, for the first time a child with communications problems could receive in one location a complete physical and psychological diagnosis. Heretofore such a total examination could have been obtained only by medical hopscotching around the country.

Several techniques were included in the design of the building to allay the normal fears of a child who is introduced to a hospital environment. The visual surrounding would appeal to children. Walls were made of glass, or covered with vivid appliques of airplanes, trains, cars and other designs that draw the attention of children.

"We live in an adult world," said Dr. Brookhouser, "but we want children who come to us to feel comfortable in a world designed for them."

Since the Institute does extensive diagnostic work and also performs corrective procedures that may require repeated minor surgeries over a period of time, there will be children in the hospital who, except for slight discomfort, are otherwise physically well. Different levels of care were foreseen in the design of the hospital. Medical apparatus, tubes and wires are all as portable as possible in order to be removed from the child's sight. Even in some cases these are connected to hidden hookups in rooms, thus leaving the children's area as free of hospital equipment as possible.

Many young children feel comfortable communicating only with a parent. For this reason separate living quarters adjacent to the main structure were constructed so that children could stay with their parents when diagnostic work permitted. This presented a far less structured environment than an acute care hospital would and is less threatening to the child.

"The emphasis on keeping the family together is inherent in the hospital's design and staff attitudes," said Dr. Brookhouser. Parents are to be involved as much as possible in every aspect of the child's care. This is a far cry from the old practice of parents dropping off their children on Monday and returning to see them later in the week during visiting hours. Separating a child from the family makes an incredible impact on the child. And in many cases, the parents need as much reassurance and information as the child does if a real healing process is to take place.

Then there is a video tape tour led by a guide dressed as a clown who goes from the Admission Office to the laboratory, the kitchen and to other areas that a child patient often never sees. In various ways the child is given a sense of active involvement in what is happening in the hospital. This includes planning meals and parties as they recover from whatever medical procedures take place. In all, it makes for intense emotional interaction between the staff and children.

For clinicians, known for their cool detachment, this indeed is a challenge, for care is more difficult to give than medicine. The entire environment is testimony to the growing concern for treating the whole child, and the success of this approach is seen in the rapid growth and popularity of the Institute.

Located in the former parents' living quarters at the Institute, the Ronald McDonald House of Omaha is now the home away from home for families of Institute patients, and, in fact, for families of children at other Omaha area hospitals. The former family living space for patients was remodeled to incorporate the Ronald McDonald design.

Boys Town first approached the authorities of the Ronald McDonald House organization in 1983. The concept of the House is to defray expensive lodging bills, keep loved ones close to the hospitalized child and allow families facing similar illnesses to share experiences and strengths. The House can serve as many as forty people at a time. Some facilities are shared, yet privacy is assured.

Funding is provided by Boys Town and McDonald restaurant owners in Nebraska and Western Iowa. Donations are also received from the public and families living there.

The first Ronald McDonald House was the product of an idea of the young daughter of a professional football player, Fred Hill of the Philadelphia Eagles. During his daughter's treatment for leukemia, Hill noted that though much progress had been made in treating children's illnesses, few hospitals provided suitable conditions for parents to be near or with their children during their hospital stay. This situation was called to the attention of the owners of McDonalds, and the first Ronald McDonald House was built in 1973. The one in Omaha was the 77th in the United States, Canada and Australia.

The original Institute construction consisted of two major components — a five story Clinical Diagnostic and Rehabilitation Center, and a Language and Learning Center. The Institute enhanced its reputation for being a national health care resource in 1979 when it established a clinical laboratory dealing with the hereditary aspects of communication disorders. In 1983 a new program of research on dyslexia was inaugurated with the objective of finding a way to identify this crippling ailment at or near birth.

Some of the world's most advanced research on hearing, speech and learning disorders takes place at the Institute. Research questions evolve from clinical problems encountered by Institute physicians. This physician-lab scientist teamwork results in innovative testing procedures. Special equipment and devices and computer technology are used to provide better patient care. Researchers also strive to improve basic understanding of the speech and hearing process so even more complex problems may be solved.

Children who come to the Institute for evaluation may suffer from ear infections, deafness, speech impairments such as stuttering, head or facial deformities such as cleft lip and cleft palate. Some have multiple handicaps. Each patient is examined by a team of specialists assembled to address the individual's particular problem, using sophisticated techniques and equipment.

Institute staff members may measure anything from a child's hearing level or sense of balance to air flow and muscle movement during speech. A patient benefits from the skills of many specialists from whom he receives treatment, but his treatment is coordinated by a single physician.

After the child has been evaluated and a diagnosis is made, rehabilitation can begin. This may mean fitting hearing aids and speech prosthesis, surgery, psychological counseling or speech therapy, or a combination. Preschool classes for the deaf, stuttering clinics, speech and language training, sign language lessons, workshops and support groups for parents — all are offered. For patients living outside the Omaha area, as well as those living nearby, Institute physicians consult with the patient's family physician for continuing care of the youth when he/she returns home.

Because Dr. Brookhouser and some of his staff double as staff members of Creighton University's Department of Otolaryngology, their expertise is also available to some adults with hearing and speech problems, but only when time and energy permit after the children are attended to.

As special needs of communicatively-handicapped children have been discovered, the Institute has responded by developing new programs. In 1980 testing of deaf students revealed that many of those with superior nonverbal IQs were not succeeding in school or participating in extra-curricular activities.

A summer program on the Boys Town campus was initiated, with academic, physical, fine art, social and computer activities to stimulate the potential in specially gifted hearing-impaired youngsters. Boys and girls from all over the United States come to take part in this summer program, then return to their hometown schools. Full reports on their participation in these summer extracurricular activities go to their teachers.

Finally, it was noted that youngsters with handicaps are very vulnerable to child abuse. They are more dependent on caretakers and less likely to recognize abuse and less able to report it. Between fifty and sixty percent of all abuse victims in the country may be handicapped children. To help such children, early in 1984 the Institute included in its program the nation's first treatment and prevention center for abused handicapped children.

You would think with this remarkable record to humanity that the Boys Town National Institute would have escaped the nitpicking and carping of the Sun newspapers before that little-lamented publication ceased to exist. Not so. In 1978 its second shot at Boys Town included the Institute.

Said the Sun: "In the months since the Boys Town Institute opened its doors it has become the target of sharp criticism ranging from poor planning to insufficient use and unrealistic goals." Comments were not documented nor the source noted.

But even the Sun saw a brighter side with this observation: "To its credit, one of the doctors, formerly at the Institute, pointed out that the Institute has an outstanding research facility and one of the best audiology and speech pathology programs in the country."

That was the whole idea of the Institute's mission from its very inception. The Boys Town National Institute is truly the most complete diagnostic and treatment center of its kind that I know of.

Make no mistake about this. Boys Town National Institute is not another "mistake across the lake."

CHAPTER **Nine**

O UR new method of caring for homeless boys, called the Family Concept, not only has worked well on the Boys Town campus but it attracted nationwide attention almost from the beginning. Our Youth Care staff was happy with the early developments of the entire program, as were the courts and youth care agencies making referrals to the Home.

Very soon we began receiving requests to extend our program to other communities with needy youths — and in the mid-1970s that included just about every agency and court we had been dealing with. Boys Town was now being recognized as a leader in the field of youth care — the flagship of the fleet.

The idea of teaching the social graces, family skills and study habits as well as learning in the classroom appealed to juvenile judges, social workers and others charged with providing good care for homeless children. Those people soon realized that we were concerned with the whole child — combining the expertise of classroom teachers, Family Teachers and clergy.

So swamped were we with requests for information about our Model that early on Lonnie Phillips and I began discussing ways of exporting it. We would create what we decided initially to call "Boys Town USA" by establishing sites in localities where most needed.

As I have reported in previous chapters, we were confident that our program could be taught to others, in large part because it did not depend on a charismatic leader in the mold of Father

Flanagan. If we could teach willing young couples to become Family Teachers, we certainly could teach a dedicated leader to step into my shoes. In other words, almost any knowledgeable and experienced child care executive could, with our support, learn to direct the program.

It has long been my idea that neglected youth in the inner city could best be taught, trained, and cared for as near their home neighborhood as possible. Let me cite an example: Busing children to schools far from their home involved too many problems to make the idea practical.

Early in my career as pastor of Christ the King parish in Omaha I was required to enroll some twenty inner-city youths. These youths would spend about two hours a day in a bus coming and going. They were unable to stay after school for special tutoring, which most of them needed, and they were deprived of an opportunity to participate in the school's athletic and music programs. Furthermore, parents of these children found it very difficult, if not out of the question, to attend Parents' Club meetings or visit individually with the child's teachers after school. How much better would it be for everyone concerned if facilities and teachers like we had at Christ the King School could be made available in the inner city.

This background thinking of mine was the motivating factor in establishing Boys Town USA sites. Teaching, training and caring for neglected youth can be accomplished with much more success, according to my way of thinking, when done in their home community. Knowing of no precedent in this kind of venture, we were bound to make mistakes — and we did. However, we learned from those mistakes. At the peak of our outward bound activities we were affiliated with 94 agencies in loosely organized joint ventures. Our first lesson learned was that in order to control the quality of our program and avoid being exploited, it was necessary that we own the property on which our program was being operated.

In January of 1976 the Boys Town Board authorized the construction of two group homes in Kansas City, Kansas. The reason for this selection was that for years more boys were referred to Boys Town from the Kansas City area than from any other single location outside of Omaha. We purchased the site recommended by the local Catholic Charities organization and began planning for a joint operation.

When the local Catholic bishop learned of this, he promptly cancelled all association with Boys Town because, he said: "Boys Town has too much money." What that had to do with caring for needy youth was never made clear. However, without full cooperation of local church authorities our efforts would suffer. We sold the property and wrote the second rule for establishing a Boys Town USA site: In advance, secure the good will of influential church authorities, Catholic and non-Catholic in the area, all important government entities, from the Governor to the Mayor, and the prevailing courts and agencies that deal with juveniles. As time went on, we learned we had to be asked to come into a community before we could successfully care for problem youth in that community. We would need to build good community relations before building any kind of facility.

One more factor was very important, and that was getting the community in question involved in one way or another. Unfortunately, some of the agencies enjoying our affiliation exploited our name and reputation, while giving our program shabby treatment. Agencies and organizations in six different states had invited us to come without making a solid commitment to our program. It was like being invited to the proverbial duck dinner, "You bring the duck." You might say that we brought the duck and they ate it.

We closed down our affiliations in Louisiana, New Jersey, Texas, Kansas and Pennsylvania without incurring a lot of negative relations in those communities. Our experience in Massachusetts was an interesting one, albeit no more rewarding than the other outreach efforts had been. A state social agency, headquartered in Boston, extended a personal invitation asking me to visit the area at my convenience and make some recommendations.

Dr. Phillips went with me. We were met at the airport by two of the local clergy, each of whom was in charge of a small home in different locations of the city. We toured the homes under their care, only to learn that each priest had his own turf to protect.

Before arriving in Boston I had made arrangements to visit with Cardinal Humberto Medeiros while I was there. Manipulations denying my access to the Cardinal gave me to understand that Boys Town really was not welcome in "Bean Town." During our ride back to the airport our two clerical escorts left no doubt in our minds where Boys Town could "pile our garbage and stack our cans." Let me say that it was more than a hint that we were not needed, and certainly not welcome to come in and share the per diem funds budgeted by Massachusetts to care for its troubled youth. Upon our return to Boys Town my report to the Board was, "Scratch Boston."

Thus after three years of furnishing our expertise and evaluating joint group home operations, it was decided to discontinue the experiment. Gradually we phased out ninety-four such ventures.

However, Dr. Phillips and I were in no mood to turn in our suits on this idea of exporting the Boys Town Model. We simply needed another brain-storming session to evaluate our experiences and incorporate them into a new approach.

Incidentally, Lonnie was plagued with the physical problem of being overweight. He had confided to me from the very beginning that before he came to Boys Town he had submitted to a medical procedure to control his weight. It had not been as successful as he had hoped. He spoke freely to me about it, and told me how the medications he was taking were affecting his energy. He requested that he be relieved of the constant pressure of the overall youth care program. Then he could more comfortably concentrate his efforts on Boys Town USA. It seemed like a good idea, and I agreed.

In a regular meeting of the Board on September 10, 1982 the name "Father Flanagan's Boys' Home - USA" was given official approval. For convenience sake the name was soon shortened to

"Boys Town USA." Calling on our previous experiences, Lonnie and I drew up the following essential rules:

* Boys Town's programs must be wanted and welcomed in writing by state and local political leaders, community church authorities, and especially the Catholic Bishop of the area.
* Boys Town must own and operate the facility to be furnished by the local community.
* Funding for each project was to be solicited in advance from local resources such as corporations, foundations, grants, and selected individuals. No Boys Town funds were to be used.
* Only youths from the state where the facility is located are to be admitted to the Boys Town program.

I've always felt that there was an advantage to have boys in the Home who came from communities in and around Omaha. We could better communicate with the boys' families, their social workers and the courts that had jurisdiction over them. This made our job simpler, and it seemed to be better for the boys. On the other hand there was always the temptation for them to run away from the Home. However, we thought the advantages were to our benefit.

Thus we were interested in an idea proposed by a case worker named John Zeeman. For many years Zeeman had been instrumental in placing Florida boys with us; sometimes as many as 80 at a time were at the Home. Zeeman suggested that the Florida State Department of Human and Rehabilitative Services might be interested in establishing a Boys Town in Florida on the terms we had spelled out. The Florida State director of this department was, indeed, interested in Zeeman's idea, as were we, and after hearing our story he was eager to cooperate in every way.

He thought a good place to locate would be in Tallahassee, the state capital. Already overrun with fund drives of one kind or another, it was not possible to find anyone to chair a drive for the Boys Town project. However, while circulating among the opinion-makers in the capital we discovered an ideal location for a cluster of five cottages. This property, which included an excellent residence and pool, was large enough for four more cottages to be built, two on either side of the existing house. The listed price was $185,000. Peter Smith, a banker with whom I had become acquainted, offered to float a loan for that amount with the option to buy the property back a year later for the same amount of money. This would give Boys Town time to demonstrate our program and test the support of the community. The Boys Town Board of Directors, on April 6, 1984, approved the arrangement with the added caution, "Go slow, one house at a time."

In the course of the next twelve months Florida's Health and Rehabilitative Service Department monitored closely our program in the one residence at 2516 Hartsfield Road, Tallahassee. Unfortunately, the glowing reports about our program coming out of the Health and Rehabilitative Services Department did not convince the leading citizens of Tallahassee to loosen their purse strings, and our goal of five cottages was not achieved at that time. However, our reputation did catch the attention of people in Orlando, Florida who extended an invitation to "Come South," as they said.

My next stop was Orlando where a different atmosphere in the community prevailed. Community and business leaders expressed a genuine interest in getting involved with Boys Town in caring for their troubled youth near their homes. A get-acquainted luncheon, hosted by the airport's manager, Jack Gillooly, was the spark needed to start the first real Boys Town USA.

A construction executive, William Demetree, made the first positive move. For his corporation he donated a ten-acre piece of property in Oviedo, a suburb of Orlando.

Meantime, fund raising began to command our time. Bob Pleuss, an Orlando attorney, agreed to chair the Boys Town USA steering committee. A fund-raising dinner, again at the airport, brought together a room full of people who were eager to hear what Father Flanagan's Boys' Home was bringing to Orlando. This marked the beginning of community involvement on behalf of our most successful site in Florida.

More luncheons and dinners, along with an invitation to play the Bay Hills golf course with Frank Hubbard and Arnie Palmer, were among the fringe benefits attendant to that first luncheon.

Another construction man, owner of a dry wall firm, offered to furnish the dry wall for our new cottages. This was Bob Vickery, a pillar in the Baptist Church of Orlando. He and I had a great time, among other things, matching Scripture texts. Our conversations must have advanced the cause of ecumenism, because when we were ready for the dry walls they were delivered.

Because of previous commitments to his own congregation, the new Baptist church in Orlando, his generosity to Boys Town was limited for the time being, but he assured me that if I were to return when his pledges were fulfilled, "We could put the Boys Town site on a paying basis," to use his words. His attitude, as well as those pioneers already mentioned, was typical of more opinion-makers of the area such as Tony Bruno, Norm Glass, Joe Gurtis, John Lord, Domenic Mancione, John Morgan, and Rick Proctor.

By the time of my retirement on June 15, 1985, sufficient local funds, in-kind services and gifts had been donated to complete three cottages on the Demetree donated property. Boys Town was prepared to furnish the trained staff to operate the homes. Now a precedent had been set. We could truthfully tell agencies around the country, "Go to Orlando and see how it works."

Some real interest in the Boys Town Model was also emerging in California. A good start was made when thirteen acres of undeveloped land in the Torrance area were donated by John and Joseph Freidrich, friends of Boys Town. It was to be used for a youth care site. The location was very accessible, yet far enough from downtown Los Angeles to avoid the problems associated with the crowded urban scene. The location hinted at Father Flanagan's idea of training troubled young people in a peaceful, rural area, away from the distractions of a runaway society. But before we could start work there, I reached retirement age.

Although there are now Boys Town USA operations in a number of cities across the nation, that land near Torrance, California waits to be developed.

CHAPTER **Ten**

U PON my return to the Archdiocese of
Omaha from duty as a chaplain in the US Navy after World War II,
my first assignment was that of Director of the Catholic Youth
Organization with residence at the Convent of the Good
Shepherd at 40th and Jones Streets in Omaha. During my five
years as chaplain at this home for wayward and neglected girls, I
was impressed with the need for additional adequate facilities for
these adolescents. Once I had recovered my bearings from the
initial shock of finding myself at the helm at Boys Town, the plight
of troubled girls became a real concern.

Introducing the Family Concept to Boys Town in 1974 and
1975 involved, generally speaking, simulating on campus as
nearly as practicable family life as it is in society. Since about half
the youth population in society are girls, it seemed to be only a
matter of time and preparation that the distaff side would be
introduced to a hitherto all male population at the Home. It was
another idea whose time had come, an idea that Father Flanagan
himself seemed to have foreseen when on November 30, 1943,
before a U.S. Senate Sub-Committee on Wartime Health and
Education at Washington, D.C. he said: "I have faith in our
American boys and girls. I say there is no such thing as a bad boy,
the same applies to our girls."

As a matter of fact, Boys Town had for some time been
operating programs involving boys and girls. The Boys Town
Institute for Communications Disorders in Children, the Urban

Program which Boys Town had rescued when Dominican High was abandoned by its supporters (more on that later), and an Achievement Plus Program, all included "youths regardless of race, creed, sex, or ability to pay."

No one had challenged the Home's right to spend trust money on the Institute, and federal law required equal educational opportunities. To insure that the Home could:

* Continue to spend a share of its funds legally on these programs,
* Proceed on a planned systematic introduction of girls to its campus,
* And proceed to construct an urban coed high school to replace Dominican High School which was scheduled for demolition to make way for the North Omaha freeway.

Some members of the Boys Town Board of Directors, still reeling from the 1972 disclosure, were not quite ready for this move. The first mention of girls needing help, with a hint that they belonged in Boys Town, was made at a Board meeting on September 22, 1975. That raised a few eyebrows along with the remark: "Boy! Are you asking for trouble!"

"Yes," I agreed, "But that's our business — solving problems of our youth."

That only provoked more skepticism until I added, "You must realize that if we had no boys at Boys Town at all the place would run like a clock." The meeting moved on.

We were not without support as we continued to prepare for the day when girls would be admitted. Shortly after my arrival at Boys Town in 1973 two Douglas County Juvenile Court judges came out to see me. Both were personal acquaintances.

"When are you going to admit girls?" asked Judge Colleen Buckley. Before I could come up with a coherent response, Judge Joseph Moylan reinforced the question with his observations about the dire need to help girls. Friendly exchanges took place without my making a firm commitment. Our visit ended with

Judge Buckley's remark, "When you need another challenge, let us know."

The need for additional facilities for girls had arrived. In Father Flanagan's day orphaned girls, more so than boys, were adopted by relatives. At that time there was an orphanage in Omaha and one in Sioux City, Iowa along with Convents of the Good Shepherd in Kansas City, St. Paul in Minnesota, Denver and Omaha where girls were accepted. But the picture had changed drastically. As these institutions were closing their doors the number of girls who needed help was on the increase. Court records showed that arrests of girls under eighteen had increased thirty-eight percent between 1968 and 1977. Forty-seven percent of the runaways between the ages of fifteen and seventeen were girls.

Delinquency among the adolescent fairer sex in the form of drugs, runaways, and promiscuity in general was beginning to match that of the boys in the mid-1970s. A potential problem loomed in that our Articles of Incorporation seemed to limit our services only to boys. This needed clarification. I asked our attorneys to petition the Court for an interpretation of the language in our Articles of Incorporation to determine whether or not we could legally admit girls to our programs. Boys Town took the initiative here because we wanted to be within the law in what we were doing. Papers were sent for comment on the case to the Nebraska Attorney General and to the Douglas County Attorney who represent people making donations to the Home. The case was assigned to District Judge James Buckley, no relation to Judge Colleen Buckley.

Attorneys asked the Court to interpret the role of Boys Town as it relates to girls. Boys Town, the documents stated, was first incorporated in 1920 as a home for "indigent and wayward boys." The language of the original Articles of Incorporation said of Boys Town: "It may have and conduct such homes, asylums, farms, and places of education at such places in the city of Omaha or elsewhere as it may deem necessary and advantageous to the causes of charity, morality and education." Attorneys for the

Home, F. Vinson Roach and John C. Burke, the latter a former District Court Judge, filed a document asking the Court to determine whether several programs which Boys Town now offers to all persons, including girls, "are within the purposes of the charitable corporation." The document said further that Boys Town should be allowed to continue offering such services to all youths, despite language in the Articles of Incorporation which seem to limit the function of the institution to the care of boys.

Boys Town's new programs, it stated, "fill an important need in our society."

"Whereas Boys Town was once a haven for male orphans, the role of the institution has changed as society has changed," the paper said. "For example, most runaways are fifteen to seventeen years old and 47% are girls. In addition, the unemployment rate of females between the ages of sixteen and nineteen exceeds the unemployment rate of males in the same age group," the document concluded.

When the Court's decision eventually came down, variations of these headlines heralded the change across the country:

"Boys Town Isn't Just for Boys Anymore" (*Omaha World-Herald*)

"Father Flanagan's Dream Has Gone Coed" (*Boston Globe*)

"Judge Opens Boys Town" (*Manhattan Mercury, Manhattan, Kansas*)

"Girls Infiltrate the City of Little Men" (*Minneapolis/St. Paul Star*)

"She Ain't Heavy Father, She's My Sister" (*Boys Town Quarterly*).

Judge James A. Buckley's decision, made public on March 9, 1981, ordered and decreed that:

Father Flanagan's Boys' Home is authorized to equip, maintain and conduct a home, or homes, for indigent and wayward boys and girls; to support and educate indigent and wayward boys and girls in such home, or homes or elsewhere and to equip and

prepare them to lead useful lives; to provide health evaluation
and treatment services for boys and girls who have or are
suspected to have communication disorders or related dis-
abilities which interfere with their education or their ability to
lead useful lives and to undertake such research as is reasonably
required to furnish evaluations and treatment for such boys and
girls; and to provide comprehensive evaluations of youths, including behavioral and academic assessments in family background, psychological and psychiatric evaluations, for the
Separate Juvenile Court of Douglas County, Nebraska and other
courts. BE IT FURTHER ORDERED that the managing officers of Father Flanagan's Boys' Home are authorized to amend
the Articles of Incorporation to provide for the carrying out of the
foregoing purposes.

Attached to Judge Buckley's determination were documents
from the Nebraska Attorney General, Paul Douglas, and Douglas
County Attorney, Donald Knowles, representing people who
made donations to the Home, that did not object to admitting girls
to Boys Town.

The Boys Town Board immediately revised the Articles of
Incorporation to include girls. When this was done the State
Attorney General's Office sent this congratulatory message to
the Board: "Given the growing public policy against discrimina-
tion on the basis of sex, we commend you for your prudent and
far-sighted action initiated on behalf of Boys Town."

Although Boys Town had been providing limited help to girls,
none had lived at its residential facility in a formal family program
prior to the Court's decision. The Family Concept Model had
been tested with girls in a residence at 3570 Davenport Street in
Omaha, with Ralph and Ethel Lassiter as Family Teachers, even
before the Court's decision. The trial run had proved to be a
surprising success.

Judge Colleen Buckley sent us five girls from her court, three
black and two white. The oldest girl, Jean, was fifteen, a chubby 5
by 5, and a real bundle of human electricity. The others were
younger and smaller. With this small group the Lassiters helped

write the chapter on "Girls" in the Training Manual for Family Teachers.

We made haste slowly, and it paid off. The girls were proud of the fact that they were pioneers in the Boys Town Model. Although they did not live on campus, they participated in a number of activities at the Home. After the first Home football game Jean came to me and asked if the girls in Lassiters' home could be cheer leaders. At the time a number of boys called themselves cheer leaders. They had the equipment, were decorated for the occasion with a repertoire of one yell, probably enough for the enthusiasm shown on the field. Clearly it was time to beef up the cheer leaders' squad, so I listened.

"Jean," I said, "How can you be a cheer leader? I'll bet you can't jump off the ground."

Well — the impromptu demonstration that followed convinced me that where there was such a will there had to be a way, so I gave Jean a green light.

For the next home game we were treated to a brief "ad lib" performance that didn't seem to stop. One of the school teachers and two Family Teachers were so moved that they came forth, volunteered to organize and train the squad — and they did. Without girls on the campus, Family Teachers and staff members had already added their own daughters to the ranks. Some were so small they were dwarfed by their pom-poms. Without realizing it we were witnessing the birth of a new era in cheer leading in this "City of Little Men."

The time had come to introduce girls to the campus. It had been my idea, and the Board of Directors agreed, to develop a "Girls Town" on our property north of Dodge Street, but without ready access to that land this development would wait for another day.

The four dormitories across the street from Dowd Memorial Chapel were vacant. They had been declared unsuitable for habitation by the State Health Department. There were those at the Home who urged we raze them and build cottages in their place. This I resisted strongly because they were sturdy structures and could be remodeled for our use, plus the fact that they had great historic value. Eagle Hall, Building One that is, was donated to Father Flanagan by the Eagles on April 27, 1941 and destroying that structure was not my idea of appreciating what this great organization had done for the Boys' Home.

This dormitory section across the street from Dowd Chapel seemed to be an ideal setting for the formal introduction of girls to the campus. So it was that after complete remodeling of Eagle Hall, two specially trained married couples launched, in June of 1984, one of the most significant changes to occur in the history of Father Flanagan's Boys' Home. Each couple cared for seven girls. For the record it should be noted that Tom and Julie Walters and Bob and Lois Sullivan were those Family Teachers.

Then there was the convent, where over thirty nuns once lived. It too was a well constructed building, and it was vacant. With a minimum of remodeling it was readied for occupancy and more girls were placed there. Three years later when a staff committee named the streets in Boys Town Village, the one leading to the convent was rather appropriately named "Convent Road." A delegation of girls who were living in the remodeled convent came to my office expressing their disenchantment with that street title. The committee was reconvened and the name changed to "Mother Teresa Lane," and so it is today.

Integration of the sexes in classrooms, in athletic events, in all phases of activity across the campus was a gradual but well accepted fait accompli. Life at Boys Town would never be the same. We started with fourteen girls, and by mid-June 1985 Boys Town's population figures showed twenty-six girls and 415 boys.

Although the number of girls was small in proportion to the total population, our athletic department lost no time in organizing sports for girls. Volley ball, basketball, cross country and track teams were the first to compete against area high schools.

Molding the raw talent into competitive teams was a challenge for our coaches. Although competing for a school called "Boys Town" invited a few whistles and catcalls, the girls were overjoyed to be involved in high school sports, an entirely new venture for them.

They did, however, draw the line on being called "Cowgirls." Boys Town teams are called the "Cowboys" but that natural correlative nickname went over with the girls like the proverbial lead balloon. Parenthetically, a donation of cowboy hats and boots to the Boys Town football team in the late '40's inspired the use of the mascot name "Cowboys." During the '40's the football team, under Coach Maurice "Skip" Palrang, was a national power-house, challenging the nation's top high school teams across the country and drawing large crowds to the competitions. The Cowboy name became well known following a Thanksgiving Day game with Aquinas Institute in Rochester, New York in 1949 with 20,382 people in attendance. Prior to this the team was known as the West Dodge Ramblers, the West Dodgers or the Boys Towners.

In a short time the change in the boys' behavior on campus was very evident. How long that would last was a matter of conjecture, but it was good to note the immediate improvement in grooming and in speech.

An interesting concern of the media at this time was: "What about the name Boys Town, now that girls are living in the Village?" Such names as "Boys and Girls Town," "People Town," and "Person Town" were among the suggestions, devoid of all color and imagination. A meeting with the girls was called and the problem explained with a view of hearing them out on the subject.

"Don't change the name," they chimed.

"We want to live at Boys Town."

Hearing from those who occasioned the problem made the determination rather easy. "Boys Town" it is.

A bit of flair was added to the next graduation day when, as Kevin Collison of the Omaha World-Herald noted, "Eighteen year old Joni Bachelor went to the podium and delivered her high school's commencement speech in one of America's most vener-able male institutions." It was another well publicized first —

graduation at Boys Town on May 28, 1983. She and four girls she had learned to regard as "sisters" were the first girls to graduate from Boys Town High School in its sixty-five year history. Her pioneering classmates were Lisa Bordogna, 17; Jeannette Hoer, 17; Cindy Koppenhaver, 17; and Diane Luce, 18.

In her speech Miss Bachelor spoke for all when she said, "Here we are, all the same and we don't leave anyone out. We are one big family."

Four of the five had been cheerleaders and Miss Bachelor was selected queen of both homecoming and the prom.

Boys Town was now coed in all activities except in the residential area. There were off-limits areas for boys as there were for girls. Evening athletic events and weekends in general were less structured, you might say, and as a result more liable to spawn behavior problems. However, the mere presence of Family Teachers at all times was a powerful influence for good. To say that a mixing of the sexes was of no concern was not realistic. But, just as every cloud has a silver lining, so each incident presented an opportunity for learning how to avoid future problems. At those particular times proper personal relationships were taught and emphasized.

Girls are no longer an oddity at Boys Town.

When a tourist strolls about the grounds on a warm summer afternoon, drinking in the beauty and spirit of the campus, that visitor may by chance come upon a girl who will stop, extend her hand for a handshake, and say, "Welcome to Boys Town: My name is Mary! What is yours? It's nice to have you here! I hope you enjoy your visit," and then continue on her way.

CHAPTER **Eleven**

I T is no secret that I have never been an advocate of busing school children out of their neighborhoods for several reasons. Disadvantages of the practice far outweigh the benefits claimed. Spending a couple of hours a day on a school bus has few redeeming features for a growing boy or girl. These young people are deprived of participating in athletics, band, orchestra and glee club activities, and special help offered by teachers after school. Parents of these young people find it almost impossible to visit with the teachers for the benefit of their sons or daughters.

It occurred to me long ago that Jesus did not lead poor people out of their lowly surroundings into high rent districts to teach them. Rather, he went into the areas where poor people lived and taught them there.

That general idea inspired me to think in terms of exporting our programs to the needy rather than vice versa. Our educational program was well adapted to the caliber of students that came to Boys Town and it was fully accredited. By chance, an inner city private school in Omaha, named Dominican High, was rumored to be in trouble. State authorities were talking about constructing a freeway which might eliminate Dominican High.

Back in 1968, the Board of Education of the Archdiocese of Omaha voted to close Sacred Heart High School, which was located in the heart of Omaha's black ghetto. Financial embarrassment of the school was the reason for this decision. Arrangements were made by Monsignor Roman Ulrich, superintendent of Omaha's Archdiocesan Schools, to transfer Sacred Heart students to the vacant school building at Holy Angels Church several blocks away. By some astute negotiating with the Dominican Sisters who had been operating Sacred Heart High School and a few handshakes by clerics with a financial grip, the school was able to function in its new location.

Needless to say, the name of the school was Dominican High, not Sacred Heart or Holy Angels High. Doors were opened in September of 1968 to Dominican High School with Sister Danielle Griffin, principal, and Father Larry Dorsey, head counselor. It was a very special school for students who had a history of failure in public and parochial schools.

It was indeed an "alternative school." Classes were smaller, permitting a personalized, supportive style of teaching. Administrators and teachers exercised enough authority to make decisions on the spot based on what each felt was best for the student. The idea was to minimize failure; these students already have tasted too much defeat. Basic skills were the core of the curriculum with self discipline the toughest course of all.

In 1972 Father James Gilg was appointed principal of the school by Archbishop Sheehan and the following year Robert Faulkner was named assistant principal. Both were ideal assignments. They complemented each other — Father Gilg is white, Faulkner is black; Father Gilg is a cleric, Faulkner a layman. Since the school had long been flirting with bankruptcy, in 1976 a fund-raising board known as the Christian Urban Education Service (CUES) was organized. This board worked closely with Father John Flynn, Monsignor Roman Ulrich's successor as Superintendent of Catholic schools in the Archdiocese of Omaha.

On August 24, 1979 Father Gilg was notified by the State Department of Roads that Dominican High School building did indeed stand in the way of the extension of the North Freeway, a divided four-lane Interstate Highway. The building must be vacated by September 1, 1981.

Where would Dominican High School go? Hasty estimates of a new building in a new location ranged around the $3 million mark. The State would pay Holy Angels parish $1,079,000, with only $702,000 allotted to Dominican High. Father Gilg and CUES asked James L. Koley to chair a committee that would work out a solution to the school's knotty problem. Koley, an Omaha attorney and prominent Catholic layman, took his assignment seriously. His committee scoured the general area of North Omaha for empty commercial buildings, parochial school buildings and convents, abandoned buildings of every kind to purchase or lease, but to no avail. If this fine inner-city alternate school was to survive a new building seemed to be the only course of action.

Meantime the $80,000 annual subsidy which the Archdiocese of Omaha had been contributing and the cash contributions CUES had been making were giving evidence of drying up. The wolf was at the door.

Self-styled spokesmen in North Omaha, of whom there were a few, stepped away from this challenge. At this point only the students, their families, staff members at the school and CUES members seemed to have Dominican at heart.

However, a silent but observing savior stood in the wings. Enter Boys Town. It was not generally known that at my instigation a number of high level meetings had taken place between two members of the CUES board and selected members of the Boys Town staff. As a matter of fact, private conversations on the subject of a possible cooperative effort between CUES and Boys Town had taken place shortly after CUES was organized. However, this had only been talk, and the subject lay dormant until now when we all could see the handwriting on the wall.

This seemed to be the time to test some of the ideas I had voiced a few years earlier about the need for good facilities and excellent teachers in the inner city as opposed to busing. At a meeting of the Boys Town Board of Directors on December 7, 1979 this concept was discussed. At a regular meeting of this Board on February 1, 1980, Father Gilg made a formal presentation of the curriculum at Dominican High. His report was an eye-opener. He said surveys indicated that 53 per cent of his students were using drugs of one kind or another, and that 59 per cent were regular consumers of alcohol in varying degrees. A number of female students were teen-age mothers.

This report left little doubt about what Boys Town's action should be. Later during this same meeting the general concept of adopting Dominican High School was approved. Board member Herbert Sampson was named to head a committee to organize the take-over. Fellow committee members were Dr. A.B. Pittman (a veterinarian), Dr. Claude Organ (a surgeon), Charles Heider (investment broker), Archbishop Sheehan and "yours trully".

Midsummer 1980 was set as a target date to complete the cooperative program. The Board decided at this time to name the new school "Father Flanagan School." It remained for us now to develop an agenda of priorities that would be a guide for all concerned. That orchestration fell on my shoulders.

The action of the Board meant the end of official church support for the school. With Boys Town's financial support, the school could now grow in areas of research, health care, vocational training, and other educational services never possible under its previous hit-and-miss financing. As I told Board members: "This synergistic combination of Boys Town and Dominican schools would generate a realistic answer to the current rage for busing."

Boys Town would export only our educational methods in this case, not our residential expertise. Later Lonnie Phillips and I were prompted to establish Boys Town USA. This would complete our immediate approach to America's youth care problems: residential and educational programs at the Home, educational programs where youth could live in their own homes, and finally residential programs where youth could live with our Family Teachers but attend their neighborhood community schools.

The first order of business was engaging an architect who could begin planning the structure while a search for a place to locate it was conducted. Normally we would ask the traditional architect for the Home, the Leo A. Daly Company, to proceed with the plans. This firm had served Boys Town so well, designing among other things the Dowd Memorial Chapel and the cottage expansion in the 1940's. Leo Daly, Jr. himself had made substantial contributions to the Home by way of cash and services. And so in the normal run of things the Daly Company would be expected to get the nod.

Knowing Leo Daly as well as I did, I felt no hesitation in presenting him with an alternate plan. Since this new construction would be highly involved with black students and black parents I suggested to Leo that it might be wise to engage a black architect. I had in mind Golden J. Zenon, Jr., who not long before had been employed by the Daly Company and whom I had known for a number of years. Leo heard me out and with class personified, agreed that Zenon was the man. On July 1, 1980 a contract was signed with Zenon-Beringer and Associates. "Goldie" and Father Gilg had their work cut out for them.

The next step was to involve the community leaders in the inner city. There were many voices in a proverbial wilderness, but there was no single outstanding individual who could speak for the local people. After meeting with Mayor Al Veys and his Planning Department people, Ed Hewitt, Dr. Phillips and I met with all the inner city neighborhood representatives and residents of the area who were interested in learning our plans. Omaha's mayor, a lifelong resident of South Omaha where he owned a business and was a staunch supporter of his community, nonetheless was delighted to cooperate with anything that would help North Omaha.

Meanwhile, Father Gilg met with individuals of the Long School Neighborhood Association and the North Omaha Community Development (NOCD) Association and was favorably impressed with the reactions expressed.

Boys Town provided the balance of funding needed for Dominican High to complete its 1979-80 school year, and on July 19, 1980 Dominican High officially ceased to exist. Omaha's alternate school became 100 per cent a Boys Town responsibility.

The most difficult assignment of all remained that of locating a suitable piece of property and acquiring it at a reasonable price.

Here the assistance of Board member Dr. A.B. Pittman, a black, was invaluable. You might know that a high degree of confidentiality was necessary in making the final decision as to location and purchasing the property. A first class high school with an athletic field and adequate parking would require about six city blocks.

Board member Herb Sampson and his committee, after much discussion, decided to offer home owners the appraised value of their homes, plus a bonus of $14,000. I was not privy to the rationale for arriving at this amount, but it seemed eminently generous to me considering the general condition of the area.

The site selected was occupied by two small neighborhood churches, twenty-three owner-occupied homes, eleven vacant rental units, eighty-four vacant lots free of encumbrances, three large pieces owned by Omaha Public Schools, and seventy-two lots encumbered with debt (taxes and assessments) in excess of market value. Many of the owners of these properties had long ago disappeared. The site was a six-square-block area located from the east border of the North Freeway to 25th Street, between Franklin and Hamilton. This, of course, was not made public until all of the property was purchased.

After shopping around for a realtor to handle this project as expeditiously and quietly as possible we selected the Maenner Company, realtors. Paul McCollister, project coordinator for the Maenner Company, was placed in charge. Armed with the figures of an independent appraisal of each piece of property, and a bonus of $14,000 for each owner, McCollister went to work. All went well until very near the end when a leak occurred and a couple of professional protesters created some needless stir. As John Bunyon would say, "Men with a muck rake are often indispensable to the well-being of society, but only if they know where to stop raking the muck."

Thanks to the relentless efforts of Dr. Pittman, with the help of some neighborhood association members, the project finally became a reality.

The pastor of one of the churches lamented the foreseeable demolition of his church building. But another Board member,

Dr. Claude Organ, convinced the pastor that with the money he would receive he could build a much nicer building in the general vicinity. He did just that.

Another lady liked the idea of the bonus, but she also loved her home and did not wish to leave the neighborhood. There was an empty lot across the street. She wanted her house moved to that lot. McCollister agreed and eventually had it done for her.

Site clearing began in August of 1981. Some opponents felt that the houses were being razed without regard for people living nearby. Rats from the demolition area would be scurrying to the rest of the neighborhood they claimed. Anderson Excavating was under contract, not only to demolish the structures on the six-block piece of property, but also to remove the trash, clean out basements, and fill with clean dirt. The machine operators were asked to watch for rats and any other unusual circumstances worthy of note as they went to work.

When the work was completed the bulldozer operators reported: "We did not see a single rat; we did see a few bull snakes."

Architect Zenon called this school the most important development in North Omaha since he arrived in 1955. He knew the area well and knew whereof he spoke.

Ground-breaking ceremonies were held November 5, 1981. On the program were Archbishop Sheehan, members of the Board of Directors and staff members of both Boys Town and the former Dominican High School as well as city officials.

Father Gilg set the tone when he said: "Our action today testifies to the faith of Father Edward J. Flanagan, who saw goodness in the eyes of every youth who came his way. This school speaks of the goodness and success that lies within every young man and woman of this country, even though they may be trapped by circumstances not of their own choosing."

Nebraska Governor Charles Thone, in a congratulatory message, saw the event as a signal of the rebirth for a large area of Omaha's Near North Side. When it was announced at a Board meeting that the cost would be $7 million, I said: "Gentlemen, on a clear day we can see the poorhouse."

We asked the general contractor, James Mainelli of Mainelli Construction Company, to hire as many minority workers and sub-contractors as possible, and he did. With a relatively small number of change orders, the school was ready for occupancy in August of 1983. Registration for the first year was held on August 29, and Flanagan High School was open for business two days later with 198 students reporting.

As someone aptly put it: "Dominican's roots survived transplant very well."

Unfortunately, Herbert Sampson who had worked so hard on all phases of the project was not around to enjoy the fruition of his labors. He died unexpectedly on September 26, 1982.

Goldie Zenon and his associates created a super structure, designed specifically around the needs of high risk students in the very midst of devastating poverty. Its sense of spaciousness, beauty and order created a respect for the surroundings. Graffiti and vandalism have no place in what the students consider "their building."

All interior areas are designed for flexibility. Teachers can lecture to a classroom of students lined up in formal array, or they can have the students move their desks into small clusters. A small cluster can be studying one phase of a subject in a "seminar room" while the bulk of the class hears a lecture in an adjoining room. This allows one teacher to oversee two activities at once.

Because all of the students come from unstable family conditions, where poverty, drug addiction, alcoholism and teen-age pregnancy are a fact of life, Flanagan High has tailored its educational and social service programs to help students complete their education and improve their chances for employment and self-sufficiency.

Planning, goal setting and critical thinking are stressed in all classes. Flanagan High is accredited by the State of Nebraska and the North Central Association of Colleges and Schools, and it offers a full line of core academic subjects — English, math, social studies, foreign languages and science, plus — and this is unusual for an alternative school — fine arts, music, drama, physical education and interscholastic athletics.

For those students for whom college is not a realistic goal the school offers a career preparation program based on getting a job, home maintenance, keyboarding and computer literacy. Advanced courses are offered in computer services, business services, construction skills, automotive services, health services, food services, human services and electronics.

There is no pretense at running a secular school. Religion is a part of the curriculum. All students take religious training each year in such courses as Reverence for Life and Family, Faith Foundations, Scripture, Moral Development, Christian Values and a choice between Catholic or Protestant teachings.

One unique element is the credit earning system. Because of disruptions in their family lives, Flanagan students often had trouble with traditional schools that required a complete semester's work before awarding credits. At Flanagan, students earn fractions of credits with each completed assignment, each passed test, and each day's attendance. This slow but steady accumulation of credits encourages students to stay in school while measuring their progress toward a diploma day by day. It also encourages them to return if they do drop out. They can pick up where they left off.

The system leans heavily on counseling. The school has developed an extensive program of responsible services for those in crisis, offering emergency financial assistance, counseling to students with family troubles, and chemical and alcohol abuse counseling from a certified chemical abuse expert. Alcoholics Anonymous and Alateen hold weekly meetings in school.

The school has its own parole officer for one-fourth of the students who are on parole or probation. The officer helps them in the difficult transition to a school setting where they are free to come and go from their previous detention.

The first classes included twelve teen-age mothers who

brought their children to school. A nursery accommodates up to twenty-eight infants, and the school offers parenting instructions to all students. Flanagan High hopes to break the cycle of teenage pregnancy and welfare dependency by keeping young people in school and improving their job prospects and teaching them the consequences and responsibilities of parenthood.

The Boys Town Hall of History, in its section on Flanagan High, contains this quote from a young girl student: "I left school when I was fourteen to have a baby. My mom didn't care. My dad is gone. If there wasn't a place like Father Flanagan High School I would never finish high school. Here my baby can play in the nursery and I am learning how to take care of her."

Flanagan's athletic teams have the nickname "Chargers," and in its first year the school's basketball team earned a berth in the State Tournament. Other athletic honors include an individual state wrestling championship, two individual Golden Gloves titles and an individual Metro Power Lifting award.

The first red letter day was May 27, 1984 — not only were seventy young men and women graduated from Boys Town High School in the afternoon, but that evening twenty-nine young men and women received their diplomas from Flanagan High School.

We must have been doing something right for in the summer of 1984 Father Gilg received notification from the U.S. Secretary of Education stating: "I would like to congratulate you on being selected by the Council for American Private Education as an outstanding American Alternative High School." Flanagan High School was named one of the top sixty private alternative schools in America.

In a corresponding letter, Robert L. Smith, Executive Director of the Council for American Private Education, referred to Flanagan High as a "distinguished school worthy of national recognition."

Father Gilg accepted the award in a ceremony in Washington, D.C. on August 29, 1984, one year to the day after the first students were registered.

Assistant Principal Robert Faulkner has summed up very nicely the school's string of successes by saying: "Our school is not a special school. It only does special things."

Chalk up Flanagan High School on the plus side of our ventures into the new and different when it comes to the care and education of homeless and troubled youth in the inner city.

And we never owned a bus.

CHAPTER **Twelve**

"Every boy must learn to pray. How he prays is up to him." —
Father Edward J. Flanagan, quoted in the Boys Town Hall of
History.

"God has a special and different plan for each of us." — Father
Robert P. Hupp, quoted in the Boys Town Hall of History.

Y OU'D think the one area where there'd be no
problems for me when I came to Boys Town would be in the field
of religion. After all, didn't a priest found the Home and didn't
another priest head it for twenty-five years?

Think again. Among all the matters waiting to be straightened
out after the Sun Newspapers' report on the Home was religion.
It stood in line, needing my attention. The Sun, among many
other things in its voluminous report, quoted an unnamed
alumnus as saying that religion "doesn't exist at Boys Town
anymore."

That wasn't quite true, but it wasn't all that far from the truth,
either. Religion had a presence on the campus, epitomized by the
grace and dignity of Dowd Chapel, and also by the Protestant
Chapel in the Field House. But few were actively supporting
religion. Religion was on a take-it-or-leave-it basis for the boys,
and given their background you can guess which choice most of
them made.

Take for instance attendance at church on Sundays, and in religion classes in the schools. A sprinkling of boys and staff members would be present in both places. To inquiries about the obvious lack of interest, the response was, "This is a free country, and one of the freedoms is that of religion." This attitude prompted the following notice — authored by the executive director — in the Dowd Chapel Sunday Bulletin, June 16, 1974:

"When regular calls to the dentist and doctor are made optional, then church attendance may follow suit. When readin' and 'ritin' and 'rithmetic are made optional, these classes in religion may become an elective. Until then religion is a required subject. Once a boy leaves Boys Town he is free to exercise all the options he wishes but while he is here he is in training. The biblical injunction, 'Seek first the Kingdom of God' (Matthew 6:33), is not a pious platitude. You have a choice of attending or not attending services Monday through Saturday of each week. Only on Sunday is church attendance required for Catholics and Protestants . . . far too many people think erroneously that freedom of religion means freedom from religion. Subscribing to this latter idea might lead you to be counted among the goats on judgment day."

Reaction to this bulletin was immediate. The next Sunday Dowd Chapel was practically filled for the students' Mass. Many counselors were on the job, although there was an element of acquiescence but silent protest in their ranks. Some remained at the main entrance as if to discourage early departures. What was very noticeable was the long line leading to the East Side confessionals. It appeared to be the first positive sign of reform. My hopes were shattered, however, when I discovered near the end of the Mass that the once crowded church was less than half-filled.

Upon investigation I found that a window, near the confessional and generally out of view from the altar, was wide open and served as an escape hatch for reluctant church goers. Closing that window and removing its crank brought an abrupt end to the unholy exit.

Two Sundays later the liturgy took a unique twist. Just before the Communion of the Mass, and immediately after the Prayer for Peace, I extended to all an invitation to offer each other a sign of peace. For no good reason that I know, a handshake was, and still is used as the most common sign of peace. Well, the boys created what seemed to me a very noisy exchange of peace gestures. They shook hands and instead of the usual, "Peace be with you," said, "Have a good day! See you later," and half of them promptly left the church.

That particular optional rubric has been shelved at my Masses from that time on. Upon meditating on the entire incident I realized that a handshake in our culture is really not a sign of peace except when one is in a boxing ring, preliminary to the first bell, or after a fight of one kind or another. However, for Americans it is a very common greeting or farewell gesture and could very well be adapted to the beginning of a liturgy, or its closing — but hardly during its most sacred moments. I was never able to explain convincingly to the boys how a handshake made sense in the middle of the Mass.

At this point I went back to the blueprints. Father Flanagan left no doubt about the importance of religious training for his family of homeless and wayward children. When Dowd Chapel was under construction in 1939 he wrote a letter to future generations for inclusion in the Chapel's corner-stone. It said in part,

> "My humble request is that those who will come after me will carry on this Christ-like work — saving homeless and abandoned boys for God and country — and will please pray for the writer of this letter, and all of those engaged in this work at this time who will long since have gone to their reward."

I was often asked how my Boys Town work compared with my former assignment at Christ the King. My stock answer was, "My former parish had geographic boundaries. This one is coast-to-coast."

By giving the study and practice of religion its rightful place, we piled even more responsibility on the shoulders of the Family Teachers. They were to accompany their boys to church on Sundays. Some Family Teachers were Catholic, others were Protestant. When the boys in their respective cottages were of mixed religions the Family Teachers in neighboring cottages planned and worked together in the exchange of boys when it came to accompanying them to church services. Arrangements were made for the few Jewish boys in residence at Boys Town to be taken to the neighboring synagogue or temple of their choice when services were scheduled.

The next move was to transfer Protestant Pastor Charles Harman to a full-time position in the Religion Department. Previously he had been assisting in the Education Department. With his help, and that of Father "Jack" Farrell, work began on a curriculum that would give religion a prominent place in our classrooms. Another goal set at this time, and that later came to fruition, was to develop a number of ecumenical services to be held throughout the year. They would occur at the opening of the school year, Thanksgiving, the beginning of Christmas vacation, the beginning of the Lenten Season, Holy Week, and at graduation.

Family Teachers were to develop an atmosphere of religion in each cottage. The boys were taught to take turns leading a prayer before meals. Every boy was given a Bible when admitted to the Home. Evening Bible readings and prayers were always ecumenical in nature. Some Family Teachers would arouse interest in the church services by asking questions about the Readings that formed part of the service — and, about the sermon or homily. One stock question always good for a lively discussion was, "Why are we here on this earth?" After hearing a variety of answers by the boys around the table a Family Teacher would usually sum it up by saying, "We're here to take care of the sick and the poor." This would open up the discussion again until one little guy asked, "Well, why are the sick and the poor here anyway?" This called for a 911 dial to one of the chaplains.

Even the Board of Directors got into the act. Realizing the importance of religion in the life of everyone and by way of supporting the efforts of the administration along these lines the following resolution was passed at the Board's regular meeting on May 19, 1975:

> "Resolved that the study of religion, ethics, or character training be a required subject in school at the Home by every boy, and that attendance at the church of his choice at Boys Town, or at a synagogue within reasonable distance, be required a minimum of once a week while the boy resides at Boys Town."

A very disturbing incident, having to do with religion at Boys Town, occurred during our Christmas Midnight Mass in Dowd Chapel in 1974. A bomb threat was phoned in to Associated Press in New York. After the reading of the Gospel a deputy sheriff came down the middle aisle in full view of an overcrowded church and handed me a note which read: "A bomb has been reported by phone to be in Dowd Chapel. It is to explode within the hour. Evacuate at once." — Douglas County Sheriff's Office.

I read the note to the assembly and asked the faithful to depart in an orderly fashion. They did. Two former disgruntled employees were seen in the rear of the church surveying the exodus. The bomb squad from the Omaha Police Department was called and after about an hour a simulated bomb was discovered in an emptied crock holy water dispenser. It was a ten inch length of two inch galvanized pipe with a nine volt flashlight battery taped to the top. Small wires, taped to the battery, were directed into one end of the pipe which was stuffed with paper, as was the opposite end.

The bomb squad dismantled the harmless device and sent it to the FBI in Washington, D.C. where fingerprints were taken. There were two likely suspects, but it was decided to pursue the matter no farther because we had much more important things to do. Incidentally, the temperature was at the zero mark and about two inches of recently fallen snow covered the ground at the time. The worshipers all left to complete their observance of the great feast of Christmas elsewhere.

In spite of the turmoil of the moment, the boys celebrated the early dismissal. The uncertainty as to what the future would bring because of the impending change to the Family Concept brought a sense of unease to the adults on the campus. But there always seemed to be a lighter side to balance the total picture. Take the little dead-end kid who arrived at Boys Town from an agency in Michigan. With long stringy hair, ragged clothes, a scowl on his face and a big toe through the end of his shoe, this twelve-year old boy was brought into my office by the Family Teacher who would make the lad feel welcome to his new home. After exchanging a greeting and extending a welcome I asked him: "What does your dad do?"

"Well," he said, "he's dead. My mother ran over him with our pickup."

"Did that kill him?" I asked.

"It sure did. Ran over him three times!" he said.

"I suppose she's in jail," I said.

"Yeah," he agreed.

"Do you have any brothers or sisters?" I continued.

"I have two brothers, one older and the other younger than me," he explained.

"Where are they?" I asked.

"My oldest brother is in jail too," he said.

At this point I felt my line of questioning about this newcomer, whose history I had not had an opportunity to read before he came, should take a different direction.

"What's your religion?" I asked.

"I don't have any religion," he snapped.

At this point I placed my hand on the top of his head and said, "Harold! As of right now you have religion."

"I do?" he said with a question in his voice.

"Yes you do," I went on. "I don't know what it is but we'll find out! Everybody at Boys Town has a religion. Everybody."

This puzzled him to the point where you could see he was thinking but had no idea what to say. Moving right on, I suggested to his Family Teacher to take him to the car wash, then to the nearest clothing store and there to fit him out with some suitable clothes. He was puzzled about the car wash deal, but cautiously went along with it all.

Much later that day these same two appeared in my office. Registering a delightful surprise at the neatly clad young man, I commented on the practical selection of attire and asked the Family Teacher, "Was this young man a big help in selecting his clothes?"

"Yes, he was. But," she added, "when we came to the underwear he asked, 'What is this?' So I explained this bit of apparel, all completely new to him. He didn't seem impressed. I went on to explain that everybody at Boys Town wears underwear."

"Is that something like religion?" he asked. "Father Hupp says everybody at Boys Town has a religion."

As important as religion is at Father Flanagan's, organization of that aspect of the Home was in a state of disarray. One ad in a National Catholic Newsletter brought over a dozen responses from priests who were interested in putting the department in order. After screening the applicants, Father James Kelly, a priest in the diocese of Albany, New York, was selected. He arrived on September 1, 1975 to begin his work by giving Catholic and Protestant religion classes equal time in our school curriculum. He established a religion training program for Family Teachers, and with Pastor Charles Harman set up a counseling service for all boys and staff personnel.

"He created a consumer feedback system for the evaluation of religious services and religious education on our campus," wrote Tom Dowd, Director of Training, Evaluation and Audit. Father Kelly developed into a good team player, communicated well with my office and provided the example needed to give religion the emphasis it deserved and continues to this day. Special liturgies, student retreats, house visits by the clergy on an organized basis, all came into being thanks to the implementation of Father Kelly. He had been a parish priest in Albany, New York prior to his coming to Boys Town. In 1983 when a shortage of priests developed in upstate New York, he was recalled to his diocese to resume parish work. Boys Town's loss was New York's gain.

The importance of religion at Father Flanagan's Boys' Home is further evidenced by the fact that the centrally located and most impressive structure on the campus is Dowd Memorial Chapel. Miss Mary Dowd of New York City donated this chapel as a memorial to her family. The cornerstone was laid on November 26, 1939 with over 2,000 in attendance at the ceremony.

Inside the cornerstone are the following:

— Photos of Mary Dowd, her parents and the Religious Brothers and Sisters at Boys Town at the time.
— Autographed photo of Father Flanagan.
— Mementos from Mary Dowd, including her rosary, an 18-carat gold ring and an assortment of religious medals.
— Large medal of the Immaculate Conception.
— A list of important dates at Boys Town from its beginning.
— Six stamps, cancelled on November 26, 1939.
— A list of the names of the 2,934 boys who had lived at the Home from December 10, 1917 to November 26, 1939.
— Six copies of the "True Voice," dated September 9, 1938 to November 24, 1939.
— Copies of the "Boys Town Times" with articles about Dowd Chapel.
— A copy of the poem, "The Cry of Children," by Elizabeth Barrett Browning.

— The Honorary Degrees conferred on Father Flanagan by his Alma Mater, Mount St. Mary's College in Emmitsburg, Maryland, and by St. Benedict's College, Atchison, Kansas.

— A letter to the "Future Citizens of the World" which read: "In this year of 1939, we are laying the cornerstone of the Immaculate Conception Church, made possible through the munificence of Miss Mary Dowd of New York City, that homeless and abandoned boys of the nation may have the opportunity of worshipping God in this beautiful edifice. The Church is costing between $178,000 and $200,000 and the boys will be benefitted through the spiritual blessings of this beautiful edifice erected in honor of the Immaculate Mother who will have gone out into the world and, through her help and intercession, made the world a better place in which to live."

Very sincerely yours,
/s/Rt. Rev. Msgr. E. J. Flanagan

The structure is Indiana Bedford stone on a concrete foundation with an exterior design inspired by the Gothic churches of rural England. The roof is light weight English tile and all gutters, down spouts, flashings, louvres, etc., are of heavy copper. Dominating feature of the exterior is the tower located above the main entrance. It is surmounted by a copper dome.

The interior of the Chapel is lined to a height of twelve feet with Indiana Bedford stone. Above this point the walls are of decorated plaster. Purlins span the space between the tresses, and between the purlins is a layer of cork that adds acoustical and insulation value.

The floor plan is cruciform with small chapels on either arm side, which originally had their own altar and statues. The statue above the right side altar, as one faces the front, was that of St. Joseph while the chapel on the left had a statue of Mary.

Just inside the main entrance, hanging on the left side of the vestibule, is a plaque commemorating the dedication of the Chapel. This plaque reads:

This Chapel is dedicated
to the honor and glory of GOD
under the patronage of
The Immaculate Conception of the Blessed Virgin Mary
A gift of Mary A. Dowd of New York City
In memory of her deceased parents brothers sister
Patrick and Mary Dowd
Thomas John James Catherine
December 8, 1940
Pray for Them

The Chapel was dedicated on January 5, 1941 by the Most Reverend James Hugh Ryan, Archbishop of Omaha, and later, on August 2, 1967, consecrated by the Most Reverend Daniel E. Sheehan, then Auxiliary Bishop of Omaha. Dedication and consecration ceremonies officially devote the Chapel to the worship of God and thus petition His divine protection. Ceremonies at a consecration are more solemn and elaborate than are those at a dedication. Essence of a consecration consists in the anointing of twelve crosses mounted on the inner walls of the Chapel. These crosses must never be removed. They are evidence that the Chapel has been consecrated. Under each cross a candle bracket is affixed. A detailed description of the Chapel as it was before the liturgical reform of the Second Vatican Council can be found in the Appendix.

When I arrived on the scene it had been thirty some years since Dowd Memorial Chapel had been dedicated. Maintenance of the structure and furnishings was always high on my priority list, but no major alterations had been made during that time.

With the changes in emphasis of things liturgical called for in the Documents of Vatican II, a renovation of the Chapel was in order.

The story of remodeling Dowd Chapel really begins with the Sanctuary, or middle front portion of the Church. The first change had to do with the main altar which was located three step levels above the main floor of the church. With all the care that could be mustered, every attempt to dismantle or move the marble altar proved futile. With the least disturbance, the marble crumbled into bits.

The relics contained in the small cavity of the middle of the altar table were salvaged and placed in a Plexiglass container to rest in the sacristy safe. The altar was eventually removed in bits and pieces, as were the canopy and backdrop, which had deteriorated beyond salvage.

The large six-foot oak, hand-carved crucifix, which had hung above the main altar under the velvet canopy, was moved to the east side of the Nave where it hangs to this day, only because no other suitable place was found for it. A new colorful Resurrection crucifix was suspended from the ceiling in the front and center of the sanctuary.

The oak communion rail was removed and a portable oak altar that had been used on occasion in the Music Hall was placed in front of and facing the pews. It rested on the first level, three steps above the main floor with the chancel organ and choir pews on either side. The Presidential chair, along with seats for the altar boys, were arranged on the next level above and behind the altar, just in front of a new matching oak seven-foot screen. This woodwork sets off the original from the new sanctuary area.

Designers from the Leo A. Daly Company, and the Harold Rambusch Studios of New York, decided to lighten up the area with paintings in bright color on the walls. After some study and thought, it was decided that the area above the wall panels in the now vacated sanctuary might be used to illustrate a panorama of events in salvation history.

On the left wall, as one faced the area, are selected events that occurred when, as one of the boys noted, "God the Father was in charge." In the fullness of time God sent His Son. Selected chronological events in His life are seen in the center panel. Finally, on the right, there is a Holy Spirit inspiring and influencing the Church. A finale, with a local flair, shows Father Flanagan beside his famous "He Ain't Heavy" statue leading his boys to the gate of the New Jerusalem, our eternal home, where the angels are receiving them.

With the new emphasis on participation in the liturgy, more light was required in the body of the Church for the congregation to read missalettes and hymn books. Poor acoustics and sometimes poor readers could make listening alone a frustrating experience. Many people, young and old, have hearing problems, too. Besides, common sense and the general consensus of psychologists indicate that the more senses one can bring to bear on a message the better is one able to remember it.

Lighting experts reported that lights in the church hung too high and did not develop enough candlepower to make for good reading. As a result all of the light fixtures were remodeled, opened up and lowered in the interest of providing better reading conditions.

Redecorating the Nave and side chapels were part of the general plan of renewal. An Indian motif was selected. The side altar chapels dedicated to Mary and Joseph, as was the custom decades ago, were entirely rearranged and redecorated.

The Blessed Virgin Chapel became the Blessed Sacrament Chapel, a place for quiet meditation and prayer. Above the gold tones of the cast bronze tabernacle, reminiscent of the Ark of the Covenant, hangs a diaphanous replica of Jesus showing his wounds to Thomas, who recognizes Him as "My Lord and My God" (John 20:38). Above and below, and on either side, are mounted cast bronzed plaques of the four evangelists: Matthew, Mark, Luke, and John.

Saint Joseph's altar chapel is now the "Boy Jesus" Chapel, with a small altar in the front for daily Mass. The entire area is a tabloid of life-size wooden carvings of Mary and Joseph finding

Jesus, at the age of twelve, in the temple area in discussion with five teachers, or Doctors of the Law.

This composition was conceived by Harold Rambusch, designed by Leandro Velasco of the Rambusch Studios, and carved by Franz Mersa in the Italian Tyrol where much of the population is engaged in carving wood for religious and secular use. The figures are carved in linden wood. This small chapel is another symbol of the Boys Town mission — adults and youth learning to communicate with each other.

The revised Rite of Reconciliation, according to the US Bishops' committee on Liturgy, (#12), encouraged the establishment and use of rooms of reconciliation. With the removal of Father Flanagan's remains from his temporary resting place in what had been the Baptistry just inside the main chapel entrance (see later in this chapter), a room was available. It is now a Room of Reconciliation.

On the one hand it is a place where the penitent, who desires anonymity, can seek reconciliation with the benefit of a screen. On the other hand, it offers the opportunity of face-to-face dialogue for those who wish to approach the Sacrament of Penance under these conditions. Option is the key word and this Reconciliation Room offers it.

In the early days of the Home, in the absence of a Chapel, Protestant church services, like those for Catholics, were held variously in the grade school band room, the gym of the old administration building, the grade school dining hall, the original post office and later in the Vocational Career Center and in the Music Hall.

On occasion, Protestant boys were taken off campus to worship in one of the area churches. It was not until 1941 that something like an organized approach to religion for the Protestant boys came into being.

Beginning on September 19, 1941, and thereafter, Protestant church services were held at the Home on a regular basis under the direction and assistance of the Ministerial Union of Omaha.

In 1950 a section of the Field House, with a separate entrance, was reserved and dedicated as a Protestant Chapel. A fixed altar and lectern, along with standard pews, comprised the main furnishings of the Chapel at that time. Nativity Chapel, it was called, so named by Sam Hereforth, Pastor of St. Paul's Lutheran Church, and his congregation in Millard, Nebraska. He was at the time conducting Protestant services at Boys Town.

With the ferment of renewal widespread in all churches in the 1970's a renovation project of the Protestant Chapel was initiated shortly after I arrived on the scene. A circular, movable altar, a lectern, a movable altar platform, a movable liturgical panel, and a Reuter pipe organ, furnished the chancel area. For maximum flexibility in seating, individual chairs replaced the pews. With a comfortable seating capacity of 200, and two services on Sunday, the Protestant boys and staff enjoyed a beautiful place of worship. The entire area was carpeted. A Baptism font was located just inside the main entrance.

A dedication ceremony was held on Sunday, September 12, 1976. Meantime, the Harold Rambusch Company of New York had been commissioned to execute a series of seven stained glass windows which arrived late and were installed early in 1977. These windows portray graphically significant events related to Christ. Naturally, scenes in the windows related to His youth. The window scenes, beginning from the altar to the Chapel entrance were:

1. Jesus, the descendant of David.
2. The Annunciation.
3. Mary visits Elizabeth.
4. The Nativity and the shepherds.
5. The Magi come from the east.
6. Jesus in the Temple at age 12.
7. Jesus brings new age to minds and hearts of his people.

A window of the Triumphant Christ was located near the entrance.

It was no surprise that a Catholic Chapel was the first one built at Boys Town, but Father Flanagan always had in his long range plans the building of a church for Protestants when a donor could be found. He envisioned locating it between the Music Hall and the new Administration Building, near the main entrance to the campus. A huge parking lot there stands empty on weekends and would provide better parking facilities than Dowd had.

During Father Flanagan's lifetime six boys died while at the Home. Since their remains were never claimed by anyone, arrangements were made to locate their graves in Holy Sepulchre Cemetery in Omaha. It was Father Flanagan's hope that some day he would build a cemetery on Boys Town property, transfer the remains of the first six boys to the Home's cemetery, and eventually be laid to rest there himself. He had in mind a site on the southeastern corner of the campus later known as the horse farm.

But his sudden and unexpected death in Berlin in 1948 posed a problem in this regard. His cemetery had not yet been built. Where would Father Flanagan's remains be laid to rest? His brother, Monsignor P.A. Flanagan, insisted that to honor "Father E.J.'s" wishes a temporary burial site be set aside somewhere on the grounds until a cemetery could be built. With the concurrence of Archbishop Bergan, and his cemetery officials, it was decided that the Baptistry, a side wing of Dowd Chapel, would be the temporary resting place of the Home's founder. And so it was.

Dignitaries from around the country came to the funeral and witnessed the entombment. Visitors henceforth could view through a wrought iron gate the marble encasement containing Father Flanagan's remains.

Twenty-five years later the remains of Father Flanagan were still in the Baptistry. It was time something be done about it. First of all, upon investigation it was learned that since Father Flanagan's death in 1948, not a single boy had died at the Home whose remains went unclaimed by relatives or friends. It was obvious there no longer was a need for a Boys Town cemetery.

More important now was the idea of a crypt, or mausoleum, for Father Flanagan. Where should it be located? Somewhere near the center of the Home, perhaps near Dowd Chapel. Could it be attached to the Chapel where visitors would have easy access?

Upon consulting with the Leo A. Daly Company, the original architects of the Home, assurance was given that a crypt could be built adjacent to the Chapel with a direct entrance from the Chapel where a side door was located. The stone would match the original structure. A green light was given to proceed with the construction.

In developing the general plan, it was necessary to design a suitable cover for the tomb, hereinafter called the "cap" of the tomb. Harold Rambusch was consulted and given authority to do the liturgical art design work for the interior of the crypt, including the windows. It turned out to be an octagonal shaped structure of 570 square feet made of buff Bedford Indiana limestone matching the stone of the original Dowd Chapel.

The tomb of Father Flanagan is centered in the structure and rises approximately three feet six inches above the floor. Concave slabs of itala rosa travertine marble, which are a continuation of the mausoleum floor, form the sides of the crypt. A one-piece bronze casting covers the top of the tomb. It is peaked in form with eight panels that point out highlights in the life of Father Flanagan, to wit:

Panel 1 with the bust of Father Flanagan reads: "Edward Joseph Flanagan, born in Rosecommon, Ireland, July 13, 1886, died in Berlin, Germany, May 14, 1948."

Panel 2 shows Father Flanagan being baptized at the Baptism Font. The date is July 25, 1886.

Panel 3 shows Father Flanagan being ordained in St. Ignatius Church, Innsbruck, Austria, 1912, with a quotation: "I want to get boys ready to go back into society."

Panel 4 is a picture of the first home on Cass Street dated 1917.

Panel 5 shows the first five boys with a quotation: "Every boy must learn to pray. How he prays is up to him."

Panel 6 is a picture of Father Flanagan facing the front, and
   over his right shoulder is General Douglas MacArthur,
   Japan, 1947, on the plaque. Over his left shoulder is President Harry S. Truman, Germany, 1948.
Panel 7 is a picture of two boys with their suitcases approaching
   Overlook Farm and the inscription on that plaque reads:
   "There are no bad boys, there is only bad environment, bad
   example, bad timing. Father Flanagan."
Panel 8 shows Father Flanagan seated with his clerical robe
   and biretta with a boy on either side of him with his arms
   around them and he says here: "This work will continue
   because God provides."
On the other sides is the inscription: "Love of Christ and Man."

The ceiling is a textured cork panel painted a medium blue.

Entrance to the crypt is gained from the main Chapel through
a hand-wrought antiquated iron gate. Letters at the top of the
gate read in Latin: "Ad Majorem Dei Gloriam." Translated: "For
the Greater Glory of God."

Twenty-one stained and chipped glass windows encircle the
shrine. There is a pattern variation in each window. A center
corona-like light fixture is suspended from the ceiling to accent
softly the top of the tomb. A hand-wrought iron priedieu matches
the gate in design.

At the head of the tomb stands a five-foot brass candlestick
bearing a candle that symbolizes the "Light of Christ" given to
Father Flanagan in Baptism, which he followed throughout his life
right into the next world.

The Father Flanagan crypt was dedicated on May 1, 1977,
marking the beginning of the Home's 60th anniversary celebration. Father Peter Dunne, Pastor of St. Margaret Mary parish, a
former Boys Town staff member and a contemporary of Father
Flanagan, eulogized the founder of the Home as "a man who saw
Christ in everyone. He was one who emblazoned the compassion
of Christ on the fabric of his time." In the absence of Archbishop

Daniel E. Sheehan, Monsignor Giovanni Cheli, permanent observer of the Holy See at the United Nations, celebrated the Mass.

Then on June 15, 1977 the Apostolic Blessing and good wishes of His Holiness, Pope Paul VI, were communicated to Boys Town. The message was sent through His Excellency Most Reverend Jean Jadot, D.C., Apostolic Delegate to the United States.

Sentiments of the Pope were summed up in these words from the Delegate's letter to me: "The legacy of Father Flanagan is awesome. One cannot begin to appreciate how much he was employed as an instrument of healing and care. We are consoled that you and your associates have been inspired to remain faithful to the vision of Father Flanagan."

We indeed were confident that we were carrying on Father Flanagan's vision in instilling a respect for religion in our youths.

CHAPTER **Thirteen**

I N the second edition of his "Romance of the Homeless Boys" which he sent out at Christmas 1930, Father Flanagan wrote:

> "In 1917 I had a dream — in 1930 I have found that vision, with thanks to God and our good friends, come true. Now I am dreaming a greater dream, and with the help of thousands upon thousands of kind, good-hearted men and women of this country, we pray to God we will live to see this greater dream come true.
>
> "The greater dream is the establishment of a large endowment fund, the interest of which will pay for the upkeep of our Home so it will be unnecessary for us to spend a good portion of our time in the appeal and collection of funds. Instead we may give one hundred percent of our time to the care of homeless boys."

In retrospect, this idea of an endowment fund as Father Flanagan described it was forty years ahead of its time. But in its early years the Fund's growth was very slow.

One event came about in 1938 which eventually turned Boys Town around financially. One was the movie "Boys Town" starring Spencer Tracy and Mickey Rooney. Contrary to the public's perception, the movie provided little direct profit to the Home. It seemed that people got the idea that Hollywood would now support Boys Town and their meager donations were no longer needed. As a matter of fact, Father Flanagan was often heard to voice his disappointment in having given his approval to have the movie filmed.

But that changed once a man named Theodore G. "Ted" Miller joined the Home's staff. What he did as a fund-raiser seems routine today, but he was a pioneer in fund raising by letter. He developed a massive mailing list, and twice a year at Christmas and Easter, he would draft a letter for Father Flanagan's signature, a letter which tugged at heart and purse strings alike. The letter never asked for much — a few dollars would be gratefully accepted — but he asked it of millions of people.

Talk about the power behind the throne. Few people, even in Omaha, knew or heard much about this stocky, swarthy man, and that is the way he wanted it. He and his staff operated in near anonymity out of a dingy office in downtown Omaha. For years the Boys Town appeal letters were the number one customer of the Omaha Post Office until Father Flanagan's Boys' Home was given a post office of its own in 1934, and thereafter all mail from the Home carried the postmark, "Boys Town."

A letter seeking donations hardly strikes today's sophisticated citizen as an innovation. But Ted Miller invented the system. He was the only one in the field at the time. Now the mail box is filled with such appeals, and they are the core of people's complaints about junk mail. Many of today's charitable organizations share consultants; their letters have a certain sameness about them. And now it is not merely a request for a donation. Letters now tell you how much to give. Just mark the proper box and mail in your check. But when Ted Miller and Father Flanagan began their solicitations by letter it was not so. It was just a simple appeal and it worked.

Under the directorship of Monsignor Wegner the fund grew while the Home enjoyed the finest in physical facilities. An expanded Vocational Career Center, new school buildings, a music hall and field house fit for a university graced the campus. A gigantic warehouse, new farm equipment, a Visitors' Center, and twenty-five cottages were all made possible, thanks to Ted

Miller's ability to capitalize on the ever increasing popularity of
the 1938 movie, "Boys Town."

Here it needs to be noted that sometimes organizations
become so involved in internal affairs that society passes them
by. This seems to have been the case with social programs at the
Home. Caring for boys in the best traditions of Father Flanagan
continued. But problems of boys in the world outside were
changing rapidly. Orphans, in the stereotyped sense of the word,
were now outnumbered by "social orphans." These were boys
who were homeless because they ran away from home or were
thrown out of their homes and in many cases lived on the street. It
was the Home's Youth Care program that reporters from the Sun
Newspapers thought should be improved.

It was the unenviable task of my administration to up-date
Youth Care to meet the new problems of youth in modern society
and at the same time never lose sight of Father Flanagan's
insistence or the need for an untouchable basic fund. In a letter to
Mrs. Harley J. Earl, who had requested information about Boys
Town, Father Flanagan wrote: "At many times we have been
hampered in our progress because I could not jeopardize the
future by incurring a debt, even though I saw additions and
improvements as vitally necessary."

The philosophy of management became the hallmark of the
Home, and the real truth about it never penetrated the minds of
the prize-winning reporters of the Sun. They were seeking only
sensational headlines. There is a world of difference between
hoarding and stewardship and it completely escaped their ultra-
liberal outlook. There are people who don't seem to understand
that money is not an end in itself. Money is meant to be a tool used
to build a better future for families and organizations. Economic
conditions in this world have always been such that a family like
Boys Town must have a surplus and not try to operate on a
break-even basis. This scenario is as old as the human race. One
need only read the first book in the Bible (Genesis 41:16) to know
this. Any non-profit organization needs a surplus if it is to enjoy
growth and long range planning, much like a large family needs a

healthy balance in its checking account if it is to live and plan for the future. Revenue from the investments of our Trust Fund at this time was providing nearly half of the operating expenses of the Home. The remaining fifty percent was obtained by personal solicitations of the Executive Director and twice-a-year mailing campaigns.

In my fund-raising treks around the country a lot of my time was spent putting out brush fires started by the Sun newspaper article. It was the same story over and over again. "I must ask you about all your money," one interviewer said. "While people are starving to death all over the world you people are sitting on a pile of money. Shouldn't you be feeding those people?"

I tried to explain that the funds we had received had been given to us by people who wanted us to care for boys at Boys Town. If we used those funds for other than operating our programs we would be violating a trust. After all, universities like Nebraska, Harvard, Stanford, Notre Dame, to mention a few, have endowment funds. Even high schools today, hospitals, museums, zoos, parks and the like have learned the value of establishing a fund to give them financial stability when the economy dips and dives as it always has.

Another reporter implied that we had to be poor to help the poor. To still another who argued that Boys Town should spend all of its fund, I countered with my dislike of deficit spending, saying, "That would be like burning planks from your life raft to keep warm." Or, to put it another way: "It's a sorry dog that doesn't bury a bone."

Much of my attention still had to be directed to our money management at the Home. Operating under the constraints of a formal budget, which the Home had never had before the days of Ed Hewitt, required constant monitoring. Hewitt had for sixteen years been Director of Finance for the City of Omaha. He had just retired from this position when I called and asked him to come and give me some direction in the matter of finances. He agreed to come for an hour or two, review our administrative policies and procedures, and give me a few ideas.

His first visit, instead of lasting an hour or two, kept him for a full day. He reported to my office with these words: "You have a real mess on your hands." After our day-long visit I asked if he would be interested in coming to work at Boys Town.

"I'm retired only two months but I'm already sick of it, so the answer is YES." Ed brought his sharp pencil along, took his position in the finance office and went to work.

In late 1975, under his leadership, the Board's Program, Planning and Budget Committee was presented the Home's first full budget. In March 1976 the budget was supplemented with the first projected income for the next three years — 1977, 1978 and 1979. Hewitt and his staff outlined the projection of all revenues reasonably estimated including campaign contributions, revenue from investments, bequests and miscellaneous donations.

"If our plan is successful," I wrote in a memo to all department heads, "you can each take a bow! If it fails, we hang together."

Hardly stop-the-press news, but it was a first at Boys Town.

It was amusing to have Hewitt, at the age of 68, come into my office and say, "There are a few old buzzards here we have to tie a can to." Now that is just a good old Nebraska expression that means "fire the bumblers." With the help of the accounting firm of Peat, Marwick & Mitchell, Hewitt prepared the Home's first budget ever. After living with Hewitt for a while everyone understood what was meant when it was said of him, "He's too honest."

The year 1974 was not a good year for investments. Besides allotting adequate money for capital improvements (including remodeling of the four dormitories which the state had demanded we remodel or close) the stock market reduced the value of our trust fund from $209 million to $183 million. Hewitt urged that we take severe corrective measures or, in two decades, we might be forced to close down. That was not the legacy I wanted to leave the Home. Hewitt's advice was heeded and we at once established a policy of strict accountability. In days gone by each little kingdom on the premises, and there were thirty-one of them according to the Booz, Allen & Hamilton study, would make direct requests or send bills to the administration building.

Those days were gone forever. Instead of thirty-one functional areas reporting to my office, there now were five: Administration and Finance, Youth Care, Education, Research and Development, and the Institute. Each department was put on a budget. Cottage budgets varied depending on the number of boys living in each. If a boy left for whatever reason, that fact would show up in the grocery budget for his cottage in a short time. Since many adjustments were needed in the early days of the Family Concept, the Board allowed my office a substantial contingency fund to cover emergencies.

Since the schools were already beneficiaries of the federal hot lunch program, some members of the Board of Directors suggested that Boys Town seek government grants for day-to-day operations at the Home. This idea received less than enthusiastic support from me because accepting federal money was contrary to the private tradition of the Home. Federal funds usually had strings attached that hamper the autonomy we enjoyed in operating our own programs. It was decided, however, that some day grants might be sought from the government to conduct research at the Boys Town Center for the Study of Youth Development and at the Institute.

It was a sad day around Boys Town when on August 26, 1978, Ed Hewitt died with his boots on. He had just finished preparing a budget for 1979 calling for the expenditure of $20,767,331.

The 1970's were difficult years for the American economy with inflation ultimately soaring to a scary thirteen percent in 1979. The pace of our donations did not increase proportionately with the rate of inflation, making it doubly difficult to operate within the budget figures and not "spend the Home broke" as a few would-be social engineers would have it.

In order to live within our means and enjoy a balanced budget for 1981 it was necessary for all Deputy Directors to effect a ten percent cut in their departments without dropping essential elements in their programs. By this time our Deputy Directors had a supply of sharp pencils with erasers and although a ten percent cut was not greeted with cheers, all complied. Remnants of the ponderous previous administration still lingered on and everybody was aware of this. In retrospect, it was one of the better things we did. All non-essential personnel were trimmed from the staff and most waste was eliminated.

It was during the years 1980 and 1981 that the Board authorized a one-time expenditure of $7 million capital funds for purchase of the land on which Flanagan High would be built and for construction of the building itself.

The budgeting process was working so well that the Board directed the Home's administration to go one step farther and develop a five-year spending policy. This meant establishing priorities that would result in honoring the Board's resolution not to dip into the Trust Fund for operations. Bequest money would be added to the fund rather than used for programs, unless otherwise directed by the donor. In short, the spending policy would have Boys Town live within its means as it watched the Trust Fund build towards the goal!

Hand in hand with our austerity program were efforts to increase donations. A new director of planning in the person of John South was hired. An outside consultant was engaged to assist in mail prospecting. People were surprised to learn that the average donation was $5.74. Little as that seemed to be there was always the demand to shepherd carefully all of our resources. Department heads as well as staff members were reminded with regularity of the need to exercise a high degree of responsibility in all things because of the trust placed upon us by our millions of average donors. Accountability and openness were the basic ethics to guide our relationship with people who were interested. This, I felt, would gain the good will of the public, something money couldn't buy.

Neighboring communities offered us their services and good will at every turn. Once central purchasing was abandoned each cottage shopped the field for household bargains, as any good family does. A number of grocery chains were approached for discounts and their response was most generous. Cleaning establishments were asked about a discount for dry cleaning and storage. Two large firms responded at once. It was not at all unusual for a dealer to offer gratis for a year or two at a time an auto to be used for student driver training. The list of benefactors, like clothing stores and yard services, went on and on. All I needed to do was pick up my telephone and help was there.

We often joked about prices in Omaha, saying there were three: retail, wholesale, and Boys Town. Many times they were in that descending order. Believe me. Omahans were good to us in more ways than one and we appreciated it.

CHAPTER **Fourteen**

---

*"History with its flickering lamp stumbles along the trail of the
past, trying to reconstruct its scenes, to revive its echoes, and kindle
with pale gleams the passion of former days."*

Tribute to Neville Chamberlain in the
House of Commons, November 12, 1940

B OYS TOWN, like every other important in-
stitution, had a distinguished history, but for nearly sixty years
every day at the Home was so busy making history that nobody
took the time to make a formal record of it.

It wasn't until the mid-1970's that we seriously turned our
attention to the things that had been accomplished in the past, our
mementos, artifacts and records.

Records were always stored in the various departments of
the Home; retained as long as they served a purpose or until
someone got a housecleaning urge. Those that were retained
were kept in helter-skelter fashion, in such disarray that perhaps
only one or two old-time employees knew they were extant and
how to locate them.

Friends and alumni kept sending us objects from the past,
something that had a sentimental meaning to the donor and

probably would kindle memories in other former residents of the Home. We'd put them somewhere out of the way with a mental note to give them some attention in the future, but before we'd get around to acting on our intentions they would be lost or stolen.

A wealth of fragmentary materials that told of the past could be found almost everywhere on the campus. Over the years many staff members had talked and dreamed of ways and means of gathering these memorabilia into a museum of some kind that would carry our living memories into the future. As time went on and more attention was given to retaining the past in a respectful manner, the number and type of available artifacts called for a spacious display.

We needed a handsome repository, available to the public, to display all those things, and we needed a knowledgeable person to arrange them in orderly fashion.

The time had come for Boys Town to establish a Hall of History.

How we financed this addition to the campus falls into the realm of make-believe.

Father Flanagan had always tried to create a favorable image of Boys Town, and the nationwide publicity and solicitation mailings were aimed at supporting his personal public relations efforts. How successful he was is illustrated by the way we were able to finance the hall of History. Here is the improbable story.

A Chicago resident was found dead in a rundown trailer park. In his will he stated he wanted a memorial to himself on the Boys Town campus. When his estate was probated, Boys Town was left just enough money to remodel a building on campus and create the desired exhibits.

The benefactor's name was Henry J. Hess, and we know very little about him. He was a bachelor who had never visited Boys Town but was known to have thought highly of the Home. In his later years he befriended a retired Chicago school teacher, one Jack Spaulding, who earlier in life had taught in Council Bluffs, Iowa. Spaulding, a personal friend of mine, became very enthusiastic about Boys Town after my assignment to the Home. In his frequent visits with the old timer he recommended that Hess leave some money to the Home. Spaulding never lived to learn the effect his good words had on the reclusive Hess.

With money available, it was now time to get to work. I appointed three co-chairmen on September 14, 1983 with instructions to bring the Hall of History to reality. The three selected John Burke, our legal counsel, as the most "co" of the three, and the committee added six more members with a broad representation of talent and experience.

The committee's first challenge was to find a site for the Hall. Various suggestions surfaced. One that received serious consideration was to remodel part of the Music Hall. The architectural firm of Bahr, Bermeer and Hacker was engaged in February 1984 to study the proposal.

A month later the firm presented its report and, to the chagrin of the committee members, not only did the Music Hall's available space seem too limited, but the cost of remodeling it was too high. Moreover, committee members concluded after thinking it over that such torturing of the Music Hall would destroy its beauty and perhaps limit its use as an auditorium for our meetings, convocations, graduations and concerts. This would never do.

The committee turned to other sites. Someone suggested remodeling the spacious area under the high school that once housed a bowling alley and now was used as a storage area — a collection point for all sorts of objects which lay in a state of total disarray.

It was soon rejected too. It was too much like a catacomb — too inaccessible to the public.

Finally, and somewhat reluctantly, the committee agreed to consider what up to now had been considered a Boys Town sacred cow — the Wegner Grade School Dining Hall. I had preferred the building from the beginning, but it seemed untouchable. It was unused and deteriorating, but the campus consensus was that nobody should mess with this memorial to the Home's second executive director.

I always thought Monsignor Wegner would appreciate having the building filled with artifacts and memories of Boys Town rather than with cobwebs and ghosts of another era.

Now that the former dining hall became the focus of the committee's attention, it might be well to backtrack a bit and explain how it came into being.

Back in the late 1930's the Home was bulging at the seams, and dining facilities, along with other services, had become totally inadequate to serve the more than four hundred boys.

On April 25, 1939 ground-breaking ceremonies were held for a new dining hall on ground between Dowd Chapel, then under construction, and the grade school. Less than a year later meals were being served. When an additional dining hall for high school students was built in 1947, across the campus to the east, the original dining hall became known as the Grade School Dining Hall.

Thus it remained until we introduced the Family Concept in 1975, when central dining facilities were no longer needed. Only the high school dining hall remained, and its use was limited to hot lunches during the school year and for an occasional banquet.

For sentimental reasons the former Grade School Dining Hall remained empty and under lock and key, waiting for the right need to come along.

The right need had now arrived, decided committee members, and the Grade School Dining Hall was selected as the site for the Boys Town Hall of History.

Immediately the Home's maintenance department was set in motion under the direction of Charles Russell. Air conditioning, plumbing, painting, carpeting and installation of windows needed attention.

With some sadness it was agreed the nostalgic colorful mural on the east and south walls of the dining hall would have to be removed. The mural depicted a montage of ships, trains, planes and other methods of transportation along with birds and animals in the wild. It was the work of an itinerant artist by the name of Cedric Von Rolleston, who in 1951 had panhandled his way to Omaha and Boys Town.

When it was learned he had artistic talents, Monsignor Wegner traded board and room for Von Rolleston's talents with a brush, to the delight of the boys. Stories are told that more than once Von Rolleston would "fall off the scaffold" in the course of his work, but everybody nodded sagely that painting murals created a fierce thirst.

On the day the mural was finished wanderlust hit the man again and he disappeared, never to be heard from again. But his mural lived on for more than thirty years. A short section of it is preserved in the rear of the Hall of History.

On the west wall of the dining hall hung a large crucifix, while on the north were mounted two large sailfish, one caught by Father Flanagan and the other by his nephew and co-worker, Patrick Norton. It was a unique, if somewhat uncoordinated, decorative motif. No wonder more than one alumnus shed a tear when upon his return he learned what had happened to his old dining hall.

Meanwhile the search for a curator ended with the appointment of Jacqueline McGlade, a former employee of the Western Heritage Museum in downtown Omaha. The monumental task of organizing the artifacts and memorabilia we already had on hand and simultaneously gathering other items fell to Miss McGlade, and she did an outstanding job.

Years ago Boys Town put a show wagon on the road, with the boys entertaining the residents of Nebraska and western Iowa towns with their enthusiastic, if somewhat limited, instrumental and vocal musical talents. Still around, but in a sad state of disrepair, the show wagon was refurbished and brightly painted for a place of honor in the Hall.

At one time our own private Greyhound bus transported Boys Town athletic teams and the concert choir around the nation on goodwill trips. Believe it or not, the bus was cut in two with acetylene torches so only the front end and the first few rows of seats remained, and it too was installed in the Hall. Visitors can sit in the driver's seat, toot the horn, and view clips of high school football games when winning was a way of life.

Preparation and preservation of these items was done by the boys themselves under the direction and guidance of Ed Novotny and his Vocational Career staff.

A professional hand was needed for the finishing touches — the plaster models of boys and Father Flanagan, the precise arrangements in orderly fashion so the visitor is exposed to a history lesson from beginning to end, the displays themselves, the labeling, the photos, the enlargements of important newspaper clippings. For this we hired the Eisterhold Llewellen Company of Kansas City. Mannequins were made by Schwartz Brothers of New York City.

After two years of feverish gathering, recording, filing and display-making, the Boys Town Hall of History was opened March 14, 1986, several months after I had stepped aside as executive director.

Not only is the museum a cornucopia of visual displays, it is an audio history as well. The tour begins with a brief orientation in the Hall's small theater, including the recorded voice of Father Flanagan and his remarks about there being no such thing as a bad boy. Audiovisual presentations that follow include:

The Boy in the Box: Billy tells his story of meeting Father
   Flanagan.
On the Road: A former Boys Town juvenile entertainer sings the
   opening show tune from the show wagon days.
On the Radio: Father Flanagan and the Boys Town band star in
   their own radio show in the late 1920's and early 1930's.
Home Movie: Audiences experience emotional reactions to the
   Oscar-winning movie, "Boys Town."
Winning One for Boys Town: Climb aboard the team bus, honk
   the horn, and see the boys in athletic competition.
Choir: The Boys Town choir sang for President Harry S.
   Truman when he visited Boys Town in 1948.

Families of Boys Town: Father Robert Hupp, executive director
from 1973-1985, brought family-style living to campus.
In My Room: Look in the mirror, press the button, and the
visitor may hear the reflections of kids at Boys Town today.
BTNI: Visitors learn about the Boys Town National Institute's
special programs for speech and hearing impaired children.

The Directors' Room at the rear of the exhibition hall contains
a showcase of memorabilia of the three former directors —
Father Flanagan, Monsignor Wegner, and "Yours truly," and
many of the celebrities who have visited the Home.

How has the Hall of History fared with the public? In 1987 the
museum received the Award of Merit from the American Association of State and Local History — a major award in its field. Since
its opening in April 1986 to the end of 1990 the number of
registered visitors annually has increased from 35,000 to
100,000.

THE STATUES OF BOYS TOWN

In the early 1930's the statue of a homeless boy greeted
visitors to Boys Town as they drove onto the grounds. It was
created by James Webster, one of the Home's boys, who drew
many of the cover designs for "Father Flanagan's Boys' Journal,"
a monthly publication.

This "homeless boy" statue rested on a simple concrete base.
It was modeled by one of the boys, fourteen-year-old Johnny
Russion, sitting on a rock in a strikingly natural pose, looking up
with arms outstretched appealing for help.

The model was carved out of clay obtained near Louisville,
Nebraska. It took Webster about four months to model, finish and
reproduce the work in plaster of Paris. Although it was painted
with a heavy sealer coat, the elements soon began taking their
toll. Each year, until he left the area, Webster would repair it.
Eventually the statue disintegrated, to rest in pieces. It remains
only in photos.

The Webster statue of a boy appealing for help has been replaced by the figures that have come to symbolize Boys Town across the nation — the "Two Brothers" statue. Today the most photographed object on the campus is the statue of a boy carrying another on his back. This statue carries the inscription, "He Ain't Heavy, Father, He's My Brother," words which capture the spirit of Boys Town better than any other — one person caring for another.

There have been two concepts of the "Two Brothers" statue, the original dating to 1948 and a more modern version in bronze completed thirty years later.

The history of the idea that was developed into the original statue is somewhat uncertain in that there are several claims as to its origin. In my visits with alumni around the country it was interesting to learn how many claimed to have modeled for the original statue. Had I been able to continue my travels this undoubtedly had the potential of becoming the most unusual "Century Club" ever. How authentic they are is difficult to pin down. We have a file of correspondence on the subject in the Hall of History between Theodore "Ted" Miller, direct mailing consultant for the Home, and Van B. Hooper, sales promotion manager for the Louis Allis Company of Milwaukee.

Hooper's company published a company magazine called "Ideals," and the Christmas 1941 issue (right after Pearl Harbor) carried a drawing depicting a soldier carrying a wounded comrade to safety with a backdrop of bombed and devastated buildings with the caption, "He ain't heavy, Mister! He's my buddy!" Ted Miller brought the drawing to Father Flanagan's attention and Father Flanagan asked permission to adapt it to Boys Town's use, which was very readily granted.

It has been said there is nothing new under the sun, so perhaps the statue concept has an earlier origin, and somebody may some day come forward with a claim. But until that happens we stick with this story. In any case, the issue is now academic, as we copyrighted the inscription in October 1977 and were issued a trademark by the Bureau of Patents in January 1978.

Any use of the original drawing was shelved during World War II but in 1948 an artist by the name of Louis Vonhajo visited Boys Town. He was commissioned to commit to canvas a picture of "Two Brothers," using the sketch as a guide.

In 1949 one W.E. Johnson, owner of a quarry in Texas, donated the rock for a statue that would depict the symbol and motto of Boys Town. Dr. Edward Montgomery, a long time friend of the Home, commissioned Ira Correll to do the work. Correll was at the time at the School of Fine Arts in Austin, Texas. Little more is known of him other than in later years he sculpted a famous Vietnam statue in Dallas.

Correll's "Two Brothers" statue was placed on a concrete foundation near the entrance to the Visitors' Center. The weather did not take kindly to this soft stone, nor did the occasional vandal. Deterioration of the statue promised to ruin it, as the boy with outstretched arms had gone down in ruin, so in February 1980 it was moved to the lobby of the new Administration Building across the south lake, safe from its attackers.

In 1967 Boys Town entered into a contract with sculptor Paul Granlund of St. Peters, Minnesota, to create a bronze memorial to be erected in Washington, D.C. It was Monsignor Wegner's idea that his work, a group called "Emerging Youth," would express the compassion and vision of Father Flanagan and his dedication to the idea of physical, spiritual, intellectual and cultural development for the boys. The figures represented adolescent boys, evolving and striving for such development under Father Flanagan's guidance.

This was to be a memorial to Father Flanagan in the nation's capital. It was to be located on a triangular piece of park land on Michigan Avenue and Fourth Street, adjacent to the entrance of Catholic University and the Shrine of the Immaculate Conception. Congress, at the request of Congressman Glenn Cunningham of Omaha, approved the site.

Granlund created a one-fourth size model in bronze, and it was presented to the District of Columbia Fine Arts Commission, which was in charge of memorials in the District. Unfortunately, the commission had just passed a resolution limiting erection of more outdoor statues in the city because of what it said was already an over-supply of statues of this type on the streets.

Granlund's sculpture never got beyond the model stage. The Fine Arts Commission was instrumental in getting a D.C. ordinance passed which prohibited further monuments and statues on city streets. Monsignor Wegner withdrew his request and searched for a home for the group. This Granlund model finally found its way to Boys Town in 1976 where it rests in the lobby of the Administration Building.

Meanwhile plans were under way to create a new bronze sculpture offering a modernized version of the statue of a boy carrying piggy-back his tired, sleeping, hungry, smaller brother.

We asked architect Leo Daly to contact an artist who had done many pieces of art for the Daly company's worldwide projects. This happened to be one Enzo Plazzotta, an Italian who had married a British war bride. Enzo did his sculpting in his studio in London and then shipped the clay models to his foundry in Florence, Italy, to fire them into bronze.

We sent Plazzotta pictures of the Correll "Two Brothers" statue and its history. We asked for a sample sketch that would represent his idea of a more modern statue to replace the original. Upon receipt of his shop drawing we commissioned him to proceed with a clay model. When Plazzotta sent word that he had a model ready for our inspection, Leo bought the tickets, and he and I boarded the British-French Concorde super jet and flew to London to see what he had created.

When he showed us his model my immediate reaction was, "I don't like it."

Plazzotta didn't understand Boys Town. His statue showed two well fed, contented youngsters. They might have been playing a game of horse and rider. It certainly wasn't a real life rendition of two forlorn boys off the streets who desperately needed a place to call home.

"They're too happy, too well fed," I said; "Their shoes are brand new. And don't put the big brother in shorts; because of our weather boys that age in Nebraska wear trousers of some sort most of the time."

I toyed with the idea of having the younger brother's shoes untied with the strings dangling from his shoes, but Leo and Enzo convinced me they probably would be broken off by souvenir hunters.

Plazzotta displayed no artistic temperament at my reaction to his first effort. He readily agreed to make the changes I suggested and several weeks later he mailed some photos of the reworked model. It was much better.

It was my idea to order two or three, but Daly convinced me we should order five. He could see I was bothered by the total price: five times $35,000, so he quickly pointed out how we would need that many, especially if we located one at Catholic University and another at Stanford.

As it turned out, when our contracts with the two universities were terminated those two statues were returned to Boys Town. The "new" statues then were located at the traffic turnaround between Dowd Chapel and the Hall of History, at the Pacific Street entrance to the campus, at the Boys Town National Institute in Omaha and on the lake side of the Center Administration Building while the last one was placed in our warehouse waiting to be taken to Flanagan High.

Pedestals for the statues are faced with green granite, each displaying a message relevant to its location: The one in the traffic turn-around reads:

He Ain't Heavy, Father, He's My Brother.
BOYS TOWN
Dedicated to helping all youth realize their
full potential for God, self and society.

Although a warmth born of familiarity had grown for the older sculpture by Correll in 1948, the new promised to be equally inspiring to our legion of admirers. The modern version was set in place in the traffic turnaround the summer of 1978. There was much agitation at the time to place the new statue where the old one had been in front of the Visitors Center. However, negotiations with the State Highway Department were already under way to change the main entrance to Boys Town, and when that happens a more suitable location might be found for the statue. Regardless of the new entrance the "Brothers" seem to have found their niche. With proper annual preventive maintenance these statues can weather for years to come the vagaries of Nebraska's climate.

NEBRASKA STATE HISTORICAL SOCIETY MARKER

The entrance to the Visitors' Center, site of the original "Brothers Statue," is now the location of a Nebraska State Historical Society Marker. The State Historical Society's marker program informs tourists and others of the meaning and significance of a place like Boys Town, and it serves as a reminder to those working at an historical site of their heritage and the importance of their work. The plaque reads:

FATHER FLANAGAN'S BOYS HOME
(The Original 'Boys Town')

Boys Town was founded as a home and school for homeless abandoned, neglected and otherwise under-privileged boys, regardless of color or creed, by Edward J. Flanagan (1886-1948) on December 10, 1917. The first Father Flanagan's Boys' Home at 25th and Dodge Streets in Omaha, Nebraska, sheltered five boys — three from the Juvenile Court and two homeless boys.

On October 17, 1921, Father Flanagan bought Overlook Farm outside Omaha, the nucleus of today's Boys Town campus. From here thousands of Boys Town residents have gone on to become productive citizens in all walks of life.

The philosophy of Boys Town is summarized in Father Flanagan's words: "Our young people are our greatest wealth.

Give them a chance and they will give a good account of
themselves. No boy wants to be bad. There are only bad environment, bad training, bad example, bad thinking."

RESTORATION OF FATHER
FLANAGAN'S RESIDENCE

Until October 1921 when Father Flanagan moved his Home
from Omaha to Overlook Farm ten miles west of Omaha, he lived
with the boys. Living conditions on the farm were primitive in the
beginning. A group of barracks-like buildings, set in a quadrangle,
held a small grammar school, trade school, dormitories, a chapel,
dining rooms and a recreation hall.

Father Flanagan's first residence was built in 1921. It was a
one-story garage converted into a two-room dwelling. That building was razed in 1926 and a new residence was erected that same
year, which today stands as a museum not far from the Hall of
History.

It is a five-bay central block structure with hipped roof and a
two-story wing to the rear. The floor arrangement is a central hall
plan with living room on the south end and a dining room and office
on the north. The rear wing contains the kitchen and housekeeper's room. The second floor has four bedrooms (one in each
corner), a bathroom and a sun room.

The original construction of the house was completed in 1927.
The west addition was constructed in 1940 as dormitory space for
the De La Salle Christian Brothers, who then occupied it at the
invitation of Father Flanagan until they were recalled by their
Superior.

This is where Father Flanagan lived until 1941 when he
moved to the residence adjacent to Dowd Chapel. Once his
original home was vacated it received only minimum care, and it

slowly fell into disrepair. It was becoming an eyesore, so in 1974 we decided to restore it to its rightful prominence. We collected as much of the original furnishings and furniture as we could round up and turned it into a museum piece of Father Flanagan's private life. It now complements the collection in the Hall of History.

In 1975 part of the residence became an alumni center, with bedroom facilities for visiting alumni on the second floor. The restoration project was completed in 1979. It stands proudly as the long-time residence of our founder and a reflection of him personally.

THE BELLS

In the course of his travels, Father Flanagan met George J. Schulmerich, a gifted young electronics engineer. Schulmerich was in the business of installing sound systems in churches around the country. The two became friends.

In 1930 Schulmerich began developing electro-mechanical bells in which tiny generators were struck by small wooden clappers to produce tones of cast bells. In the course of time, the contemporary carillon was born. Acceptance of this new instrument was not easily come by at first, but slowly the walls of tradition began to crumble.

Knowing the problems of the young inventor, and intrigued by the idea of electronic bells, Father Flanagan agreed to have Schulmerich install the bells so that Mary Dowd, who was interested in purchasing them for the Chapel, could hear them on site. This was a major break for Schulmerich and brought him many other commissions.

By the time I arrived at the Home the carillon required extensive repairs, so much so we decided to replace them with new bells. In 1976 a new Schulmerich Basilican VI model carillon with appealing musical tones and low budget clock-controlled operations was installed in Dowd Chapel to be heard across the campus.

BOYS TOWN ALUMNI ASSOCIATION

Some of my best friends are Boys Town alumni. They are spread all over the country, 17,000 strong, and they are a proud lot — proud to have lived and learned at Boys Town and proud of the Home's nationwide reputation of excellence. To them, Boys Town is "home."

But making friends with all of these dudes is another story. At first the prevailing local area chapter resisted every change they saw taking place at Boys Town. Almost to a man they were opposed to change.

"What was good for us is good enough for today's boys," was their battle cry. "We never did it that way before. For sixty years everything ran smoothly, and you come in as a total outsider and want to mess with success."

One of the most vocal opponents to our new approach to youth care was an alumnus who served on the Board of Directors. He collared me one day after a Board meeting and we stood toe-to-toe beside his car for nearly two hours. I couldn't seem to make a point with him. Some months later I got the idea of asking him to be master of ceremonies at a Boys Town banquet when we dedicated our Boys Town Institute. He accepted, probably because this was a new program with a youth mission that could hardly be denied, and because it was divorced from the campus location. Little by little he bought the Family Concept and now is a staunch supporter.

As I traveled the country speaking to alumni groups, almost everywhere I went I'd find one guy who claimed to be one of Father Flanagan's original five boys. I considered forming that Century Club — for the 100 members of the original five. One fellow didn't claim to be one of the originals, but he did say he was "one of the original five altar boys." If that claim made him happy, who was I to argue?

One right move in the eyes of Alumni Association members was the appointment of Tom Burnes as the first full-time Alumni Association executive director. He had been employed by an agricultural firm in Minneapolis. We opened the first permanent alumni office for him in the Father Flanagan residence.

When Burnes got tired of taking the heat from disgruntled alumni visitors I suggested he bring them to my office and I'd give them a sales pitch. I made a few converts, but to this day, occasionally an alumnus will visit the campus, stop by the Alumni Association office, shake his head and mutter to himself, "Girls."

CHAPTER **Fifteen**

IN many respects the Boys Town Village Police Department and Fire Department grew up together. Father Flanagan, who in the beginning seemed to wear every hat he could find, was absent from the Home on numerous occasions, soliciting support, financial and otherwise, as his responsibilities demanded. This meant that in his absence a trusted person had to be in charge.

The first such person upon whom Father Flanagan relied heavily, even when he was at the Home, was Ken Corcoran, who had come to the Home in 1930. When something had to be done and there was no one else to do it, Corcoran would rise to the occasion. He taught in the classroom, was athletic director and settled all sorts of everyday problems. But most of all he represented order and discipline to the boys, and the seeds of the future police department were sown by this man.

In 1936 Corcoran was placed in charge of the Gate House, something of a security and guide station at the main entrance. The telephone switchboard also was located there.

In 1943 Ted Miller, Director of Development and Mailing, persuaded Father Flanagan to hire Maurice "Skip" Palrang, a highly successful high school athletic coach in Omaha. More about Palrang in the next chapter, but Father Flanagan appointed him director of athletics and coach, which fragmented Corcoran's authority, and he eventually left the Home for another job.

Security was at loose ends until 1945 when Father Flanagan

hired Larry Kennedy to take charge of campus security with the added responsibility of providing safe transportation on and off campus for himself and the Sisters who worked at the Home.

Kennedy had graduated from Boys Town High School in 1937, and after having been employed in the business world he returned to the Home. Besides his security duties he worked in the Mailing Division and assisted at the Gate House.

In February, 1947, as the new buildings were being completed in a wide arc from the old Administration Building to the Field House, along with the first twenty-five cottages, Kennedy was appointed Director of Public Safety.

Prior to that time a special watchman was on duty overseeing the grounds at night. Kennedy's Safety Patrol was on duty seven days a week, twenty-four hours a day, but his department was also in charge of the Souvenir Shop as well as having some duties in the Purchasing Department. He had a staff of nine, including six security personnel and three telephone operators.

From the number of additional duties placed on Kennedy's shoulders it was apparent that security was not yet really a high priority item. Finally in 1971 a local security company was hired to augment the Boys Town Public Safety Department.

This company was responsible for checking cars and trucks that came onto the campus, along with other supervisory chores. Most of what these men did could be accomplished from their patrol cars, and that's where most of them stayed.

This was the setup when I came to town, and I wasn't overjoyed with it. As I related in an earlier chapter when I described the theft of my bicycle as security and safety personnel stood by, my faith in their dependability began to waiver.

"Kennedy's Keystone Kops" — and let me tell you a story that might explain why I gave them that name: One Saturday morning shortly after I came here a report came to my office that two little fellows had skipped out overnight — a little black kid from Ohio and a little white guy from somewhere in Texas.

Not only were they gone, but also missing was an old surplus truck we had purchased from the U.S. Post Office for delivering mail around campus — a truck with the steering wheel on the right and, similar to old milk delivery trucks, one in which the driver stood rather than sat behind the wheel. It was such a cripple that it spent more time in the auto service department than on the street. It was parked outside the garage to be repaired when shops opened on Monday morning.

I suggested to our cops that there might be a connection between the two missing boys and the missing vehicle.

Oh no, they assured me. Reportedly the truck wouldn't run and besides, those two runaways were too small to drive it. No way could they have taken it.

Well, about nine o'clock Sunday night I received a call from the Chief of Police in Sioux Falls, South Dakota. He was laughing, and he said, "We have a couple of your cowboys up here. Could they really be yours?" Our athletic teams are called "The Cowboys" and so calling them cowboys was not unusual. When he gave me their names I immediately identified them as the two who had hit the road.

"How'd they get there?" I asked.

"They were driving a little beat up former mail delivery truck," he said.

"How could that be?" I persisted; "Neither is tall enough to handle the steering wheel and reach the pedals at the same time, and besides, that truck was not fit to drive according to the reports I had received."

The Chief of Police chuckled as he explained: "One of my officers noticed this strange looking old truck painted white with the steering wheel on the right side being driven down Main Street by a little black boy. We have only a few blacks in Sioux Falls and this one was so small that my officer took a closer look. Besides, there was no license plate on the vehicle.

"He stopped it and very professionally asked the driver for his driver's license. Of course, he didn't have one. About that time a little towhead pops up from the floor. He had been down there working the gas pedal and brake while his partner in crime did the steering."

They told, then, how they had siphoned gas a few times along the way and spent most of the time driving. When the officer asked them what they thought they were doing so far from Boys Town, the Texas kid snapped, "We're up here buyin' cattle." In days before he came to Boys Town he had accompanied his rancher-father on cattle buying trips and he had heard his dad say that before.

I asked the chief to put the runaways in the cooler overnight and I'd send someone up for them the next day. Monday morning I announced to my safety team that two of them were to go to Sioux Falls, one to return the two boys and the other to drive the truck back.

"But the truck isn't fit to run," one of them protested. "Take one of those boys with you," I said. "He can show you how to get around in this world."

At a meeting of the Deputy Directors in my office in March 1974 I suggested that the security at the Home should come in for a complete overhaul. It was decided that since Boys Town is an incorporated village in Nebraska and our law-and-order problems could be of the big league variety, a full-fledged police force should be our goal.

Herb Sigurdson, Youth Care Deputy Director, said that one of his acquaintances in California might be convinced to come and assist in building the kind of department we needed. He had the necessary qualifications, we were told. This was before we had an opportunity to psyche out another of his proteges, Mike Casey! After a number of interviews by those of us who had major responsibility for security, this man was invited to join us. In May 1974 Sid Smith was named our first Chief of Police with recommendations to develop a first class police force.

Smith retained Larry Kennedy to assist him, but terminated the contract with our security company. In the four years Smith was in charge, among the elements of genuine law enforcement he introduced were a written reporting system, a standard uniform for all officers, respectable salaries, the certification of some officers at the State Police Training Academy at Grand

Island, Nebraska; hiring a licensed investigator in the person of Michael Mench, and an organized Police Cadet Corps to complement our existing Fire Cadet program.

Smith also moved the Central Police Station from the Gate House to share quarters with our Civil Defense Unit in the warehouse. All in all, Sid Smith put the Boys Town Police Department on the map.

We had hoped Smith would stay with us permanently but instead he left us in 1978 to return to California and a promotion in his chosen field of police work. We hated to see him go, but after a diligent search we were doubly fortunate in being able to fill his position with another competent chief in Robert Allbritton, a retired Navy Chief Petty Officer from Alabama. He was sworn in as Chief of the Boys Town Police Department in March, 1978. It was his special mission to fine-tune a Police Department that eventually became one of the most efficient village police forces in the State of Nebraska. What makes our police force unique is the specialized training required to operate in a "City of Little Men" — also "little women."

As police functions grew, the department's quarters in the warehouse became more and more cramped, and in 1981 Allbritton made arrangements to move his department to the former Boys Town Clinic, which had been vacated in 1976 when the Alexian Brothers, who had operated the Clinic, were called to other assignments.

The former Clinic would henceforth be known as the Boys Town "Town Hall," with offices to accommodate all police activities on the campus and in cooperation with neighboring jurisdictions.

Boys Town has been an incorporated village under Nebraska statutes since 1936, and as such our main thoroughfares are public streets. With the majority of our population consisting of teenage boys and girls it was not surprising that unsavory characters would look to our citizens as being ripe for their drug distribution business.

It was important to me and to our police that they be armed, as are most other law enforcement officers. Chief Allbritton asked for this authority, pointing out that occasionally his men had to deal with public law breakers of every kind who wandered on our premises. Dr. Lonnie Phillips was adamantly opposed to this idea, arguing that residents of Boys Town could be handled without the use or threat of sidearms. He was even opposed to police using marked cars. This created a big rhubarb between Lonnie and myself; it was the one subject over which we had a few heated arguments. After reminding him again of the old buccaneer and his pancakes we moved on.

Phillips was entirely correct in his assessment of what we might call "in-house" problems. However, we were living in the real world, not on an island or in a fairyland. Normal people don't carry sidearms around their homes. Neither will our Family Teachers. Our police? That's different. Public buses traveled our streets. Our athletic contests were open to the public and visitors by the thousands toured the Home each year. Every criminal element in society has access to our public streets and public buildings. A sign in the back of church says it all: "All you who enter guard your purse and coat! Not everyone who comes to this church has been converted." The bearing of sidearms and the use of marked cars is as valid at Boys Town as in any other village in Nebraska. Not everyone who walks the streets of any village does so to protect the local citizens and their interests.

Just as important as safeguarding the boys and employees of the Home from outside predators is the constant need to keep order within the Home itself. Most of the boys who come to Boys Town have had some experience with drugs and can react at any time. Every officer must take the Family Teacher Training Course so that he knows the philosophy of youth care and can work closely with the Family Teacher who calls when a youth is out of control in a house. The police are trained to remove the boy from the home peacefully to a neutral situation where the Family Teachers are able to apply their sophisticated methods of handling problems. In almost every case the boy can be cooled off and returned to his cottage. If he persists in his wild behavior he is taken to the Douglas County Youth Center for further determination of his future fortunes.

Ours is an excellent police force. As a matter of fact, it has been declared one of the best and well-equipped of the nearly four hundred village police units in Nebraska. This honor came from the National Crime Information Computer and its companion organization, the Nebraska Crime Service.

The Boys Town Village Police are also involved with the Police Cadet program. Much work needs to be done with this group in the matter of developing details consistent with the schedule of the Home at large. Some sort of drill team is in prospect, along with a training course to educate cadets to assist in directing parking traffic at athletic and school sponsored events.

And our police do wear sidearms.

FIRE DEPARTMENT

Although the Volunteer Fire Department antedated the Police Department at Boys Town, the two in a sense grew up together. After long dependence on "bucket brigades" and hose carts, Father Flanagan eventually organized his first Volunteer Fire Department in 1946. This fledgling group was equipped with a hand-pulled hose cart and a box of fire extinguishers. Earl Melia, Chief Engineer at the time, was the first Fire Chief. His baptism of fire, you might say, came during the next Christmas vacation when on January 3, 1947, fire broke out in the attic above the fifth floor of the building that housed both the grade and high schools.

Built in 1922, it was the first permanent structure on Overlook farm. When fire was discovered during the noon hour, members of the Volunteer Fire Department and nearly every other resident of the Home went into action. They fought the blaze with hand extinguishers and small hoses until the arrival of a company from the Omaha Fire Department and one fire truck from Millard.

Melia supervised and coordinated the actions of his own bunch and the visiting firemen. An off-hand remark by one of the residents summed it up succinctly when he said: "Everybody works at our Home."

No injuries were reported but damage to the building was estimated at more than $100,000. The main lesson we learned was to make everybody at the Home more fire conscious.

During that first year the Boys Town Volunteer Fire Department answered twelve calls. As the Home grew so did the demands on the fire and safety contingent. More and better equipment was purchased. The first motorized fire engine came for the department in 1947. But it wasn't until 1964 that the Home was in a position to purchase a used water tanker.

Duties of the department varied until the late 1960's when Fire Chief Paul Sing, who had taken over these duties after the death of Earl Melia, was given added responsibilities as representative of the Civil Defense program. Upon his death in 1970, his widow, Mable, was appointed Acting Director of Civil Defense.

When Sid Smith was hired in 1974 to direct the village safety program along with that of Civil Defense Director, John Sing, Paul's son, was named Acting Fire Marshal. John had a lot to learn, and he set about teaching himself by taking advantage of every course and seminar available. One of John Sing's first noteworthy efforts was to introduce an employee safety program and workers' compensation for employees of the Home. Shortly thereafter he organized the Fire Cadet program. These boys went on to win State Fire Competition championships each year from 1979 through 1985.

Begun in 1977, these events featured teenage fire fighters from volunteer and full-time fire departments across Nebraska. Some one hundred boys competed each year in hose rolling, hose connecting, water bucket races, air-pak races, hydrant races, and ladder and hose hoisting. John Sing designed the program and usually had at least a dozen of his Boys Town fire fighters participating for the Home. The event never claimed the media attention as did a state championship in football, basketball, baseball or track. However, it was very exciting for the contestants and the public safety lessons it taught were invaluable.

When Smith left for California in 1978 his titles and duties were combined in the "Village of Boys Town Fire Department," and John Sing was named Chief. In 1978 Sing organized and equipped a Rescue Squad, and two years later he organized a Water Rescue Response Team that began building an enviable record in the Omaha area. It was frequently called upon by law enforcement agencies to retrieve drowning victims or to search for objects such as stolen cars and other contraband abandoned in area lakes and rivers. The Boys Town Water Rescue Response Team has often seen duty scuba diving in the treacherous Missouri River.

Early in 1985 the Boys Town Fire Department signed the first mutual aid agreement with neighboring village fire departments, thus assuring better protection for all concerned.

PHILAMATIC CENTER

In the 1940's, after several years of searching for a suitable location to display his extensive collection of stamps, currency, coins and other items, a man by the name of Dwight O. Barrett met Father Flanagan. The rest is history. Boys Town was the beneficiary: Mr. Barrett, a retired mechanical engineer came to Boys Town and designed a suitable museum to house his collection.

On July 1, 1951, through the generosity of Mr. Barrett and one Mrs. John R. McCall, who donated the funds to build the museum in memory of Mrs. McCall's deceased husband, the Philamatic Center opened. Mr. Barrett chose the name "Philamatic" for the Center because it is a combination of the terms Philatelic (collection of stamps) and Numismatic (collection of money). The name "Philamatic Center" was subsequently copyrighted by Mr. Barrett. He was curator of the Center until

1959 when he retired, and was curator emeritus until he died in 1964.

Since its founding in 1951 the Philamatic Center's collection has increased from two hundred frames of stamps, coins, and other items to nearly six hundred fifty frames, 28 by 44 inches. The collection of stamps and coins continues to increase through the generosity of many contributors. Not only are its collections special, so is the design of the Center. Glareless lighting and humidity controls at forty to fifty percent, as recommended by the U.S. Bureau of Standards, are the best climate for preserving papers. Coins, medals, tokens, and currency are displayed in such a manner that both sides of the same display can be seen in the same frame. Special die-cut cardboard holders make this possible. Some of the unusual items to be viewed are:

* A 600-pound solid ball of stamps (featured in Ripley's "Believe It or Not")
* World's largest paper money display — over 9,000 notes
* The only existing block of four Uniontown, Alabama Confederate stamps
* An exhibit of obsolete paper-money where visitors are invited to find their own town's scrip
* A stamp with the denomination of $50,000
* Bank notes — all major issues of U.S. banknotes, Continental currency from the Revolutionary War
* U.S. Treasury display of counterfeit notes and high value notes including a U.S. $100,000 specimen note
* Coins of all denominations. A one-pound (12 oz.) coin from the Bahamas
* Full set of U.S. Gold Coins
* Medals and medallions from all over the world
* American Indian arrowheads and artifacts
* Set of filigreed silver ingots of the 48 contiguous states of the USA

* Set of filigreed silver ingots of the Presidents of the U.S.

* And many more items with an estimated value of $1.5 million.

Until April 1974, the boys at the Home used tokens in place of regular coins and currency in transactions on the campus. In September of that same year legal tender replaced the tokens — just another step into the real world.

In 1979 the Boys Town collection received the American Philatelic Society's most prestigious honor, the John W. Luff Award. It was presented to William W. Wylie, consultant to the Boys Town Philamatic Center. Making the presentation for exceptional contributions of philately was James T. DeVoss, executive secretary of the society.

In the mid-1980's Boys Town made stamp news again with the issuance of a four-cent U.S. Postal Service stamp honoring the 100th anniversary of the birth of Father Flanagan.

A Father Flanagan stamp was approved by then Postmaster General William Bolger in October 1984, but was not unveiled until May 8, 1986. By this time Albert V. Casey had succeeded Bolger.

Getting approval for the stamp wasn't easy. In fact, it was about as difficult as dealing with the Washington, D.C. Fine Arts Commission in its opposition to a Boys Town statue as described in the previous chapter.

It wasn't that the Postal Service objected to a stamp commemorating Father Flanagan's achievements; in fact, the stamp was issued as part of the Service's great American Series, which included such notables as Pearl S. Buck, Harry S. Truman, Thomas H. Gallaudet, Carl Schiry and others. The problem seemed to be with the number of requests for stamps by countless organizations and groups and the denomination of the stamp.

Our efforts at accomplishing this began in 1976 when William E. Ramsey, Deputy Director of Development, contacted the Omaha postmaster, John P. Munnelly, for advice and assistance. Ramsey had joined the Boys Town staff in April, 1974, after careers as radio and television newsman, public relations director at two colleges, and a total of five years experience as an executive at two advertising agencies. He, over a period of time, assumed Jim Brown's position in the public relations department and, being a local well-known personality, he received an immediate favorable response from the postmaster. However, it wasn't until 1980 that Nebraska's delegation in Congress took up the task of lobbying for the stamp. Four years later we heard from Postmaster General Bolger. Although I left the office of executive director in mid-1985, I was asked to continue the Home's efforts on behalf of the stamp.

At the time, first class mail required a 22-cent stamp, and in a letter to Postmaster General Casey I argued for an 11-cent stamp, pointing out: "In my opinion, a four-cent stamp would be of little practical use. On the other hand, if it were an 11-cent stamp it could be used in our tens of thousands of first class mailings. And since Father Flanagan of Boys Town enjoys an international reputation, a significant public demand for this stamp could be expected."

Casey responded by saying it was too late to change plans. He wrote: "The denomination for the stamp was selected some time ago, the engraving has been made and the printing plates manufactured. To change the stamp's value at this point would entail great expense and make it impossible to issue the stamp on the planned date." Who would ever have thought that but a few years later the 25-cent stamp would be raised to 29 cents thus giving the Father Flanagan stamp new life.

We accepted the decision and the new four-cent stamp picturing Father Flanagan was unveiled by the Postal Service on May 8, 1986. It was the first stamp honoring either Boys Town or its founder.

In a news release, the Postal Service suggested meeting the 22-cent stamp requirement by combining the Father Flanagan stamp (four cents) with the Postal Service's George Washington-Washington Monument stamp (eighteen cents). Both stamps were of the Great American Series and commemorated two men who were founders of great concepts and ideals.

The First Day of Issue of the Father Flanagan stamp took place July 14, 1986, in a ceremony in the high school dining hall. Presiding was Mitchell H. Gordon, senior assistant Postmaster General. The Strategic Air Command Elite Color Guard from Offutt Air Force Base made the presentation of colors, and the Most Reverend Daniel E. Sheehan, Archbishop of Omaha, gave the invocation.

The main speaker was John H. Griesemer, Governor of the U.S. Postal Service. Guests included Stanley T. Payne, general manager and postmaster of the Omaha division; John Tillson, postmaster of Boys Town, and Christopher Calle, of Stamford, Connecticut, designer of the stamp.

The printed program carried this message: "The United States Postal Service is proud to issue this postal stamp as a tribute to the devoted humanitarian, Father Edward Joseph Flanagan. Designed by Christopher Calle, the stamp becomes the latest addition to the Great American Series."

Thus concluded a fitting tribute to a man who knew the meaning of the word compassion, and dedicated his life to a demonstration of it.

The Philamatic Center is a busy tourist attraction. We all appreciate the public relations value this Center brings itself in the form of good will and ultimately as a potential fund raiser.

Gifts to that collection continue to mount. The display of this collection is just another way of telling the public that we are grateful for any and all gifts to the Home.

VOCATIONAL CAREER TRAINING PROGRAM

When Father Flanagan began his boys' home in 1917 he believed strongly that troubled youth in his care needed to be taught a trade. And for such a youth, work with his hands was as valuable as any intellectual pursuit. As a matter of fact, every boy needs an academic education and a vocational education because the two go hand in hand. Some want to enroll in a college or university; others go directly into the work force in the real world. Here again Father Flanagan was far ahead of his time. He had a trade school when trade schools were not in vogue.

In line with his legacy, the Vocational Trade School at the Home today ranks among the finest. This Center is variously called the "Vocational Career Center" and the "Trade School."

In order to keep up with the ever changing climate in industry, teachers at our Trade School meet at least twice a year with an advisory group of representatives from the trade they are teaching. This insures that the students keep abreast of the latest advances and also helps in linking students with jobs upon graduation.

Under the direction of Ed Novotny, himself a Boys Town alumnus, the Vocational Career Center, in the 1980's, taught as many as nineteen trades and occupations. Novotny had come to Boys Town at the age of thirteen and was graduated from its High School in 1943. Five years later he returned to work at the Home and eventually became principal of the Vocational Career Center.

Among the regular career subjects were: air conditioning, heating and sheet metal, auto body repair, auto mechanics, baker, barbering and hair styling, business education, construction I and II, culinary arts, drafting, driver education, electricity-electronics, general mechanics, graphic arts, industrial arts, metals, welding, and horticulture.

The last named, horticulture, had been a minor part of the program for several years, but it received a tremendous boost with the dedication on October 21, 1981 of the Vernon F. Dale Memorial Greenhouse.

The greenhouse was a gift from Vernon and Earline Dale of Onalaska, Wisconsin, where they operated a sporting goods store. They had visited Boys Town in 1975 and, interested in plants and the out-of-doors, gave special attention to the Home's horticultural program. They saw the program needed a home of its own.

Vernon Dale died in 1976 and his widow donated funds in his name for the greenhouse, which was built by students of the

Vocational Career Center's construction classes and students of the Horticultural Center. It stands between the Hall of History building and the Father Flanagan residence museum, and it provides one of the best horticultural education programs in the area.

In March 1948, about two months before his death, Father Flanagan reiterated his evaluation of vocational training in words to which we still subscribe wholeheartedly:

> "Trade training has a most beneficial effect on the boy. There is something exhilarating to a boy in being able to do something with his hands — making something with tools — creating something useful. This is character building and oftentimes the solution of a boy's behavior problem. I note that most of our behavior problems here at Boys Town are with boys who have not been taught much, who can do nothing with their hands, whose minds are, therefore, not easily attracted to useful things, and who have too much time on their idle minds."

Mickey Rooney admires a painting of the Boys Town symbol (1976).

With Secretary of State Henry A. Kissinger and Ambassador William W. Scranton, former Governor of Pennsylvania (1976).

Ted Williams brings a smile to the lips of Bobby Paylor while Father Hupp looks on (1983).

Louise (Mrs. Spencer) Tracy, founder of the John Tracy Clinic for the hearing impaired, attends the dedication of the Boys Town National Institute (1975).

Mother Teresa pays a visit to Boys Town in 1976.

With President Gerald R. Ford in Denver, Colorado (1978). Photo by Tom Masamori

Danny Thomas expresses his best wishes while an obviously thrilled Johnny Laratta smiles to have his picture taken with such a celebrity.

Hank Aaron signs autographs for his fans. Photo by Tom Plambeck, Omaha World-Herald

"Big O" Oscar Robinson attends the Booster Club Banquet as its guest speaker in May, 1978 and receives a Boys Town statuette from Father Hupp.

This four-cent stamp honoring Father Flanagan was issued by the U.S. Postal Service in 1986.

Father Hupp takes his seat as President Ford's Special Delegate to the United Nations, October - December, 1976. Photo by Max Machol

To my dear friend, whom I love Rev. Hupp Pearl

The irrepressible Pearl Bailey, America's "Good Will Ambassador" to the United Nations and a good friend (1976).

Frank Szynskie brings the Boys Town Choir to visit the United Nations when Father Hupp was there.

Back where the revolution in youth care began, with the boys and girls of Boys Town, Nebraska.

CHAPTER Sixteen

H UNDREDS and hundreds of Boys Town
boys enlisted in the Armed Forces during World War II, the
Korean and Vietnam and Gulf conflicts, to defend the very principles on which our country was founded. Thirty-nine of our alumni
made the supreme sacrifice.

They knew the principles for which they fought were sound
because as residents of Boys Town they had been taught to
govern themselves in an atmosphere that emphasized the basic
freedoms guaranteed them by the Constitution of the United
States.

Eugene Leahy, a former judge and former Mayor of Omaha,
once referred to Boys Town as a "mini-United Nations." It was a
tribute to the fundamental human rights he saw being taught and
practiced at the Home.

Part of this discipline and training was learned in the extra
curricular activities of the Home, to wit: on the playing fields and
in the choir loft.

Father Flanagan, hardly an athlete himself, was convinced of
the importance of athletic competition and supervised recreation
in the life of a young boy. He knew that physical activity not only
built strong bodies but also drained off that excess energy every
boy has that sometimes gets him into mischief.

In 1943, during World War II, Father Flanagan hired a man to
run the athletic program at Boys Town who, over the next
twenty-nine years, became second only to the founder himself in

his influence on the boys. His name was Maurice H. "Skip" Palrang. He served the Home as athletic director, coach, teacher and counselor, and it has been said that no individual at Boys Town, other than Father Flanagan, has had a greater impact for good on more boys than did Skip Palrang.

By the end of World War II Boys Town had completed an ambitious building program that saw the construction of twenty-five cottages, Music Hall, Administration Building, High School, Dining Hall and Trade School, at a cost of $2,900,000. Father Flanagan and Skip Palrang also wanted to build a field house, but the federal government disapproved the request at the time because of a shortage of building materials needed for the nationwide veterans' housing program.

But in 1947 the government relented and approved construction of the field house, along with a boiler house, laundry and auditorium. Work began immediately, since Father Flanagan and Skip Palrang had already designed the Memorial Field House, as it was to be called, awaiting the green light.

The structure was modeled after facilities at Purdue University and Michigan State University. The main arena, 300 feet by 150 feet, had permanent seating for 2,500 with an additional 6,000 temporary bleacher seats. It would have a dirt floor at first, and much of the interior was left unfinished under the original construction plans.

Four years later the building was completed, with a basketball court for interscholastic competition, running track, facilities for indoor baseball practice and tennis and volleyball courts. A partition was built to separate that segment of the Field House from another gymnasium with two intramural basketball courts, gymnastics area, a wrestling room, swimming pool, handball and racquetball courts and classroom and office space. It was a beauty — by far the most complete indoor athletic facility in the Omaha area at the time.

Francis Cardinal Spellman of New York City came to Boys Town for the dedication on May 8, 1949, and he gave all the new postwar buildings a special blessing.

Twenty-nine years later, in 1978, we gave the Field House the name it deserved: "Skip Palrang Memorial Field House." But that took some time; during his lifetime Skip would not consent to my wish to name it after him.

Meanwhile, Skip Palrang became a legend at Boys Town. He coached football, basketball and baseball from 1943 until his retirement in 1972, the year before I became executive director. In addition, he was a teacher, holding classes in Spanish and science.

His athletic teams gained a national reputation, with the football team traveling over the country to play the best high school teams available. During his tenure his Cowboy eleven played in twenty-one states and the District of Columbia.

He was a pioneer in developing T-formation football, still the standard of many high school, college and professional teams, and he was recognized in both high school and college circles as an authority on the subject, publishing a book on it.

His football record at Boys Town was an impressive 201 wins, 66 losses and 12 ties, and his teams won two State Class A football championships. In basketball his record was 240 wins and 96 losses; while in baseball his Omaha American Legion "McDevitt" junior team won the National Championship in 1939 and his Boys Town teams won two State Championships.

My first meeting with Skip was during my years as athletic director of the Catholic Youth Organization in the late 1940's. From that time on I followed him through his successful years. He was a tall, ascetic type of a man with a lined face and deep voice that at once commanded respect.

His great success with Boys Town's special kind of boys was based on the fact that he could convince the boys that he had their welfare at heart. He was tough, all business, and seldom minced words. He could and did lay down the law with the boys. From time to time Father Flanagan spoke to him about his salty language. Father used to take his daily stroll, reading his Breviary (prayer book) along on the sidelines during football practice.

According to Skip, Father Flanagan's presence there tended to limit the coach's vocabulary.

Skip claimed strong language was all the kids from the streets understood, but Father Flanagan argued that they would benefit by being addressed with proper expletives.

Aside from what Skip said, or how he said it, boys knew he cared. He was fair. Wally Provost, retired sports editor and columnist for the Omaha World-Herald, once wrote of him: "Skip Palrang was a master of taking either a Fauntleroy or an aimless tough and putting him on the road to manhood."

One of my regrets was that Skip retired after the 1971-72 school year, shortly before I came to Boys Town. The feeling was mutual. One day he came into my office — I remember him rolling the edge of his trademark pork-pie hat around in his long fingers saying he had retired too soon.

"If I had known you were coming I would have stayed on," he told me. He went on to say his retirement pay was hardly enough to live on and could we use him around the campus?

"Could we use you?" I asked. "You bet we can. We'll pay what your Social Security allows if you will just walk the halls of the high school twice a day. I want the boys to know you're still with us."

In addition, Skip was an excellent teacher as well as coach. I reminded him he could substitute teach in English, Spanish and science. Besides, Skip was a watchmaker and repairman — it was his hobby. He had a small room in the Field House where he used to spend leisure hours at his repair work. He had a key and he could come and go as he pleased.

"One more thing," I said. "The Field House should have your name on it."

He had been pleased with everything I said leading up to that. Now he frowned. "Over my dead body," he said, and I could tell that he felt such a thing would never sail after some of his experiences at the Home.

Despite his legendary status as a coach and athletic director, he always avoided the limelight as much as possible. "Maybe that's how we'll do it," I said. "Over your dead body." And that's how it happened soon after his death.

Jim Spencer, who had been Skip's top assistant, was the logical successor to head the athletic department and he was up to the task. He had his work cut out for him because the last winning year in the Athletic Department was 1965.

Just prior to that time Monsignor Wegner's health began to fail miserably. He was gradually weakened by one surgical operation after another and as his health waned, so did discipline around the Home. One Friday night the starting quarterback did not show up for a regular scheduled game. Seems he had a date. The incident was not an isolated one. It was only indicative of the tone of dedication throughout the Home.

To add to the coach's woes, a new type of boy was being admitted from the drug infested areas of the streets, and the total enrollment of boys on campus was being reduced from 787 in 1973 to a goal of 400 or less. It was no wonder that Boys Town submitted a request to be released from the tough Metro Class A Conference League to compete with Class B schools, more our size.

An added problem plaguing the Athletic Department was the fact that the average stay of a boy was much less than it had been in previous years. To develop competitive teams with players who were in the system an average of only two years was asking a lot. But Spencer was able to get our teams back on a break-even basis and with better days ahead Jim stepped aside and turned the coaching chores over to a younger generation.

Skip Palrang died of a heart attack on February 8, 1978 and seven months later to the day, September 8, 1978, a dedication was held to change the name of the Field House to the "Maurice H. 'Skip' Palrang Memorial Field House." Near the entrance a large plaque erected in tribute to him reads: "Athletic director, coach, teacher, friend . . . to thousands of boys who became better men because they were touched by his wisdom, leadership and patience. He expected and got every player's best effort. He asked no more. His record of success showed that it was enough."

MUSIC AND CHOIR

From the earliest years of Father Flanagan's Boys' Home, music played an important role in the boys' education. The choir, as a separate entity, began to take shape in 1941 with the arrival at the Home of the newly ordained Father Francis P. Schmitt. In my book he became in the Music Department what Skip Palrang was in athletics, a giant in his profession. He was a perfectionist, but every boy who sang a note in his choir really admired him. When former choristers returned to the campus for a visit they would, without fail, seek him out and he always had time for "his boys."

In an amazingly short time Father Schmitt's Boys Town Concert Choir became internationally famous, touring the United States and a number of foreign countries for concerts before packed houses of appreciative music lovers. The first tour occurred in the fall of 1946 and with but one exception continued each year through 1984.

National tours included concerts in Washington, D.C., and cities in all forty-eight contiguous states, except Louisiana. International tours included ten days in Cuba; six weeks in Japan; and five provinces in Canada at one time or another. Before the advent of television the Concert Choir performed for all radio networks, especially at Christmas time, with a message from the Executive Director. When television came to life it appeared on Ed Sullivan's "Toast of the Town," the Milton Berle Show, Kate Smith Show, the original "Today Show" with Dave Garroway, Mike Douglas Show, CBS Christmas Midnight Mass for several years, and lesser local and public TV appearances too numerous to mention.

There were appearances with the Omaha, Buffalo (New York) and Hartford (Connecticut) symphonies, and in over fifteen renowned Concert Halls across the country from Carnegie Hall to the San Francisco Opera House. Special events, perhaps enjoyed most by the boys, were the appearances at Disneyland in Anaheim, California, and Disney World in Orlando, Florida. The boys appeared on ABC-TV "The Osmond Show" and at half-time of countless football games and between baseball doubleheaders from Nebraska to Los Angeles.

Private tutors accompanied the choir on all tours to keep the boys apace in their classroom work. Volumes could be written about the experiences enjoyed and the lessons learned on these tours.

It's interesting to note here that there were various singing groups throughout the Home with approximately two hundred boys involved. There was the "Duck Choir" made up of boys who were just learning to swim in the music world. The next step up were those in the "Soup Choir." I never really discovered the origin of that title; here you may use your imagination. At any rate, out of this group were separated members for the "Chancel Choir" made up of sopranos and altos, and the "First Choir" comprised of high school tenors and basses — lads, for the most part, whose voices were changing or had already changed. Forty boys, more or less, were then selected for special training to go on tour as members of the famed "Concert Choir."

Early in his career Father Schmitt created an award, the prestigious St. Cecilia Medal, named after the patroness of music, and awarded it to outstanding musicians in the choral and instrumental fields with whom he associated.

The Boys Town Alumni Association honored Father Schmitt in 1979 by installing a plaque in the lobby of the Music Hall which reads:

> "Father Francis Schmitt developed the finest boys' choir in the United States. Becoming a member was as great an honor as a boy could attain. The 'first squad' was readily strengthened by members of the second string choir, a competitive plan intro- duced by Father Schmitt that not only improved the choir but

> also helped motivate the boys. Members of 'his' Boys Town
> Choir and all the boys who knew him and loved him take pride in
> sharing this special honor with Father Schmitt, patient teacher of
> talent."

Father Schmitt helped many young men become not only fine concert choir singers, but also gentlemen and good citizens.

Unfortunately, after this colorful and productive career, Father Schmitt was caught in the chaotic web that befell Boys Town in the wake of the Sun Newspaper articles. He and I had been good friends through the years — my ordination preceded his by one year — and shortly after I arrived at Boys Town he came to my office for a visit. He was a worn and weary man. Among other things we discussed the future of the Concert Choir. He even suggested that choir tours be discontinued. I would hear none of that because it seemed to me that this Concert Choir was one of the finest good will ambassadors the Home ever had. My reading of his suggestion was that he himself was too exhausted to continue preparing for these tours and actually conducting them.

This man was far too valuable an asset of the Home as a liturgical musician and teacher to be lost in the maze of changes. Between the two of us we worked out a sabbatical arrangement which would allow him to relax and do some writing, while keeping touch with the boys. It was during the next year or so that he wrote a scholarly book entitled, "Church Music — Ten Years Later (After Vatican II)." It is a masterful analysis of what has since been called "Church Music Trashed."

Norb Letter, who came to Boys Town in June 1946 from Daggett, Michigan where he was Superintendent of Schools, was Father Schmitt's assistant. On March 1, 1975 he was promoted from his position as director of the Concert Choir to director of the Music Department. His wife, Evelyn, had been the secretary in the Music Department and worked as a tutor and substitute teacher in the department. She retained her position.

Frank Szynskie, known to his friends as "Moe," then

succeeded Letter as director of the Concert Choir. He was well qualified for the job. He had started his musical career when he came to Boys Town after the death of his mother. He joined the choir as a boy soprano in 1941 and sang with it until he graduated from Boys Town High School in 1947. His fellow Boys Town residents soon learned that this little blond who sang soprano was angelic only from the larynx up; the rest of him was all boy and a yard wide. His ability to emphasize the fact that he was a member of the Church Militant earned him an additional nickname, "Duke."

He enrolled at St. Benedict's College in Atchison, Kansas and completed his studies in music at the University of Nebraska in Lincoln. After the Korean conflict, where he served as an Army chaplain's aide, he returned to Boys Town to teach music and continue undergraduate study at the University of Nebraska in Lincoln and Creighton University in Omaha. Once on the staff of the Music Department at Boys Town, he worked his way to the top. Mr. Letter directed the Music Department and "Moe" directed the Concert Choir in the finest tradition of their mentor, Father Francis P. Schmitt, who incidentally in 1959 received from Pope John Paul II the honored title, "Monsignor."

STREETS AND SIDE STREETS

It was never necessary for me to look for trouble. More of it found me than I could conveniently handle. However, occasionally I would leave my office if only to regain my balance and enjoy a little fresh air. One day, after making a cursory tour of the street where all of the cottages were located, I referred to it as the "Gaza Strip." I saw enough on that first tour to call for a closer inspection, which I made a short time later, only to learn how accurate the name really was. It wouldn't help our image to advertise the conditions there. It occurred to me then that a more respectable name should adorn that street because soon the devastation there would be cleared up. As a matter of fact, all of

the streets needed names. After all, most villages have designations of some kind for their streets, I thought.

Boys Town had been an incorporated village in Nebraska
since 1936 with a public thoroughfare. It had most everything that
an ordinary village might have — schools, gymnasium, swimming
pool, post office, bank, churches, clinic — but no jail, and no
street names. Of course, some of the boys thought the whole
place was a jail in spite of the fact that we had no fences around the
place or bars on the windows. But street names and house
numbers to match? Not at all. A home address implies roots,
stability, self-identity, whereas a cottage with no address does
not quite do it.

For the boys, living in a home with a street and house number
heightens one's sense of personal identity — "125 Maher Circle"
sounds better than "Cottage 25." Streets could be named after
persons who were important in Boys Town history, giving them
some added recognition. And finally, visitors, residents and staff
at the Home would find street signs and house numbers a great
convenience.

We needed a committee to make recommendations along
these lines. With the Village Board's approval, I gave Clarence
"Mitt" Stoffel, Jr. the nod to chair such a committee and select
members he could work with to accomplish this assignment. In a
short time "Mitt" submitted the following list of Boys Town
veterans he had solicited to serve with him: Father Schmitt, Skip
Palrang, Pat Norton, Ed Novotny and George Pfeiffer. It did not
take long for these stalwarts to come up with a list of twenty-eight
street names and designations. "Father Flanagan Boulevard"
was a natural for the campus main street, a long thoroughfare that
runs in a wide U-shape from the Home's main entrance to Dowd
Memorial Chapel.

Then came a great mix of titles such as boulevard, drive, lane,
circle, loop, way and plaza. Stoffel reported that all streets were
named except the short one separating the Music Hall and the
High School. He said that his committee could not agree on a title
for that short street so they decided, tongue in cheek, to call it the

"Grand Loop." My comment was that it should be named after the chairman of the committee.

"Over my dead body," he said. Well, I had heard a remark like that before, so it was not until after Mitt died that the street in question was tagged "Stoffel Road."

Mitt richly deserves a greater recognition. He was a contemporary of Palrang in the Athletic Department. He served the Home no less as an educator and confidant of the boys. Physically he was a mighty man with a heart to match. For me he was a pillar of support during the difficult days of change in our philosophy of youth care. I leaned on him heavily and often.

Now that Father Flanagan Boulevard and Stoffel Road have been identified, here is a street directory of what was once the "City of Little Men":

Alexian Drive — The Alexian Brothers operated our medical clinic from 1956 through 1976.

Bucher Drive — Commander Lloyd "Pete" Bucher was Captain of the USS Pueblo, which was illegally seized by the North Koreans, and one of our very illustrious citizens.

Crawford Street — Harold P. Crawford, Superintendent of Boys Town schools from 1944 to his retirement in 1973.

Dowd Drive — Miss Mary Dowd donated Dowd Memorial Chapel as a memorial to her family.

Doyle Drive — Kansas City millionaire who contributed much for Boys Town trade school in the 1930's. Donated funds to build grade school football stadium in 1940.

Franciscan Circle — The Franciscan Sisters served the Home from 1940 - 1976, working in the clinic, the kitchen, the laundry as well as clerical work.

Giannelli Road — Guiseppe Giannelli, a highly decorated alumnus, was killed in the service of his country. He won many honors for bravery and is buried in Arlington National Cemetery.

Grodinsky Circle — William "Bill" Grodinsky, an attorney for the Home, a member of the Board of Trustees, great friend and benefactor.

Gutowski Road — John Gutowski, former Omaha city attorney, was active in assisting alumni.

Heroes Way — Honoring those alumni, living and deceased, who distinguished themselves in the service of our country.

Kuhn Drive — A tribute to Father Leo Kuhn, an alumnus, and to the other youths who left Boys Town to serve as priests in the Lord's vineyard.

Lachimia Road — Joe Lachimia was one of the Home's first employees and devoted himself to the Home in the capacity of tailor and counselor.

Maher Circle — Thomas Maher, with serious behavior problems, was typical of boys who came to the Home. He ended up an honor student and returned to his home community where he made excellent progress. He met an untimely death in an auto accident.

McBreen Circle — Patrick McBreen, one of the Home's first counselors, was a "jack-of-all-trades" around the campus.

Mertz Circle — Walter Mertz, an alumnus, was stricken with muscular dystrophy in the prime of life but remained active in alumni affairs until his death.

Miller Drive — Theodore "Ted" Miller was the first director of fund raising. He was a great friend and inspiration to all the boys.

Mahoney Drive — Ike Mahoney was an assistant in the athletic department for years who had a great rapport with the boys, having come from modest means himself.

Monsky Drive — Henry Monsky, a prominent Omaha attorney, was a life-long friend of Father Flanagan and one of the Home's earliest benefactors.

Mother Teresa Lane — A tribute to Mother Teresa of Calcutta who visited and left her missionary spirit on our campus. Originally named Convent Road for the Sisters of St. Francis who worked on our campus, it was changed at the request of the girls of Boys Town who lived on the street.

Norton Drive — Patrick Norton, Father Flanagan's nephew, held many administrative positions and dedicated his entire life to the Home.

Oddo Drive — Tony Oddo, as a resident, always dreamed of owning a hamburger stand. He became a successful Omaha restaurateur and was an original member of the Boys Town Booster Club.

Overlook Park Road — A memorial to the Original Overlook Farm where present day Boys Town was started.

Plewa Plaza — Dr. Frank Plewa, who fled Europe with his parents to escape Hitler, was the first head of Social Services. His wife, a concert pianist, taught music to the boys.

Sudyka Circle — The Sudyka brothers were two of the first five boys to come under Father Flanagan's care in 1917. The street is named for the elder brother, Bill.

Thomas Road — John Thomas was a lifelong employee. He created much of the wood-carved memorabilia seen throughout the Home.

Walsh Drive — Father Edmund Walsh served as interim director after the death of Father Flanagan until the appointment of Father Nicholas Wegner. As the long time assistant to Father Flanagan he was highly regarded as friend and confidant of the boys.

CHAPTER Seventeen

FATHER FLANAGAN was years ahead of his time in the matter of human rights. His built-in ecumenical spirit pre-dated Vatican II by at least forty years. It was routine for him to invite outstanding individuals from all walks of life, entertainers to entrepreneurs, to visit the boys and acquaint them with their accomplishments. When it came to admitting and caring for boys, he was indeed color-blind.

To highlight this unique aspect of the Home and call it to the attention of the public, we thought a special award would be another way to distract people from the lingering damage done the Home by the Sun Newspaper, and to focus on our positive programs. Really, it was to be a community relations project. We would call it the Father Flanagan Award for Service to Youth.

We needed an attention-getter. How better could this be accomplished than by giving an award to a well known figure who had made a notable contribution to the youth of our country? My staff, with Bill Ramsey calling the shots, brainstormed the idea and drew up these criteria which I presented to the Board at the November 1975 meeting:

* The person must have made a significant contribution to the youth of our nation and continue to further influence young people by an exemplary public and private life.

* This contribution may have been made in any area of endeavor as long as it was and continues to be supportive in any way of youth.

* The honoree must be living, able to accept the award in person and visit with the boys on campus.
* The award is to be made on an occasional and not oftener than annual basis, this to avoid forcing a presentation and thus diluting its message.

Any member of the Board or of the Home's administrative staff could suggest candidates. These would be given to an ad hoc committee of the Board to screen and make recommendations.

Presentation of the award would be made at a luncheon or banquet to which the opinion makers of the community and the general public would be invited. A brief but well-planned program accompanied presentation of the award, a bronze statuette of the "He Ain't Heavy, Father" symbol of Boys Town.

Although the award was offered to persons who were extremely popular and busy, not one hesitated to come and accept it and graciously mingle with the boys. It was my privilege to contact the proposed recipients without relying on a booking agency.

The ad hoc board committee was extremely cautious in making its recommendations lest we single out for admiration and emulation someone who might later betray our ideals. Many people were considered including sporting greats, prominent leaders in youth care, and others but not all were recommended. Special care was taken to screen out individuals with perceived sexual improprieties, especially pedophiles, persons with questionable management abilities and drug connections, just to mention the most glaring rejects.

Following is a list of recipients of our Father Flanagan Award for Service to Youth:

1975: MRS. SPENCER (LOUISE) TRACY — The widow of the actor who starred in the movie, "Boys Town." Mrs. Tracy was a heroine in her own right, working on behalf of the hearing impaired. She was founder and president of the John Tracy Clinic, named for her son who was born deaf, in Los

Angeles. She attended the blessing of the Boys Town National Institute and had high praise for it, saying it promised to become one of the most complete diagnostic and treatment centers in the world.

1976: MOTHER TERESA OF CALCUTTA — This international symbol of goodness and compassion dedicated her life to working with "the poorest of the poor" in the slums of Calcutta. During her visit to our campus everyone noted how she vibrated with joy and love. Her eyes sparkled and her smile broke out from the inside, unlike the paste-on grins of many celebrities. We could readily see that God was using her to write a love letter to the world. Three years after receiving our award she was selected for the Nobel Peace Prize.

1977: BOB HOPE — A long-time acquaintance of Father Flanagan's, Bob Hope was cited for his annual Christmas entertainment tours of military bases around the world. Hope began touring military bases in 1941 and was still at it thirty-six years later when honored. His philosophy was always the same: "Young or old, you can't do better for your physical well-being than laugh. It makes valium look like a placebo."

1978: DR. MILDRED JEFFERSON, Boston,   president of the National Right to Life Committee — On accepting the award, she said, "It is not for myself, but for the thousands and thousands and thousands of those who are dedicated to Right to Life." She excoriated those who would take human life, either through abortion or euthanasia under the guise of a distorted philosophy of "improving the quality of life."

1979: DR. JONAS SALK — The citation read: "For the development of the Salk vaccine, which for a quarter of a century has protected youth from the crippling disease of polio." "Thank you all," said Dr. Salk in accepting his award. "All day I have been trying to figure out the magic of Boys Town. You can't take it into a laboratory or dissect it, or measure it, but it is no less real. It is something as intangible as relationships and family feelings."

1980: ROBERT and DOROTHY DE BOLT — Parents and humanitarians, nationally known through the book, "Nineteen Steps Up the Mountain," which tells the story of their nineteen children, thirteen of whom were adopted. The adopted children were special because they are physically or emotionally "challenged." The De Bolts founded Aid to Adoption of Special Kids (AASK) to encourage others to adopt "unadoptable" children. Given love, understanding and intelligent care, the most "challenged" child can and will be made whole, was their message.

1981: DANNY THOMAS — Founder of St. Jude's Children's Research Hospital in Memphis, Tennessee, and one of America's most popular entertainment personalities. On a winter night in 1940 Danny Thomas prayed to St. Jude Thaddeus, patron saint of the hopeless, to be rescued from his despair. His pledge was to some day erect a shrine or home for those who had none. At the presentation, Thomas said: "We are Lebanese, directly descended from the Phoenicians. We go so far back. First there was God, then us. It is a great honor for me to receive this award."

No award was given in 1982 or 1983, reflecting our determination to select a winner only when in our opinion one was deserving.

1984: JULIUS ERVING — The famous "Dr. J" of basketball was honored because of his outstanding positive example to the youth of America, especially his public role in encouraging youngsters to stay in school and stay off drugs. One of the most famous players in National Basketball Association history, his citation read: "He serves as one of the most significant, positive role models for the youth of this nation." In response he said: "God has said, 'As a man thinketh in his heart, so he is.' I am what I think. I am not what I eat. Clothes do not make the man, thinking makes the man, therefore I keep my thought processes active and open to the voice of God."

BOYS TOWN BOOSTER CLUB

For years there was talk among the alumni who lived in the
Omaha area about organizing some kind of "pep club" to encourage and support the athletic program at Boys Town. Dr. Frank
Carlotta, class of '40, a chef in his own right, featured his
spaghetti dish at a dinner held in Millard, Nebraska to which only
members of the football and basketball teams were invited. Assisting Carlotta prepare and serve the dinner were Tom White,
Tony Oddo, John Gutowski and Gus Shiro.

The enthusiasm shown by the boys at this gathering was all it
took to goad Dr. Carlotta into forming what he called "The Boys
Town Athletic Boosters." Articles of incorporation were filed on
April 28, 1966 with the following signers:

Dr. Lee C. Bevilacqua	Dr. Frank Carlotta
John A. Gutowski	W. W. "Wally" Keenan
Arthur Knapp	Eugene A. Leahy
John P. Mainelli	Tony Oddo
Donald W. Ryan	C. "Gus" Schiro
Harry Smith	

On 21 June 1966 the first election of officers was held with
the following results:

President:	Eugene A. Leahy
Vice President:	Dr. Frank Carlotta
Secretary:	John A. Gutowski
Treasurer:	Donald W. Ryan

Objectives of the corporation, as stated in the by-laws, were
to:

* Support the athletic activities of Boys Town High School and
  Grade School as well as other programs of Father Flanagan's
  Boys' Home;

* Honor the Boys Town athletic teams and also individual athletes whose performance and achievements were
  outstanding;
* Establish a fund by means of membership dues and contributions from business firms, professional and business men, and
  other individuals, to carry out objectives of the organization;
* Contribute toward scholarships for worthy athletes in
  graduating classes at Boys Town.

It was voted at the first meeting to change the name "Boys
Town Athletic Boosters" to simply "Boys Town Boosters."

Each year thereafter a banquet was held in the early spring at
which all boys involved in any athletic program at the Home, and
their coaches, were the honored guests. A guest speaker would
dwell on highlights in his own career, deliver an inspirational
message and then open the floor to questions. Hearing some of
the young exhibitionists was often worth an admission price.

Guest speakers, as you will see, were all of the big league
variety. Just to meet them, hear them, and obtain their autographs was always a real thrill for the boys:

1967: DAVID BLACKWELL, local sports announcer, was
speaker at the first official athletic banquet, held at Piccolos in
Millard, Nebraska. His incisive observations and caustic humor
won the hearts of all in attendance and set a precedent that bode
well for the future of the Boosters. After the banquet the boys in
attendance suggested that hamburgers, not steaks, be served in
the future.

1968: GEORGE CONNOR, twice All-American tackle at
Notre Dame University and named All-Pro in six of his eight years
as a player with the Chicago Bears, told his listeners to apply to
life the lessons learned in sports and urged "participation for
participation's sake. When you have a tough decision, just think
back to the sport you played and apply the lessons you learned
there," he said.

1969: ROCKY MARCIANO, as a youth, was an all around athlete and once received a tryout as a catcher with the Chicago Cubs. During World War II he served overseas in an amphibious unit. On September 23, 1952 he became the World's Heavyweight Boxing Champion by knocking out Jersey Joe Wolcott in the thirteenth round, a title he held until 1956 when he retired as the undefeated champion. Most notable among his victims in his march to the title was Joe Louis, whom he knocked out in eight rounds in Madison Square Garden on October 26, 1951. He defended his title successfully six times and upon retirement had amassed a record of forty-nine fights, forty-three of which were by knockouts. He was never defeated in professional competition.

1970: BILLY MARTIN was the prime attraction at the fourth Annual Booster Banquet on May 8, 1970 at Peony Park. Martin, star second baseman of the New York Yankees from 1954 to 1965, played in twenty-eight World Series games, compiling a .333 batting average. He signed autographs for all of the boys attending the Booster Club banquet and did so with the color and comment of a champion. He said that he felt right at home having been reared from his earliest years in an orphanage. "Boys," he said, "you can be as good an athlete as you want to be, if you are willing to work hard enough."

1971: EWING M. KAUFFMAN, owner and president of the Kansas City Royals baseball team, was a successful athletic business man. His address gave the boys insights, too often neglected in a young man's early education. He set the stage for public recognition that evening of two men who meant many things to the hundreds of athletes at Boys Town who had come under their guidance for the previous quarter of a century, M.H. (Skip) Palrang, and William (Willie) Ojile, his right-hand man.

1972: ROGER STAUBACH, quarterback for the Navy football team and later for the Dallas Cowboys. He won the Heisman trophy as a junior and set Naval Academy football records that will stand for a long time. Among other honors he was named AP and UPI back of the year and won the Maxwell trophy. He captained the All Star squad in Chicago in 1965. In 1971 as a Dallas Cowboy he moved to the top of the class of NFL quarterbacks, completing 59.7 percent of his passes for fifteen touchdowns. He suffered only four interceptions. He was named the Most Valuable Player in the Super Bowl that year and was voted the Cowboys' Most Valuable Player by his teammates. He won the BB Award as outstanding player in the NFL. His message to the boys centered around the great importance of religion in a person's life.

1973: DICK BUTKUS, was Most Valuable Player in leading the University of Illinois in a Rose Bowl victory over Washington University in 1963. As a first round choice of the Chicago Bears, he was the only middle linebacker to step into professional football with a starting assignment. He was named the defensive Rookie of the Year and All Pro in 1965. His reputation as one of the roughest defensive players in football belied his friendly, outgoing, likable personality off the gridiron. His message to the boys reflected in every way his personality off the field.

1974: JESSE OWENS, a quadruple Gold Medal Winner in the 1936 Olympic games in Berlin, where he showed great character by ignoring the fact that he was snubbed by Adolph Hitler. He was a legend in his own time as a strong humanitarian and a role model for United States athletics. He frowned on professional sports for giving young people a mistaken idea of the value of sports. "What's important," he said, "is giving a child a code of ethics and teaching him respect. The goal of victory is essential but victory itself is insignificant."

1975: KEN GEDDES, a Boys Town alumnus from Jacksonville, Florida, was one of those boys who arrived on a bus with a note pinned to his chest that read: "Deliver to Father Flanagan's Boys' Home, Nebraska." He starred as a linebacker at the University of Nebraska and played pro football for the Los Angeles

Rams and Seattle Seahawks. "My experience at Boys Town taught me that I owed something to society to do all I could to help. I am trying to take a little bit of Boys Town around the country to the kids," he said.

1976: DAN GABLE, considered the greatest amateur wrestler in the world, starred for the University of Iowa, won the Gold Medal at 149.5 pounds in the 1972 Olympics and won titles in the Pan-American Games-and World Championships. His message to the boys: "A healthy mind goes with a healthy body."

1977: ERNIE BANKS, longtime outstanding shortstop with the Chicago Cubs. He was Most Valuable Player in the National League two consecutive years, 1958 and 1959, although his team never played in a World Series, and he was elected to the Baseball Hall of Fame in 1977. Beyond his baseball skills, he is remembered for change in the battlefield of social hatred in Chicago, "where the combatants learn from him there is a better way than the hater's way." He convinced, not by his vocabulary, but by his decent lifestyle that real gentlemen come also in colors other than white. What better message for youthful athletes?

1978: OSCAR ROBINSON, All-American basketball player at Cincinnati University and for twelve years an All-Pro in the NBA with the Cincinnati Kings and Milwaukee Bucks. Wilt Chamberlain said of him: "If I had my pick of all the players in the league, I'd take the Big O first." No wonder the boys listened to him.

1979: DOUG BUFFONE, played thirteen years as linebacker and defensive captain of the Chicago Bears, starting his pro career under the legendary Coach, George Halas. He held the Bears' record for consecutive games — 142. He was honorary chairman of the 1978 Easter Seal Drive in Chicago. His memories of the game were not all about winning and losing. Dedicated to participating in civic and community affairs, his message was summed up as, "there is real life after football."

1980: VINCE FERRAGAMO, former Nebraska Cornhusker quarterback and hero of the Los Angeles Rams' first ever Super Bowl victory, was co-captain of the Nebraska team that beat Texas Tech in the Astro-Bluebonnet Bowl. He established himself as one of Nebraska's premier quarterbacks when he set the Husker record for most touchdown passes in a season — twenty-two.

1981: JERRY FAUST, spoke at the Boosters banquet only a few days after being named head football coach at Notre Dame. For twenty-one years before he succeeded Dan Devine as coach of the Fighting Irish, Faust built an astonishing reputation as coach at Cincinnati's Moeller High School. His record was 172 wins, 17 losses and 2 ties. His football philosophy was an emphasis on basics: "Blocking, tackling and praying." His message to his players was: "The power of prayer is unbelievable," and on his locker room walls is a sign reading: "God plus effort plus dedication brings victory." He spoke words that boys could understand.

1982: ROSS BROWNER, defensive end for the Cincinnati Bengals, broke every school defensive record at Notre Dame. His senior year he won both the Outland and Lombardi trophies, recognizing him as the nation's Number 1 defensive player, and he was named the Maxwell Football Club's college player of the year. He was a first round draft pick in 1978 and was the defensive star in the 1987 Super Bowl game against the San Francisco Forty-Niners. His message: "I am a strong believer in self-motivation. My major goal in life is to make some worthwhile contribution to society."

1983: TED WILLIAMS, one of baseball's all-time greatest hitters, was the last player to hit over .400. His career spanned twenty-five years, ending in 1960 when he hit .316 at the age of forty-two. He served nearly five prime years in the military during World War II and the Korean War as a fighter pilot. He was voted the American League's Most Valuable Player in 1946 and

1949, and was named to the "Greatest Living Team Ever," and to the Hall of Fame. He was a major league manager, but later retired to Florida where he hunts and fishes. His message: "Be your own man, and never give anything but your best in whatever you do."

1984: FRANCO HARRIS, tabbed one of the greatest players in pro-football history, was a running back with the Pittsburgh Steelers and played in four Super Bowls. He set twenty-nine National Football League rushing records. In the book, "Football's Greats," he is described as "probably the hardest fullback of his era to bring down, and should be remembered as one of the very best." He is known as one of professional sports' most active persons in working charities. He has helped children's hospitals and the Boys Scouts, served as chairman of the Pennsylvania Governor's Council on Fitness in Sports and received the Humanitarian Award from New York's Association of the Blind. His message: "Never be too busy to do a good turn for someone in need."

1985: GORDIE HOWE, who started his professional hockey career with the Omaha Knights of the U.S. Hockey League in 1945, went on to achieve greatness with the Detroit Red Wings of the National Hockey League. He played an incredible twenty-five years with the Red Wings, retired, then returned to the game with the Houston Astros and Hartford Whales of the World Hockey association as player and manager. He played with his sons while with the Whalers and was nearly fifty years old when he finally retired for good. He was twelve times named All-NHL, was the league's Most Valuable Player six times, and played in nineteen Stanley cup playoffs. His message: "Set your goal in life high, and never take your eye off of it."

CHAPTER **Eighteen**

RATHER late one night near the end of August 1976 my residential phone rang. Dick Herman was on the line. Herman, an Omaha businessman, had long been a key person in the Republican Party and he was a close friend of President Gerald R. Ford. After a few pleasantries — Dick had been a personal friend of mine for years — his voice took on a serious tone.

"The Ford Administration is looking for a delegate to the United Nations General Assembly next month," he said. "The 'Year of the Child' is coming up and we need the right person to represent the United States in this important session. Would you consider such an appointment?" I was flabbergasted, to say the least.

"Hello," I said. "Are you sure you have the right number?"

"Yes," he continued. "The President wants someone to tell the world what the U.S. is doing for its youth."

My immediate reaction, after catching my breath, was, "No, a thousand times no!"

We bantered for some time and the best reason I could muster for not considering his offer was that I was too busy at the Home to be going to New York each week for three months.

Dick wasn't one to give up. "Let me talk to the President about that and I'll get back to you," he said. "It may not be as time consuming as you think." And thus we ended the conversation.

By that time I was convinced that I could not do justice to my responsibilities at Boys Town, were I to accept an assignment that meant being absent five days a week for three months. And with that I perished the idea from my mind.

The next evening I received a call from one Julius Walker, an officer in the U.S. State Department. He explained that he and Herman had visited about this appointment with the President and that Father Flanagan's Boys' Home enjoyed an international reputation. They stated that the executive director of that Home was the logical choice of the President to represent our country in the preliminary plans for the "Year of the Child." They all wanted a general practitioner in youth care rather than some college professor type who would theorize about it.

I listened intensely, was a bit flattered, told Mr. Walker so and for a moment my resolve began to melt, but then I regained my senses and reiterated my commitment to Boys Town.

"Five days a week for three months is too long to be gone," I repeated, thanked him for the courtesies and terminated the conversation as gracefully as I could.

This, I was sure, would be the end, but I had no idea what it meant to be "leaned on." There seemed to be some part of the word "No" that was unintelligible.

On the third evening my phone rang again. This time it was from the White House and the caller was W. Tapley Bennett, a career diplomat from Georgia and a personal friend of former President Jimmy Carter. He identified himself as the newly appointed Assistant Ambassador to the United Nations; the Ambassador, he informed me, is William W. Scranton, former Governor of Pennsylvania.

Bennett, with his soothing Georgia manners, turned up the heat a bit with the suggestion that my presence in New York at the United Nations could be limited to three days a week. I enjoyed a very interesting exchange of pleasantries with him. My counter then was that if one day a week would be satisfactory I would accept. With a great amount of reluctance, saying that he couldn't see how one week's work could be covered in one day, he concluded by saying, "I'll mention that to President Ford."

That was on a Friday night. The following night at about eleven o'clock my phone rang again. This time it was one Doug Bennett, the President's Personnel Officer, as I recall.

"I'm just coming from a meeting with President Ford and Ambassador Scranton. They said that if you could be present at the United Nations one day a week you would probably have a better attendance record than the two Senators."

He was referring to the practice of appointing to the U.S. Delegation, in alternate years, two senators and then two representatives, one from each party. This particular year Senator George McGovern (D) of South Dakota and Senator Howard Baker (R) of Tennessee were members of the U.S. Delegation to the United Nations.

Now the reality of it all struck me. President Ford had agreed on my terms. The rest was up to me. Before I had really come to grips with the new chapter in my career my phone rang again. This time it was Sunday afternoon and the caller's name has escaped me. It was a summons to the State Department in Washington for a day-long briefing on Tuesday, which happened to be the day after Labor Day. The FBI immediately began an extensive background check for a security clearance, a requirement for Senate confirmation of my appointment.

The briefing, conducted by the State Department and aided by a number of ambassadors from trouble spots around the world, was attended by Ambassador Scranton, Assistant Ambassador Bennett, myself and a number of consultants to the U.S. Delegation. For me, it was a very interesting, at the same time sobering experience. My work was cut out for me, and I was no longer in a state of shock. As I returned to Boys Town it dawned on me that I was no longer sitting in the bleachers watching a gigantic international peacekeeping team; I was now approaching the playing field.

The United Nations, I knew, had not always been a favorite among many Americans. There are politicians — and private citizens, too — who have wished the UN would abandon its highfalutin ways and posh headquarters in New York City's East Side and go somewhere else — anywhere else.

If my memory serves me I recall Winston Churchill once saying, "The UN is not expected to bring peace to the world. Nobody can do that. It is only to keep the world from blowing itself to pieces." If he didn't say it somebody should, because that rather succinctly says what the UN is all about. Senator Daniel Patrick Moynihan of New York, a former ambassador to the UN, is reported to have described the General Assembly as a "Cave of Winds" where nations could shoot off their mouths rather than their guns. Certainly, it is not a perfect meeting place for the world's nations but it may have to do until something better comes along. It is a great stage for world dialogue.

Like almost every other facet of life, the public is fed a much larger helping of news about its bad side than of its good. The United Nations has done immeasurable good since it came into being on October 24, 1945, barely six weeks after the end of World War II. The first session of the General Assembly was held in London on January 10, 1946. It was later that the organization moved into permanent quarters in New York City.

The UN's purpose was lofty indeed. It was based on the principles of the Atlantic Charter, a document signed by the twenty-six Allied Nations fighting Germany, Italy, and Japan during World War II. This document envisaged a peace that would promise the following to all peoples: Security from aggression, freedom to choose their own government, access on equal terms to the trade and raw materials of the world, improved labor standards, freedom from fear and want, and freedom of the seas. The nations of the world, the charter asserted, "must come to the abandonment of the use of force."

Certainly the nations of the world frequently fell short on that score. But the UN has also recorded its share of successes. The Security Council and General Assembly are the most visible parts of the organization and the squabbling in those two bodies was often more than the public could stand. However, numbered among its thirty-six committees, commissions, and agencies are several which have quietly served humanity well.

High on the list of these are the World Health Organization, which has brought better health measures to scores of backward nations; the Food and Agriculture Organization, aiding in better crop production; the International Monetary Fund and World Bank, which has financed Third World efforts toward improving the environment, health, food, industrial development and human rights; the United Nations Children's Fund (UNICEF); Office of the High Commission for Refugees; Commission on the Status of Women; Commission on Human Rights; and even the weather.

UNICEF, especially, has been a tremendous success in its efforts to combat disease, malnutrition and illiteracy among the world's children.

More than a dozen times the United Nations has successfully carried out peace-keeping missions, notably in the Middle East in 1949, 1956, 1973 and 1979. The Korean conflict was a UN operation.

But probably the United Nations Security Council's finest cooperative actions have come recently, during the Persian Gulf crisis following the invasion of Kuwait by Iraq. With the Soviet Union and United States working in harmony for the first time, the UN imposed economic sanctions on Iraq before launching a unified military action against Saddam Hussein's aggression. The support of nearly all UN members left Iraq standing alone before world opinion.

The United Nations began with fifty member nations, added nine in the next ten years, and stood at 134 when I was asked by President Ford to serve. The figure reached 159 in 1990.

From the general instructions given during our briefing it seemed to me that most of my time would be spent with the "good guys" in the Social and Economic Committee, otherwise known as Committee 3. Despite widespread criticism of some activities of the UN in the early 1970's, I felt comfortable accepting a challenge to help children of the world through this international body.

Senate approval of my appointment came swiftly, and all of a sudden I wore the hat of a "U.S. Delegate At Large" of the United States to the United Nations. This was confirmed at the arrival of a magnificent, framed document which read:

GERALD R. FORD
PRESIDENT OF THE UNITED STATES OF AMERICA
TO ALL WHO SHALL SEE THESE, PRESENTS
GREETINGS;

Know Ye, that reposing special trust and confidence in the Integrity and Ability of Reverend Robert P. Hupp of Nebraska, I have nominated, and, by and with the advice and consent of the Senate, do designate him a Representative of the United States of America to the Thirty-first Session of the General Assembly of the United Nations, and do authorize and empower him to execute and fulfill the duties of his commission according to law, with all the powers, privileges, and emoluments thereunto of right appertaining, during the pleasure of the President of the United States.

In testimony whereof, I have caused these Letters to be made Patent, and the Seal of the United States of America the two hundred and first.

By the President:
/s/Gerald R. Ford

/s/Henry H. Kissinger
Secretary of State

The thirty-first session of the UN General Assembly was called to order at 10:30 a.m., September 21, 1976. Ambassador

Scranton held a meeting of the delegation at 9:00 a.m. in the U.S. Mission building, across the street from the UN Building.

It was my introduction to Ambassador Scranton's staff and to his method of making assignments. Generally speaking, such a meeting was held each morning before the United Nations went to work at 10:00 a.m.

As it happened, Scranton spent much time at the State Department in Washington, Bennett represented him in the Security Council, and I sat in the General Assembly meetings. Several consultants were usually seated behind me including Bob Rosenstock, one of our attorneys. There were three seats in the United States section. I was instructed to move from my position to the Number One chair when Scranton and Bennett were absent. This provided for some rather exhilarating moments as time passed because I was at liberty then to invite one of the consultants to occupy the seat to my right.

Who better could grace the position than our "Good Will" ambassador, Pearl Bailey, who enjoyed a better attendance record than many. She shared my secretary, Rita Brown, in the U.S. Mission, and the result was that we soon became very close friends. You never had to wonder about where you stood with her — or where anybody else in her legion of friends and acquaintances stood. One of the great nightclub performers of her time, she spent much of her life on the road. Her recent extended trip through the continent of Africa made her very conversant with representatives from that part of the world. When she died suddenly in the fall of 1990 at the age of seventy-two, the press said of her: "She was a tireless entertainer who transcended racial barriers while singing and dancing to stardom in a career spanning seven decades." She was all that and more.

She was patriotic to the core and a hard-working diplomat, whether working the floor of the United Nations or mingling at receptions with representatives from the Third World countries.

One morning, after one of the many receptions to which she accompanied me, she came in and said, "I'm getting tired of all those meatballs they keep serving at these receptions." That's when I suggested that her popularity with the host and the usual entourage prevented her from getting beyond the first line of hors d'oeuvres to the soul food.

On my bookcase stands a photo of Pearl Bailey with the inscription: "To my dear friend, whom I love, Rev. Hupp. Pearl Bailey, UN 1976."

President Ford picked a winner when he named her a representative to the UN and her death meant the loss of a great American.

In 1976 there were six main organs of the United Nations:

> 1. *Security Council*
> 2. *General Assembly*
> 3. *Economic and Social Council*
> 4. *Trusteeship Council*
> 5. *International Court of Justice*
> 6. *Secretariat*

My general assignment was with the Economic and Social Council, with additional duties in the General Assembly. Working under the General Assembly, Committee 3, as it was known, coordinated the economic and social work of the UN, along with related specialized agencies known as the United Nations "Family of Organizations." My efforts were to be expended in the Human Rights Division, specifically with the rights of children. Whatever free time I had was spent in the General Assembly, which technically could only make recommendations to the Security Council without power to enforce them. In the absence of Scranton and Bennett, my duties in the General Assembly were to monitor speeches, deliver speeches, cast votes and deliver explanations when feasible in sponsoring and cosponsoring resolutions. Everything I said and did in any capacity required advance clearance by the State Department. That is to say, I was an instructed delegate. That was a good idea; it kept all of us on the same wave length in our relations with other countries.

Although I was essentially third string behind Scranton and

Bennett, it wasn't at all unusual for the presence of these two to be demanded elsewhere, which put me on the field, in a manner of speaking. The first time this occurred was after I had been there only three weeks. Andrei Gromyko, the Soviet foreign minister, was to speak to the General Assembly at 11:00 a.m.

Scranton reminded me that he might be late and that I was to take his chair until he arrived. Bennett was at the Security Council. At the appointed hour, with Scranton nowhere in sight, I took his seat. I invited Pearl Bailey to join me. We were ten rows from Gromyko. You baseball fans — if you can imagine him being at home plate, we were about where the second baseman plays. It was quite evident that he was watching us very closely as he delivered his talk. More than once he gave us the evil eye, as they say, seemingly disturbed that Scranton wasn't there to hear him insult the United States of America.

The next day's New York Times reported Gromyko to be in ill humor because the distinguished U.S. Ambassador was not present for his speech. Normally, when the ambassador from one of the Big Five of the Security Council — United States, Soviet Union, Great Britain, France and China — was on the podium ambassadors from the other four would honor him with their presence. This time it was a "black person and a man of the cloth for the United States of America." After reading the paper the next morning I went to Scranton and said, "I'm here only a couple of weeks and already I'm in trouble with the Russians. I may need some allies if I stay much longer." He laughed.

Another time when I sat in for Scranton I was instructed to cast a vote for the U.S. against a resolution that had to do with mineral rights at sea. President Amerasinghe called for a vote. My instructions were to vote "No," so I pushed the red button. Votes were appearing rapidly on the large lighted board above the President of the Assembly. My vote was the only red one as all the others were coming up green.

Pearlie Mae said to me, "Are you sure you pushed the right button?" "Yes," I said, as I pointed to my instructions. By this time all votes had been cast and Amerasinghe was calling for a final check before locking in the votes for a count. I turned and asked Bob Rosenstock, our attorney, "Am I reading these instructions correctly?"

"Yes," he said. "This is one time you are right and the rest of the world is wrong."

The votes were no sooner locked in when two black delegates from Uganda, I believe, rushed over and challenged me: "How come you voted 'No' to that resolution?"

Before I could say a word Pearlie Mae said to them, "Why don't you fellas go back and sit down! You're winnin' everything anyway."

They turned around and left without a word. With Pearlie Mae and one good attorney at my side, how could I go wrong?

Another day I was again in line to handle the chores of our Ambassador, who had indicated earlier that he might be late because of an appearance he was to make at the Security Council. Well into the morning, without warning, I heard the president of the Assembly say in very official tones, "We shall now hear the distinguished delegate from the United States offer his proposal."

Scranton had not yet returned, so with script in hand I proceeded to the podium. Just before arriving at the end of the outside aisle where I would turn to the podium, Scranton met me and without breaking stride, took the document from me and delivered it. After that meeting Amerasinghe, who had not seen the handoff take place, asked in a lighthearted way, "What's going on there with you people in the United States?"

"Well," I said. "Just a little football play we threw in there."

Once in a while, on special occasions, our delegation would invite a few guests for lunch at the U.S. Mission. Henry Kissinger, the Secretary of State, was there occasionally. He has quite an accent as you know but I noticed little if any accent in his parents' speech as I sat with them at one of these luncheons. It made me wonder how Henry came about his.

On one occasion at one of these luncheons I sat with a Middle East delegation. I tried my best to strike up a conversation with one or the other at my side. Finally the delegate at my right turned directly to me and, loud enough to command the attention of all at table, demanded: "Will you please tell me what the hell you are doing here?"

"You bet I will," said I. "You asked the right fella. When you want water you go to the well."

I pointed to the Boys Town badge I wore on my coat, said a few calm words about Father Flanagan's Boys' Home, and then our connection with the upcoming "Year of the Child." A few milder questions then from around the table seemed more like peace gestures to dissipate the steam of the explosion than quests for information. However, an environment more conducive to proper digestion returned to our table and another inroad had been made to the Middle East.

Incidentally, I always wore my clerical collar with a Boys Town badge on my suit coat. No one ever fussed about the fact that I was a clergyman. There could have been other clergy there, but none could be identified as such by their wearing apparel.

At a reception given by one of the African countries, after the customary political and social gestures to the host and his retinue, I discovered that I was the only white person at the party. Looking around for someone with whom I could strike up a conversation, I noticed two young delegates, seemingly enjoying life to the fullest, and they were speaking English. When the opportunity seemed right I introduced myself and asked, "Have you ever heard of Boys Town?"

"No," they said.

"Maybe you have heard of Father Flanagan's Boys' Home?"

"No," they said again.

"Well, how about Spencer Tracy and Mickey Rooney in the movies?"

"Oh, yes," they said, and we were off then to a very pleasant conversation.

A number of our delegates lived in the same hotel, the Beekman Towers, a few blocks east of the U.S. Mission Building and the UN Building. It was not unusual for a few of us to walk together to the Mission for our 9:00 a.m. meetings. One morning Pearlie Mae was a half block ahead of me and I was hurrying to catch up. It was raining and, just before I was close enough to say something to her as she was crossing the street, she slipped in one of New York City's notorious potholes. I rushed up to help her, as did a near-by policeman. As she gained her composure, she had a few uncomplimentary things to say about the New York Democrats and their potholes.

The cop asked, "Do you need some more help in getting her to the office?"

I said, "She ain't heavy, she's my sister."

How it got there I don't know, but that incident ended up in the New York Times the next day.

Another rainy day, as we walked along the East River, Pearlie Mae complained about all the garbage, logs and other junk floating on the river's surface. She turned to me and said: "I bet even you could walk on that water."

Finally on December 6, 1976 the culminating reason for my being a member of the U.S. delegation had come. The moment had arrived for my speech on youth and it was listed under this title in the day's agenda:

"Statement by Reverend Robert P. Hupp,
United States Representative in Committee Three,
on Policies and Programs Relating to Youth.

This was my speech:

"By the year 2000 — the turn of the century — every country in the world will be literally taken over. Taken over by the youth of today. Will the takeover be orderly or chaotic? Will it improve upon the human rights and values which we cherish and try to improve today? Or will it enforce an every-man-for-himself philosophy?

"The seeds for both have already been sown. It is given to us to encourage the growth of the good seed and to minimize or even stamp out the bad. I say 'it is given to us' to recognize the job that needs doing and to do something about it. It is a gift that may not be given again.

"Youth problems are universal — have always been — varying only in nature and degree. Adult responses to the problems have unfortunately all too often fallen to one or another category of the Cassandra/Pollyanna/Griselda axis. Cassandras cry: 'The problem can't be solved.' Pollyanna asks: 'What problem?' and Griselda says: 'Let's all be patient, it will solve itself.'

"None has worked. So many of youth's problems are the inevitable tragic result of 'good men doing nothing.' That good men and women doing something can have a positive effect on our youth is happily all about us. In our own country — in the private sector alone — we observe the good works and dedication to youth of such great institutions as the Boys Clubs, the Boy Scouts, Girl Scouts, Big Brother, Big Sister and so many more.

"At a recent luncheon given by Dr. Kissinger I was asked by one of the guests, 'What are you doing here?' Whereupon I responded, 'I am one of the United States delegates to the United Nations General Assembly.' His next question was 'Why you?' My response was something like this: 'I am the Executive Director of Boys Town, a home in Nebraska for disadvantaged boys, with almost 14,000 alumni. We have a symbol that is very well known throughout the United States — even some foreign countries — that dramatizes as well as anything could, one human being caring for another. It illustrates a young boy carrying a smaller youngster on his back and saying, 'He Ain't Heavy, Father. . . He's My Brother.' This image is understood in every language, and since much emphasis in this session of the United Nations is on human rights and all of its ramifications, our government thought it was too good to keep to ourselves. We care about people and this image communicates that idea.

"The kinds of problems youth have all over the world are fairly universal. Let me tell you briefly how we at Boys Town became involved, and what one approach, our approach, to them is.

"Exactly fifty-nine years ago this December 10, a good man, Father Edward J. Flanagan, befriended five homeless boys in Omaha, Nebraska, by finding them a home, providing them with hope, and the realization that someone really cared about them. Father Flanagan's dream about helping youth became a reality as countless thousands of other concerned people wished to share the dream and provide its fulfillment.

"Boys Town is a fulfillment, the dream come true. There are Boys Towns in other countries, many styled after the original Boys Town, which, as Mickey Rooney says, is the heartbeat of them all. We have a constant dialogue with many of them, exchanging ideas and impressions, the concept of brotherhood among youth and not necessarily in the form of Boys Town. How encouraging, how beautiful, the words: 'He Ain't Heavy, Father, He's My Brother.'

"At Boys Town we are enjoying a new era, in that we now simulate as never before living conditions of a boy in a typical family in society so that he can develop and mature in a normal manner and atmosphere. We care about his development — physical, mental, cultural, spiritual — so that he can and will become a responsible citizen.

"At the Home, freedom of religion, not from religion, goes back to the founder himself, who said: 'Every boy must learn to pray. How he prays is up to him.'

"Our new commitment is even more important for the future of mankind than is our new era at the Home. No longer are we satisfied only to care for disadvantaged and troubled boys and girls. We have launched into two large projects of trouble prevention.

"The Boys Town Institute which will open next year will address itself entirely to diagnosing any and all physical factors that relate to learning and communication disorders in pre-school boys and girls. A very significant number of boys and girls today are problems in society because they have hearing, sight and speech difficulties that were not cared for in early life. The earlier the detection, the greater the possibility of a cure, or at least an adjustment for a proper direction in life. This aspect of intervention is all the more important in today's world because one of the great problems between youth and adults is one of

communication. Listening is a very important part of
communication.

"The other important commitment, the details of which have
not yet been completed, is the Boys Town Center for the Study
of Youth Development. This Center will attempt to search out
the root causes of such problems as drugs, child abuse, parental
rejection, youth rebellion and the rest in an effort to present to
the whole world some methods of prevention.

"This world body, the United Nations, can do so much to
assist our young people in their anguished years of growing up —
anguish which would seem to be an extension of birth itself.
Growing has always had its difficulties, its pains. There has
always been a generation gap, although we did not know what to
call it. Today's youth problems are immeasurably complicated by
something that has been called 'future shock.' Author Alvin
Toffler describes future shock as 'that stress and disorientation
that all individuals suffer when they are subjected to too much
change in too short a time. It can make us ill, physically and
mentally; it robs us of the power to decide, deprives our children
of the roots we took for granted.'

"It is so heartening to me, a newcomer to the General
Assembly, to see the high priority given to human rights, and
especially to the rights and needs of our world's children.

"I return to my original question: Will the takeover of every
country in the world by its youth be orderly or chaotic? Will it
improve upon human rights and values, or will it enforce an
'every-man-for-himself' philosophy? I have spoken briefly now of
my experience in trying to communicate with American youth,
and my belief that communication with today's youth is necessary to bring about their important role in the future. It goes
without saying that enlarging channels of communication with
world-wide youth is also my concern, and that of my government. We support whole-heartedly the effort to make the United
Nations volunteer program an operational unit for communication with youth. We believe that it is time to go beyond resolutions — there are already more than thirty-five of them dealing
with youth; and it is time to go beyond studies — there have
been more than a dozen major studies on youth organized by the

Secretariat in the past seven years. It is now time for
implementation.

"My delegation believes that implementation can best begin
through the program of the United Nations volunteers and
through the efforts at the regional level for youth and youth
organizations to participate in their national and regional planning
for development."

So ended my speech. This was the first time the United
Nations had ever heard of something like our Family Concept,
and it was well received. I remember the ambassador from
Finland, a lady, who chaired the session, was especially com-
plimentary. It seemed to be an entirely different approach from
anything we had been hearing. The whole concern seemed to
have been with "what's going on today," while I was looking to the
future. It made me feel like one of the crowd.

Mine was the final speech of the 1976 General Assembly
session. Although we were subject to recall during the remainder
of the UN session, should the international situation warrant it, I
for one wrote finis to one of the most exhilarating and educational
experiences of my entire life. Meantime, "back home at the
ranch," as we used to say a full-time job was calling — and I went.

You read all about it in the previous chapters.

CHAPTER *Nineteen*

"I will not forget you.... I have held you in the palm of my hands."
Isaiah 49:15. (Selected by Father Hupp for his Golden Jubilee of
his ordination as a Catholic priest.)

THIS CHAPTER was not written by Father
Hupp. I have written it. I have collaborated with him in his
memoirs of his days as Boys Town's savior (my word, not his),
and when it came time to list the honors he received for his
leadership at the Home, I insisted the chapter be written by me.

If I know him — and I think I do — his list would be so brief it
would not accurately reflect the high esteem in which he is held by
others. Those "others" include the general public, which does not
know precisely how he turned Boys Town around but in a general
way understands he did something extraordinary, and child care
professionals, who unabashedly copy the system he developed
during his tenure.

I say "developed during his tenure," not developed by him.
The latter way is not Father Hupp's style. The system was
developed as a team effort — by experts whom Father Hupp
hired and consulted, and then gave a long leash. Not complete
freedom, but a long leash. He was never afraid to credit his people
for their accomplishments.

The honors that came his way are a reflection of the success
of his methods.

Father Flanagan's Boys' Home is a national treasure. In 1973, it was in serious danger of having its illustrious reputation severely damaged through a well intentioned but out-of-date management style. I think there would always be a Boys Town; it would have survived the Sun Newspaper's report, but not as the flagship of youth care it became.

That is the legacy of Father Hupp.

After eighteen chapters of how he operated, told in his own words, the reader by this time knows a great deal about him. But the following anecdote tells how others see him. These are the words of Father James E. Gilg, spoken at Christ the King Church on May 20, 1990, on the occasion of the fiftieth anniversary of the priestly ordination of Father Hupp.

"I recall a very grateful moment in my life when the three qualities (of Father Hupp), namely, mind, heart and will, combined to literally save the day for myself and all those connected with Dominican High School (see Chapter 11). It was 1:00 p.m., November 20, 1979, and I was sitting face to face with Father Hupp in his office at Boys Town.

" Archbishop Sheehan had called me the day before suggesting that I go visit with Father Hupp about our plight at Dominican High School as we faced the necessity of relocation and a very uncertain future.

"I was expecting some very guarded words from Father Hupp, some vague references to 'perhaps' or 'maybe' or 'we'll see.' But instead I was almost knocked off my chair by the clear, focused, determined message that I heard. Boys Town would adopt Dominican High; there would be a new school; we would have a future; and we would be able to do the kind of job we could have only dreamed of before. And all this would happen because of one reason:

'It is the Lord's work,' said Father Hupp.

"Nothing else mattered; nothing would stand in the way. Of course, being a man of extraordinary political astuteness, Father Hupp reminded me that it would take a long time to actually accomplish this vision, but it would be done. Just leave it to him.

"And we all know that it was done, in spite of many obstacles, many doubts, many meetings, many arguments, many delicate negotiations, and even some occasional misunderstandings."

As for the misunderstandings, Father Gilg went on to address two other Father Hupp qualities — his humor and his common sense:

"How frequently his use of homespun wisdom at an official strategy session or event dissolved the tension in a room, or brought discussion back to the task at hand, or helped everyone come to a manageable consensus."

In my case, I first met Father Hupp during his days as athletic director of the Catholic Youth Organization (CYO). No, I wasn't one of his basketball players, like Dr. Claude Organ. I was in charge of the sports department of the Omaha World-Herald on Sunday nights, and on busy summer nights we never worried about getting proper coverage on CYO baseball games. We knew we could count on Father Hupp to gather up pages of statistics, box scores and game details, and bring them to our office.

I have lived in Christ the King parish for many years, although I am not a Catholic. But I have been inside many times, attending funerals, weddings and consecrations. It is a magnificent structure, school and grounds, an appropriate memorial to the priest who founded the parish when it was nothing but a vacant lot.

So much for saying some things about Father Hupp he would never say about himself. In the previous chapter he told of his experiences at the United Nations. But that appointment was just one of the many honors and awards that came his way. Here are some of the others:

1973:   Honorary Alumnus, Creighton University. Lifetime member, Knights of Columbus (presently State Chaplain). Fraternal Order of Eagles, Outstanding Service Award and Lifetime Membership.

1975: Jewish Community Center Award of Appreciation

1976: Clergy Knight of Holy Sepulchre of Jerusalem. University of Note Dame Award Man of the Year, Omaha Council Bluffs Chapter. Board of Directors, United Way of the Midlands.

1977: Honorary Doctor of Letters Degree, University of Nebraska at Omaha.

1978: Board of Trustees, City of Hope. Defense Advisory Committee for Women in the Service.

1979: Distinguished Service Award, UN Association of the USA Executive Board, Mid-America Council, Boy Scouts of America. National Idealism Award, City of Hope.

1980: Honorary Doctor of Laws, Catholic University. National Advisory Committee on Neurological Disorders and Strokes Appreciation Award. Franklin Credit Union for "devoted and invaluable service to low income minority community in Omaha." Honorary Doctor of Humane Letters Degree, St. Mary's College, Emmitsburg, Maryland. Brotherhood Award, National Conference of Chrisians and Jews.

1981: Distinguished Nebraska Award from Nebraska Society of Washington, D.C. Youth Consultant for the Government of Cayman Islands. Board Member, Special Olympics.

1982: Civilian Aide to Secretary of the Army and Chief of Staff for the State of Nebraska.

1983: George Washington Club Award to Outstanding Individual "who has contributed to his community and gained national prominence." Honorary Lincoln City-Rancher Award by Lincoln County, North Platte Nebraska Historical Society.

1984: Award from Child Psychologists of Nebraska "for consistent commitment to the children of the State of Nebraska." Board of Directors, International Hearing Foundation.

1985: Thomas Shields Award for Promoting Catholic Education. Golden Gloves Community Service Award for personal and inspirational leadership in sports. Certification of Recognition from US Families of America. Named Monsignor in recognition of "his exemplary life's work as a priest."

1986: Distinguished Service Award from the Kansas Association of Child Care Workers "in recognition of contributions to the field of residential care services to children, and commitment to professionalizing child care workers." Membership Newcomen Society.

1987: Sportsman of the Year, Douglas County Ducks Unlimited (presently State Chaplain).

Some remarks from the various awards and honors:

United Way of the Midlands: "Father Hupp brought Boys Town into this community wide charitable organization, making it possible for Boys Town staff members to contribute in concert to the United Way through payroll deductions if they so desired."

City of Hope National Idealism Award: "The City of Hope has pioneered in psychosomatic approaches, personalization of patient care and family centered medicine." Its facilities include forty-three buildings on ninety-three acres of land in Duarte, California, making high quality, free care available to patients from throughout the nation suffering from cancer and leukemia, heart, blood and respiratory afflictions, diabetes and other disorders of heredity and metabolism.

University of Notre Dame Man of the Year: The award is given annually to "an individual who has made a substantial contribution to the local community, particularly in the field of Catholic education."

In accepting the award, Father Hupp said: "In today's complex and confusing society, Boys Town, and other places like it, are more needed than ever. We have made a new commitment to expand our help to troubled youth. We are in the throes of a new era of service to youth, a service that will prepare youth, better than ever, for a future of hope. I have the same faith as my friend and fellow priest, Father Flanagan, had. He faced every situation, as he often said, 'with courage and trust in God.' "

Women in Military Service: In accepting this award, Father Hupp noted that "American women have served this nation in its armed forces with 'ability, adaptability and stability.' Today, more than 400,000 women are on active duty, Reserve or National Guard members of the Army, Navy, Air Force, Marine Corps and Coast Guard. Women are partners with men, comprising over ten percent of the total number."

Fortunately, the steady stream of the awards slowed down shortly after Father Hupp's retirement; fortunately, because his office walls and desk top have little space left for additional plaques, certificates and statuettes.

Father Hupp reached retirement age for Catholic priests on July 3, 1985, his seventieth birthday, and his retirement from Boys Town was effective June 15, 1985.

Friends of Father Hupp raised funds to build a house for him, designed by Leo Daly, for his retirement years, to be located on the east side of the Boys Town lake and opposite the Administration Building, once called "the mistake across the lake." However, this plan never materialized. Father Hupp now lives in quarters near the Administration Building constructed originally for visitors attending meetings at the conference center.

Several years ago the Archbishop of the Omaha Archdiocese asked Father Hupp to prepare a chronicle of his days at Boys Town. From this labor grew the realization that a simple recitation of dates, names and places was not nearly enough; that a narrative in his own words about those exciting days should be put together, to be published in book form as a historical document of events as he experienced them as an inspiration to future generations of people wanting to best serve the world's homeless, neglected and abused children — the ones he has embraced as "social orphans."

Father Hupp's words to the Newcomen Society on April 25, 1985, a few weeks before his retirement, summed up his recognition of the Home's historical significance and his charge to those future generations:

"The story of the past decade at Boys Town has been a story of change and growth — responses to meet the complicated and challenging needs of today's troubled youth. I am proud to have been a part of this exciting era.

"However, I have no doubt there are more changes ahead in Boys Town's future. We must never be content to stand still — the needs of troubled children are too great. The flame that Father Flanagan lit in 1917 must burn brighter than ever, offering hope to thousands of children who awaken daily to a world of hatred, fear, humiliation and pain.

"As Father Flanagan said: 'The work will continue, you see, whether I am there or not, because it is God's work, not mine.'"

HOLLIS J. LIMPRECHT

EPILOGUE

Time is a difficult task master.

When I stepped aside as Executive Director in June of 1985 because I had reached our Archdiocesan priests' retirement age of seventy, there were still a number of major items on my agenda for improvements at Boys Town. The calendar interfered with my intentions.

An ambitious follow-up program of our graduates made sense to me. It would give some evidence whether or not we were accomplishing our mission of turning out good and productive citizens. To the extent that we were not reaching our goal it would show where improvements were needed and could then correct our shortcomings in education and training. At the same time we would be ready to give a personal response to those who question us about the merits of our program.

Our alumni seem to fall in one of three categories:

1. Those who have become truly outstanding citizens,
2. Those who still have not found their niche in life,
3. That legion in between these two extremes who have returned to society as creditable human beings in every imaginable field.

Generally, those in the first category, and others who have found here the only real home they ever had, comprise our active Alumni Association. Beefing up this organization seemed to me the vehicle for a realistic follow-up program.

Once Father Flanagan's crypt was completed, the alumni who originally had been opposed to the idea of moving his remains, fell in love with the idea of a crypt. They insisted that a similar one be built for Monsignor Nicholas Wegner who had done so much to insure the future of the Home. The Leo A. Daly Company agreed that it could be done without disturbing the beauty and integrity of the Chapel. Blue-prints were drawn, specifications were prepared. But time ran out. His remains still lie in Calvary cemetery in Omaha.

The most grandiose plan of all involved a Girls Town across the highway. The Board of Directors and Monsignor Wegner once planned an institute for retarded children there, but it failed to materialize. Before work could be begun on an extension of our campus to the north, the Nebraska State Department of Roads would need to complete the widening of Highway 6 (West Dodge Road) and rebuild our main entrance. Then with the redesigned entrance there would be easy access between north and south campuses. This had to wait.

And finally, I thought some day we ought to have a golf course. There are a few who scoff at the game saying it's only a game for the rich. There may be some truth to this, but I am one hacker not in that category, nor are the thousands who crowd local golf courses from sunup to sundown during the golfing season. It was my idea to have a nine-hole golf course southeast of the new Administration Center building, downstream from our South Lake. This would enhance the beauty of our Pacific Street entrance, but most of all would offer, among other things, the potential of a vocational educational program in golf course management and maintenance. Who knows, we might even unveil another Lee Trevino. At least those of our boys and girls who wished to learn this sport would have the opportunity to do so. We had a high school golf team at the time. It played on a local course. The Leo A. Daly Company completed plans for such a course . At about the time I was ready to make the move a local newspaper critic got wind of it and without benefit of an interview accused me of building my own country club. The inference, of course, was the course would be a place for the Executive

Director and his staff to play golf while the boys would caddy and shag balls. The idea of a golf course was shelved for a later day when the media might get off my back.

Well, Rome wasn't built in a day. Nor is the work of Boys Town completed. Father Flanagan himself insisted, "This work will continue because it is God's work, not mine." My situation now might be likened to that of Henry Kissinger when he said to the students at Georgetown University shortly after his term as United States Secretary of State ended: "Being out of office I am now rapidly approaching infallibility."

APPENDIX

DESCRIPTION OF DOWD MEMORIAL CHAPEL BEFORE VATICAN II

As we mentioned in Chapter Twelve, the structure of the chapel is Indiana Bedford stone on a concrete foundation with an exterior design inspired by the Gothic churches of rural England. The roof is light weight English tile and all gutters, down spouts, flashings, louvres, etc., are of heavy copper. Dominating feature of the exterior is the tower located above the main entrance. It is surmounted by a copper dome.

The interior of the Chapel is lined to a height of twelve feet with Indiana Bedford stone. Above this point the walls are of decorated plaster. Purlins span the space between the tresses, and between the purlins is a layer of cork that adds acoustical and insulation value.

The floor plan is cruciform with small chapels on either arm side, that had their own altar and statues. The statue above the right side altar, as one faces the front, was that of St. Joseph while the chapel on the left had a statue of Mary.

The main altar, mensa and predella, were of Bottocino marble, which also was used for the side altars. Relics in the main altar were those of Sts. Agatha, Justa, Martha, Nereus and Severus. The floor of the Nave and Narthex, as well as the floors in all the vestibules, were of hand made tile developed in patterns of color. Black axle grease was added to the mortar to give it a dark color. Floor of the chancel, the side altars, and the sanctuary are of Travertine marble with an inlaid pattern of Rouge de rance marble.

The sanctuary was paneled in selected oak. A small wall-inlaid mosaic of the Madonna and Child (Spes Nostra Salve - "Hail Our Hope") and the Sacred Heart (Praebe Bili Mi Cor Tuum Mihi - "My Son, Give Me Your Heart") are from the Vatican's mosaic works which Monsignor Wegner brought from Rome some time after the dedication. The communion rail, narthex screen, chancel choir stalls, gallery choir stalls, nave pews and transept pews are all of oak.

The backdrop behind, and the canopy over the main altar, was of imported velvet and the cross and corpus hanging over the canopy was of hand carved oak, an Italian piece. All of the sanctuary and chancel furniture is richly hand carved.

The priests' sacristy, on the west side of the sanctuary, is connected by an ambulatory back of the altar to the boys' sacristy on the east. Adjoining the priests' sacristy is a workroom.

Double confessionals are recessed in the outside walls of both side chapels.

Just inside the main entrance, on the left, was a highly adorned Baptistry with a marble font in the center. On the right side of the entrance is a wrought iron gate which leads to the choir where there is a 64 rank Reuter organ that has 3,892 pipes. It was designed by Professor Flor Peeters, who had been director of the Royal Flemish Conservatory, Antwerp, Belgium, though his primary base was Mechelen. It was some time after the original installation that the organ was completed. It was paid for by the choir.

On a small rest, called the "Ruck-Positiv" division of the pipe organ, extending from the choir loft and over the center aisle, is a marble statue of St. Cecilia, as her undeteriorated body appeared when it was exhumed in 1599. It represents the position of her body as viewed by Maderno, who was present at the exhumation — lying, neck-cleft, in the bathhouse of the Cecilia family. The body is beneath the high altar of St. Cecilia Trastevere. St. Cecilia is the Patroness of Music.

Adding a special touch to the Chapel are the fourteen Stations of the Cross, engraved from castings of pure aluminum, sculptured by Mrs. Eugene Kormendi, who was commissioned by Father Flanagan to carve the pieces and complete them for installation by Good Friday in 1947. She is probably the first to fashion a major sculpture work out of aluminum. Her husband, Dr. Eugene Kormendi, did the wood statue carvings in the Chapel which included the Good Shepherd, Sacred Heart, Curé of Ars, John Bosco, Little Flower, St. Joseph, and the Blessed Virgin Mary. He also did the ceramic Madonna on the choir stairs. It was cast in the Boys Town ceramic shop.

When Dowd Memorial Chapel was donated, Father Louis Demers, an assistant to Father Flanagan, was chosen to select the subjects of the stained glass windows. A description of the windows:

SANCTUARY

Eight grisaille type windows of rich color, with symbols on the Epistle side of the four Minor Orders and on the Gospel side of the three Major Orders and the Episcopacy.

SIDE ALTARS

Two grisaille type windows on each side containing symbols of the Blessed Virgin Mary taken from the Litany of Loreto: Morning Star, Spiritual Vessel, Mystical Rose, Seat of Wisdom.

TRANSEPTS

Two figured windows on each side dividing the three lancets each and dedicated to the following saints:

Epistle Side:

St. Isaac Jogues, S.J. — North American Martyr
St. Joseph, Spouse of the Blessed Virgin Mary — patron of the Universal Church
St. Francis of Assisi — Founder of the Franciscan Order

St. John Baptist de la Salle — Founder of the Christian Brothers
St. John Bosco — Patron of Catholic Charities

Gospel Side:

Bl. Kateri Tekakwitha — North American Indian Maiden
The Immaculate Conception — Patroness of the U.S.
St. Bernadette Soubirous — Visionary of Lourdes
St. Rose of Lima — First Canonized Saint of the New World
St. Cecilia — Patroness of Music and the Archdiocese of Omaha
Serv. Mother Magdalen — Foundress, Poor Clares in U.S.

NAVE

Ten figured windows of three lancets each, the center lancet representing the Joyful Mysteries of the Rosary on the Epistle side, and the Glorious Mysteries of the Rosary on the Gospel side. Each of the remaining twenty lancets is dedicated to saints chosen from each of the past twenty centuries of Christianity and their names appear in the respective windows. The twentieth century representative is a model French boy who died shortly after making his First Holy Communion, and who some day may be canonized.

Epistle Side - Centuries	*Gospel Side - Centuries*
1. St. John the Baptist	11. St. Emerit
2. St. Januarius	12. St. Benezet
3. St. Tarcisius	13. Blessed Herman Joseph
4. Ss. Justus and Pastor	14. St. Peter of Luxemburg
5. St. Patrick	15. St. Casimir
6. St. Columbia	16. St. Aloysius Gonzaga
7. St. Isidore	17. St. Martin de Porres
8. St. Hubert	18. St. Gerard Magella
9. St. Edmund	19. St. Gabriel Possenti
10. St. Edward	20. Guy de Fontgallant

The theme of the Facade Window in the choir loft is expressed in the Scriptural text: "Suffer children to come to me, and forbid them not; for such is the kingdom of God" (Luke 18:16).

The lower half of the window, composed of six lancets, represents Christ blessing the children of a devout group of fathers and mothers gathered in the streets of Jerusalem near the Temple.

The upper half of the window, symbolic of the kingdom of God and of those things necessary to enter it, shows six knights clad in the armor of God as described by St. Paul in his epistle to the Ephesians (6:14-17) Stand, therefore, having girded your loins with truth, and having put on the BREAST-PLATE OF JUSTICE, and having your feet shod with the readiness of the GOSPEL OF PEACE, in all things taking up the SHIELD OF FAITH, with which you may be able to quench all the fiery darts of the most wicked ones. And take unto you the HELMET OF SALVATION and the SWORD OF THE SPIRIT, that is, the word of God."

The four cardinal virtues of Prudence, Justice, Fortitude and Temperance are represented respectively by a serpent, scales, sword and fire being extinguished by a stream of water.

Above these are four gold shields in rose-figured sections, representing the Queen of Heaven who is invoked as: Tower of David, Tower of Ivory, House of Gold, and Ark of the Covenant. These towers are also symbolic of Christ's words: "In my Father's house there are many mansions" (John 14:2).

The top sections of the window represent God's royal supremacy and providence by a gold crown and a blue orb, and also as the beginning and end of all created things by the Greek Alpha and Omega.

The Holy Spirit, third person of the Blessed Trinity, is represented by a dove and flames of fire under which forms He appeared respectively after the Baptism of Christ by St. John and at the time of his descent upon the Apostles at Pentecost.